REGENTS CRITICS SERIES

General Editor: Paul A. Olson

LITERARY CRITICISM OF
DANTE ALIGHIERI

Other volumes in the Regents Critics Series are:

Literary Criticism of
Dante Alighieri

Translated and edited by

ROBERT S. HALLER

UNIVERSITY OF NEBRASKA PRESS · LINCOLN

Acknowledgments for the use of copyrighted material appear on pages 187–188, which constitute an extension of the copyright page.

Publishers on the Plains

UNP

MANUFACTURED IN THE UNITED STATES OF AMERICA

Regents Critics Series

The Regents Critics Series provides reading texts of significant literary critics in the Western tradition. The series treats criticism as a useful tool: an introduction to the critic's own poetry and prose if he is a poet or novelist, an introduction to other work in his day if he is more judge than creator. Nowhere is criticism regarded as an end in itself but as what it is—a means to the understanding of the language of art as it has existed and been understood in various periods and societies.

Each volume includes a scholarly introduction which describes how the work collected came to be written, and suggests its uses. All texts are edited in the most conservative fashion consonant with the production of a good reading text; and all translated texts observe the dictum that the letter gives life and the spirit kills when a technical or rigorous passage is being put into English. Other types of passages may be more freely treated. Footnoting and other scholarly paraphernalia are restricted to the essential minimum. Such features as a bibliographical check-list or an index are carried where they are appropriate to the work in hand. If a volume is the first collection of the author's critical writing, this is noted in the bibliographical data.

PAUL A. OLSON

University of Nebraska

Contents

Introduction

The reading public of the turn of the century, which developed a great admiration for Dante, was well served by the publishers of inexpensive editions for the general reader. The Temple Classics printed the Latin works, including the *De Vulgari Eloquentia*, the Letter to Can Grande, and the *Eclogues*, in their small and useful format, with the English translation on facing pages (1904). W. W. Jackson translated the *Convivio* (1909) with a style and (given the available texts) an accuracy which is a model for later translators. Paget Toynbee edited the *Letters*, including the Letter to Can Grande, in an edition (1920) which is both accurate in its scholarship and useful in its notes and translations. Writers such as Ezra Pound and T. S. Eliot, along with a literary public which had some Latin and a smattering of Italian, could read not only the more famous and imaginative works, the *Comedy* and *The New Life*, but also the more obscure and scholarly works which form the corpus of Dante's writings.

At present, however, these earlier editions and translations, even when in print, can no longer serve their earlier purposes. The definitive editions of the *Convivio* by Busnelli and Vandelli, and of the *De Vulgari Eloquentia* by Marigo,[1] have recovered and corrected so many readings that only new translations are likely to be accurate. And the major reading public has no longer been trained in Latin, finding therefore Dante's observations in the *De Vulgari Eloquentia* about the nature of Latin, or Italian, or Provençal, completely opaque if not meaningless. If Dante's critical writings are to be understood in the present by the present reading public, primarily students, it must be with the aid of a commentary which will clarify those points which depend upon the forms of Latin and vernacular poetry no longer directly accessible to the readers.

1. See below, "A Note on the Translation," for full bibliographical details of these editions and those mentioned in the paragraph above.

Furthermore, recent scholarship in Dante and in medieval literature has discovered that an exacting attention to the cultural milieu
of the poetry and the criticism will make drastic changes in the
perspective from which it is viewed. Any modern edition aimed at
modern readers cannot make the patronizing and romantic assumptions of an earlier time about the significance and truth of the
writings. The present edition and translation aims to fill a gap in our
understanding of what writers in the Middle Ages were trying to do,
and how their art adapted the learned classical tradition to the
requirements of a Christian and vernacular culture. Making Dante's
critical writings accessible should provide a corrective to certain
assumptions about the history of criticism which have arisen out of
the neglect or partial understanding of the important medieval
texts.

THE CONTEXT OF DANTE'S CRITICISM

In recent times, the writer or anthologist covering the history of
criticism usually pays least attention to the period of over a thousand
years between Longinus and Sidney. He may either leave it out
entirely as void of literary speculation, or acknowledge the existence
of certain commentaries, treatises, and apologies only to dismiss
them as departures from the classical tradition and therefore irrelevant to the perennial problems of poetic art—or even doubtfully
relevant to medieval poetic practice.[2] To explain this curious

2. W. J. Bate, in *Criticism: The Major Texts*, enlarged ed. (New York: Harcourt
Brace, 1970), p. 7, claims that there was a "comparative indifference to literary
speculation during the Middle Ages"; his attitude is typical of the anthologists.
One exception is *The Great Critics*, ed. J. H. Smith and E. W. Parks, 3rd ed.
(New York: W. W. Norton, 1951), which has excerpts from Dante's criticism.
Among the historians of criticism, the fullest and most sympathetic discussions of
Dante and of his contemporaries can be found in George Saintsbury's *History of
Criticism and Literary Taste in Europe from the Earliest Texts to the Present Day*, 2nd ed.
(Edinburgh: W. Blackwood, 1959), and in Allan Gilbert's *Literary Criticism: Plato
to Dryden* (Detroit: Wayne State University Press, 1962). Most other historians
treat medieval criticism with a condescension which arises from the belief that it
could not have been used by practicing poets except for mechanical and empty
exercises. See, for example, C. S. Baldwin, *Medieval Rhetoric and Poetic* (New York:
Macmillan, 1928), pp. 269 ff.; C. H. Haskins, *The Renaissance of the Twelfth Century*

anomaly, he need only appeal to the incompatibility of the piety which dominated the Middle Ages with the true aims and content of poetry: those who wished to read and write poetry during that period would either have had to distort its content so as to slip it by the eyes of the censor, or would have been forced to reduce it to a meaningless exercise in the manipulation of rhetorical devices. These necessities would account for the allegorical commentaries which arbitrarily assign bland and far-fetched moral values to the myths and figures of classical poetry, and for the poetic textbooks which mechanically list the figures and colors by means of which an essentially meaningless narrative could be ornamented, expanded and contracted, or distorted from its natural order. Their circumstances, so the argument continues, forced medieval critics to be either dilettantes or fanatics: they had either to deprive poetry of meaning, or to fool themselves and others about its meaning. In either case, they committed the cardinal critical sin: they separated poetic meaning from the form in which it was expressed.

If one critic from the period is admitted into a history or anthology, this place is usually given to Dante Alighieri, whose criticism, because it is written in explanation of his own highly respected poetic practice, cannot so easily be dismissed as irrelevant. This is not to say, however, that the same charges have not been brought against him as against his medieval colleagues. Some of his devotees have helped to bring his criticism into disrepute by taking his critical principles as a license to find in his poetry the subjective and esoteric revelations of private mystical experiences. The poetry itself is so personal and so filled with human interest that critics may easily doubt the sincerity and importance of Dante's critical professions, attributing them to coyness or to pious self-delusion: by finding allegorical significance in his poetry, Dante could impose a spurious moral upon its experiential and affective content; by articulating as an afterthought the divisions and strategies of his poems, he could make them seem didactic when in fact they were expressive. At any rate, such critics say, his explanations are so

(New York: World Publishing Co., Meridian Books, 1957), pp. 107–8; and E. Faral, Les "arts poétiques" du XIIᵉ et du XIIIᵉ siècles (Paris: Librarie Honoré Champion, 1924), p. xv.

mechanical, and the gap between surface beauties and deeper meanings so great within them, that Dante can, as a critic, be classed with his contemporaries, and treated accordingly.[3]

Arguments which depend upon the ignorance or pious self-delusion of past ages are inherently suspect, however appealing they might be to modern prejudices. It is therefore not surprising that sympathetic modern scholarship has been able to answer all the charges leveled against medieval critics, Dante among them. Allegorical interpretation, and the theory which lies behind it, has been shown to depend upon a high, not a low, valuation of poetry itself, to be a development of, not a departure from, classical practice, and to be a disciplined, not an arbitrary, mode of criticism.[4] Allegorical interpretation depends, in the first place, upon the belief that poets are authorities, that the truths they express, by means of allegory, are identical to those found in the philosophers, scientists,

3. The argument in Italian criticism over the question of how to distinguish "poetry" and "non-poetry" in the *Divine Comedy* was, in essence, a dispute about the applicability of Dante's own critical terminology to his work. Benedetto Croce and Francesco De Sanctis, who were largely responsible for setting the terms of the dispute, wished to dismiss from the poem those passages required by allegorical theory and by the moral and theological levels of meaning; see Croce, *The Poetry of Dante*, trans. Douglas Ainslie (New York: Henry Holt and Co., 1922), pp. 5–6, passim, and De Sanctis, *History of Italian Literature*, trans. Joan Redfern (New York: Harcourt Brace, 1959), 1:178–263. For discussion of this dispute, see Egidio Guidabaldi, "Poesia e non-poesia negli ultimi quarantanni di critica dantesca," *Civiltà cattolica* 110, no. 4 (1959): 42–52; and Helmut Hatzfield, "Modern Literary Scholarship as Reflected in Dante Criticism," *Comparative Literature* 3 (1951): 289–309.

4. The major documents in this reappraisal of allegory have been Jean Pépin, *Mythe et allégorie: les origines grecques et les contestations judéo-chrétiennes* (Paris: Editions Montaigne, 1958), which established beyond dispute the continuity and pervasiveness of allegorical interpretation in the ancient world; Jean Seznec, *The Survival of the Pagan Gods*, trans. B. Sessions (New York: Random House, Pantheon Books, 1953), which established the artistic usefulness of the mythographic tradition; D. W. Robertson, Jr., *A Preface to Chaucer* (Princeton: Princeton University Press, 1962), which connects the practice of allegorical interpretation, scriptural and poetic, with the practice of poetic composition; and Rosamund Tuve, *Allegorical Imagery* (Princeton: Princeton University Press, 1966), which explores the actual results, in the period just after their composition, of the attempts to interpret medieval allegorical works.

and moralists. This high regard for poetry has been traced back almost to the dawn of poetry itself. The myths of Homer and Hesiod were from the beginning regarded as repositories of metaphysical and moral ideas, and the same belief in the hidden truth of fables which produced commentaries on the poetry of the past informed its composition at any time in the classical period. What medieval commentators added to the classical tradition was a historical dimension, derived from the nature of scriptural allegory. Scripture differed from poetry in being the true history, not fable, and in becoming allegorical because its fulfillment in later history required its reinterpretation.[5] This fulfillment paradoxically both confirmed and defied expectation, preserving the meaning of the events leading up to it by redefining the frame of reference in which they are to be understood. Medieval commentators, by combining the static allegories of the poets with the scriptural method of historical reinterpretation, developed a discipline for incorporating events both mythical and historical into a scheme of truth.

The values thus imposed upon symbols in poetry or Scripture may seem arbitrary because they are not necessary inferences from the nature of the symbolic object, and may seem even more arbitrary in assuming references to ideas and things not intended by or even known to their authors. But the allegorical method is not in fact arbitrary; it requires the preservation of the intent of the original context while assuming that part of that intent was to express the truth. If allegorical values are not necessary inferences from the nature of objects, they must be reasonable inferences from the intent of context in which the objects appear. If according to commentators the lion in Scripture sometimes means Christ, sometimes an evangelist, and at other times the devil, this is because a riddle, a vision, and a simile in Scripture take a lion as the strong from which sweetness came, as a living creature whose face is among those surrounding the throne of glory, and as a danger waiting in the

5. The original and radical nature of medieval scriptural commentary, and its development in accord with rigorous and consistent principles, is lucidly presented in Henri de Lubac, *Exégèse mediévale: les quatre sens de l'écriture* (Paris: Aubier, 1959–1964). See especially pt. 2, vol. 2, pp. 182–255, where the relationship between scriptural and nonscriptural allegory is discussed.

streets, and because the truest referents for these concepts are the three meanings mentioned above.[6] If Egypt, to use Dante's example, may stand for the misery of sin, or the corruption of the world, this is because by an accident of history Egypt was the place of bondage from which the Chosen People escaped to journey to their Promised Land, and because the ultimate fulfillment of the promise of the Exodus came with the redemption of Christ, the grace which releases man from sin and brings him to eternal glory.[7] By the same token, Virgil's prediction of an extraordinary birth in the Fourth Eclogue, and his prophecy of an eternal Empire in the *Aeneid*, could not have been intended as references to the birth of Christ or to the founding of the Church; but since these two events followed his prophecies in time, and since their conditions corresponded to those described in the poems, it was not unreasonable to make Virgil into a prophet of Christ.[8]

The discipline of the allegorical method, whether applied to interpretation or to composition, required, therefore, a method for establishing the intention of a context; and this method was supplied by the discipline of rhetoric. Rhetoric was, in this sense, a study of the properties of the real world as these are assumed and manifested in the forms of human expression.[9] A writer in any discourse which aims to inform, persuade, or move someone assumes that something is possible or impossible, desirable or undesirable, known or uncertain, and that it is so to some person or persons at some point in time. A formal rhetoric sets forth the general qualities which things

6. These passages are respectively from Judges 14:18, Ezekiel 10:14, and Proverbs 26:13. The freedom of Christian exegesis, which rejoices in finding many symbols for the same meaning and many meanings in the same symbol, is expressed by Saint Augustine, *De Doctrina Christiana* 25.35–27.38.

7. See the *Letter to Can Grande* 7.

8. This identification was especially important to Dante, whose conception of the Empire was dependent upon the correspondence of the Pauline "fullness of time" with the Virgilian return of the Golden Age. See Charles Davis, *Dante and the Idea of Rome* (Oxford: Clarendon Press, 1957), pp. 117–21.

9. The radical nature of medieval assumptions about language has been given a preliminary exploration by Marcia Colish, *The Mirror of Language: A Study in the Mediaeval Theory of Knowledge* (New Haven: Yale University Press, 1968), with an extended treatment of Dante's poetics.

in the real world must possess if these assumptions are justified. If men express their joy and sorrow, fear and hope, love and hate, then the objects of those passions must really exist and must have such qualities and effects as are presupposed by the passions. If men can complain and pity, then events must have elements of justice and injustice in them. If men express admiration and contempt, then beings must exist whose beauty or ugliness, honor or shame, justify such expression. A rhetoric textbook which pairs the forms of expression with the qualities of objects makes explicit what is obvious and almost tautological in the nature of human expression; for this reason ancient rhetoric seems sometimes an unenlightening and dry study.

When used mechanically, rhetoric can be the empty art it sometimes seems. When used imaginatively, however, and as a tool of analysis rather than as a repository of formulas and recipes, it produces interesting insights for the poet or the commentator. Rhetoric says, for instance, that the objects of fear are those things which someone regards as possible, imminent, and harmful. If it can be shown that a person is an eternal soul rather than a temporal physical being, then it can also be shown that no event in the external world should be feared: the harm to the soul is internal. Rhetoric says that happiness is the possession of goods and the capacity to use them. If nothing in the world can be truly possessed nor used without harm to the soul, then the paradoxes of the Beatitudes, which say that happiness lies in poverty, are true. This kind of rhetorical analysis tends to confirm allegorical readings by showing that the literal objects of passion and belief do not fulfill the formal qualities required of them so well as do the suggested spiritual references. It is possible to extend this analysis to questions of rhetorical style. The book of Genesis, for instance, can be found to come closer to the requirements of the sublime style of rhetoric than do the epics and orations of the ancients because its subject is truly grand and its style fitting to its subject. By the same reasoning, Dante could call his most sublime poem by the lowly name of "comedy," using the terms of a classical rhetorical theory to justify a practice that seems to defy the classical canons which, paradoxically, it really confirms.[10] (And it should be remembered, in this regard, that the adjective "divine" was affixed to the poem by later admirers whose adulation exceeded their appreciation for Dante's paradoxical reasoning.)

Rhetoric, then, establishes the subjective value of a thing, as it is known or felt by some person, while allegory establishes its objective value in a system of truth. A poem brings the two together by fitting a rhetorical stance to a thing and to the significance of the thing. But this significance itself is the product of the part which the thing has played in some earlier work where by aiding or impeding the discovery or possession of the ultimate goods of man, it came to stand for one of the agents or instruments or ends in the scheme of all such discoveries. The rhetoric of the particular works in a tradition thus determines the allegorical significances of things available to a follower of the tradition; and this follower will in turn indicate his choice among possible significances by assigning a thing a value in a particular purposive action. Rhetoric makes plausible and consistent the judgments and volitions of individuals involved in an action, while allegory, the objective significance of the objects of knowledge and feeling, permits the action to be incorporated into the purposive schemes to which all human actions belong.

Allegorical meanings do not exist apart from the texts of the tradition which created them except in the form of dictionaries which merely list all the uses of a symbol in that tradition.[11] Rhetoric, on the other hand, is a set of formal possibilities which may be studied without reference to particular texts. When they came to write poems or comment on texts, medieval poets and exegetes could explain allegorical meanings by referring to earlier writings in which the same god or person or object had appeared. They could discuss the form in which this meaning was expressed by referring

10. See the *Letter to Can Grande* 10. These paradoxes have been well defined by Erich Auerbach in "Sermo humilis," in his *Literary Language and Its Public in Late Latin Antiquity and in the Middle Ages*, trans. R. Mannheim (New York: Random House, Pantheon Books, 1965), pp. 25–81.

11. And Dante was quite conversant with such dictionaries as the *Trésor* of his old mentor, Brunetto Latini, or the *Magna Derivationes* of Uguccione of Pisa.

to the elements of rhetorical theory which were an abstract model of human expressive possibility. They did not always feel the need to make the relationship between allegory and rhetorical form explicit; but this does not mean, as is sometimes alleged, that they thought meaning and form were unrelated.

Indeed, any close examination of the allegorical meanings which Dante, in his criticism, assigns to texts makes clear the extent to which the relative value of an element in such meanings, though not the element itself, is determined by a rhetorical stance. Rhetoric, says Dante, is either left- or right-handed, taking the form of either dissuasion or persuasion, irony or congratulation, contempt or praise, and these forms will have objects suitable to them.[12] It is reasonable, therefore, to see the "noble lady" of *The New Life* as Philosophy, a fit object for the love and praise expressed in the poems.[13] No one is more worthy of standing for Christ than Cato, says Dante, for the heroic dignity which Lucan attributes to his relationship with his wife Marcia is equivalent to that of the marriage between Christ and the human soul.[14] The ancients considered their divine wisdom and song the gift of Apollo, who thus became suitable for Dante's invocation when he was about to sing his divine vision.[15] The Garden of Eden in Scripture, like the Golden Age of the ancient poets, was the original and natural milieu of perfect man, to which he could be restored by regeneration; it was thus a fit symbol for that just empire which would result from the spiritual renewal of human society.[16] And one need not stop with the passages which Dante himself explains; the critics listed in the Bibliography below have all demonstrated that any passage in Dante which is explicated according to the method suggested by his critical writings will yield meanings of an allegorical kind which are perfectly specified and prepared for by the rhetorical forms in which they are expressed.

12. *On Eloquence* 2.14.2.
13. *Banquet* 2.12.5–8.
14. *Banquet* 4.28.13–19.
15. *Paradise* 1.13 ff.; *Letter* 18.
16. *Purgatory* 28.139–44. See also Dante's *De Monarchia* 1.11, which identifies the Virgilian "Saturnia Regna" with the coming of the Empire and consequently of a single world government.

Though it would be impossible for a modern poet to follow these principles, they by no means deserve the contempt to which they have been subjected. They made possible the composition of new poetry which could contribute usefully to the discovery and confirmation of the purposive pattern of which all actions, in poetry as in life, were instances. They allowed a poet to express the truths of metaphysics, ethics, and science and thus to claim the authority accorded to other disciplines. They gave poets priority in the demonstration of the concord between the nature of man and the order of the universe, for poets were the most eloquent users of the forms of language which expressed this concord. They assured the continuity of the poetic tradition by affording the means of confirming the authority of ancient texts and preserving the usefulness of ancient mythology and history for the writing of new poetry. Modern principles sometimes limit the meaning of poetry to such formulations as can be derived from its internal workings, place the authority of poets in their right to an individual vision, and thus assure the existence of two cultures, the one dealing with clearly formulated and useful general truths, the other with obscure individual truths of limited relevance. There is no reason to regret the pluralistic and relativistic conditions of modern life which make these principles necessary and older principles impossible. But there is no reason either to look down on the attempts in the past to assert the continuity, authority, and dignity of poetry.

These virtues of poetry were no more self-evident in Dante's time than in our own, however, for even when the principles were possible, they were not necessary. There were men of learning in the Middle Ages, for instance, who refused to grant the authority of poetry. With Saint Paul and Plato, they might hold "fables" in contempt. Or they might simply wonder why the poets should be read if the teachings of poetry were the same as those of theology, ethics, and science, which could be taught more directly and lucidly by the methods of those disciplines themselves. There were others who, while willing to grant authority to the classics in certain areas, doubted the usefulness of imitating them. A Christian could write devotional or doctrinal poetry without using the machinery and mythology of the pagans; and it would seem superfluous and anachronistic, a quaint exercise in irrelevance, merely to repeat with slight variation what had been excellently done over a thousand years before.

The medieval humanists developed their theory of poetry to answer these objections, and Dante's criticism shares with them their apologetic purposes.[17] But his criticism goes further, and answers an objection to his practice raised by the humanists themselves. Many of these doubted the desirability, or even the possibility, of writing true poetry in the vernacular. Latin had been the language of learning for over a thousand years. The precision and lucidity to which the various sciences had been brought could not be transferred overnight into the vernacular. Latin was also the language of art. The definitions of rhetorical schemes and tropes assumed the inflections and syntax of Latin; prosody depended upon its phonology; and distinctions in levels of diction were based on Latin vocabulary. It was the learned readers of Latin who conferred authority and dignity on poetry, new as well as old. Readers of vernacular rhymes, lacking access to the classical tradition, could be pleased only by artless and ignorant entertainments.

Dante's criticism and practice, then, is both representative and radically new. He wished to preserve the values of humanism, but in a medium not approved by most of his humanistic allies. Had he written in French or Provençal, which had longer and more dignified vernacular traditions, his job might have been easier. But even in France and Provence, the clear trend to vernacular poetry had not found apologists who could satisfy a thoroughgoing humanist, with his eyes on the dignity of the past. It is easy in the present to see that in choosing the vernacular Dante chose to move in the direction of the future, but it is very hard to appreciate the difficulties which such a choice entailed. He could have accepted and asserted the dignity of the vernacular as separate from the classical tradition. Or he could have acknowledged the inferiority of the vernacular, and undertaken to improve it by subjecting it to the rules of classical art. But instead, he took on a more difficult task, namely, to demon-

17. By far the fullest and most representative such apology available to readers of English is *Boccaccio on Poetry*, ed. C. G. Osgood (New York: Bobbs Merrill Library of Arts no. 82), 1956.

strate that there already existed a vernacular art, equal in dignity to and continuous with the classical tradition. He granted the validity of the humanistic argument against vernacular poetry in agreeing that an art without rules was unworthy of the name of art; but he denied the minor premise by declaring that the vernacular had rules of its own fully as rigorous as those of Latin poetry. In other words, he assumed the existence of what Erich Auerbach has called "vernacular culture,"[18] even while his critical writings brought this culture into existence.

A culture is formed from a collection of scientific and artistic writings by a body of ancillary learning which unifies it and assures its continuity and availability. Classical Latin culture, in this sense, was the product of those educators, commentators, and compilers who, from the first century through the thirteenth (and beyond) made it certain that each new generation of students would understand how Virgil and Horace, Cicero and Valerius Maximus, Tacitus and Suetonius, Seneca and Boethius were parts of an interconnected whole.[19] They made the study of grammar, logic, and rhetoric, along with the other so-called liberal arts, the common and necessary introduction to all the authors of the tradition. They surrounded each text with glosses which applied these arts to it, proceeding from a philological discussion of its constituent members to the establishment of a surface sense from which could be derived a "sentence," a more general meaning with practical application to life. In the process they emphasized the interdependence and common standards of all the authors by pointing out allusions,

18. In his important essay, "The Western Public and Its Language," in his *Literary Language* (above, n. 10), pp. 237–38. The understanding of Dante's purposes expressed in this present introduction owes a great deal to Auerbach's exploration of the problem of literary language for vernacular poets.

19. The most thorough presentation of those qualities of ancient culture which account for its pervasive importance in Europe through the seventeenth century is contained in R. R. Bolgar, *The Classical Heritage and Its Beneficiaries* (Cambridge: Cambridge University Press, 1964; rpt. Harper Torchbooks, 1964). The specific manner of the transmission of classical culture in the Middle Ages is best described in G. Paré, A. Brunet, and P. Tremblay, *La renaissance du XIIIe siècle: les écoles et l'enseignement* (Paris: J. Vrin, and Ottawa: Institut d'études médiévales, 1933); C. H. Haskins, *The Renaissance of the Twelfth Century* (above, n. 1); and, for Dante, Bruno Nardi, *Dante e la cultura medievale* (Bari: G. Laterza, 1942).

explaining passages with quotations from other writers, measuring
the excellence of each against the same standard of eloquence, and
determining the dignity of all persons, real and fictional, according
to the same general standard of decorum. Thus they showed how
works in all genres contributed to a common body of received ideas
in all areas of learning. The student would learn to take for granted
the interdependence and unity not only of the authors, but also of
the elements of culture. Politics was a function of style, ethics the
product of metaphysics, and wisdom the result of mastery of an
interpretative method which applied equally well to an ancient or
a modern document. Since all the cultural documents of the Middle
Ages were in Latin, Dante's contention that there could be, and
indeed already was, a vernacular culture would seem to such a
student bold in the extreme, and impossible of proof.

Certain undeniable facts stood in the way of Dante's establishing
the truth of his contention by argument alone; but such arguments
as he had available, he used. If many writings in the vernacular
seemed unworthy of a culture, he could argue that these works
should be distinguished from the products of true "experts in
eloquence." If even the remaining works seemed to lack art, since
for example they could not observe the rules of Latin prosody or
since they did not observe all the classical decorums, arguments
could establish the consistency and rationality of the rules they did
follow. If the limited scope of these few works would seem to restrict
the relevance of vernacular culture to a small number of cultural
activities, and if the novelty of the medium would seem to prevent
one learned in Latin culture from applying his knowledge and skill
to them, arguments could demonstrate the continuity and com-
patibility of the two cultures and thus justify their alternative or
simultaneous application to cultural problems. Such arguments
would make Dante's claim plausible, if not prove it.

Arguments could not supply vernacular culture with works of
magnitude and scope comparable to those of Latin, nor with the
body of ancillary learning which a culture required. Therefore,
from the beginning of his career as a poet, Dante undertook to
supply these necessities of culture even in the process of presenting
his arguments. It is hard to classify many of his works as either

"critical" or "creative," for each work calls attention to the elements of art which it contains, and presents arguments whose truth is contingent upon the existence of the work itself. Each new work assimilated to vernacular culture earlier works whose cultural significance had not previously been appreciated, while incorporating into the vernacular elements of Latin culture whose applicability could not have been recognized. It was his ambition to rival Virgil as a poet, but also to rival him as a cultural force. Therefore he was not content to let others be his commentators, as Servius or Macrobius had been for Virgil; he rather supplied the critical apparatus for his own works (and incidentally attracted to his work more commentary in two hundred years than Virgil did in a thousand). The most useful introduction to Dante's critical works, therefore, is that which takes the form of an explanation of the respective places of these works in his program for the establishment of a new culture.

THE CULTURAL SIGNIFICANCE OF DANTE'S WORKS

The New Life (1292–1295) was the first of Dante's sustained works, and the first which manifests the direction of his new vernacular culture. As an occasional and artistic commentary on the thirty-one lyric poems it contains, it is a work which assimilates the forms already to be found in the vernacular. The *vidas* and *razos* of the Provençal tradition were "lives" and "explanations" which grew up around the lyrics of the troubadours, giving them unity, human interest, and artistic plausibility.[20] Whereas the *vidas* and *razos* were frequently rather simplistic in their assumptions about the relationship of art to the life which produced it, Dante's descriptions of the stage or crisis in his young love for Beatrice, and his discussions of the forms, devices, and divisions of his art, copy this simplicity on the surface while teasing the reader into a recognition of the classical complexity of his theme.

In its form and strategy, the work deliberately models itself on

20. On the *razos* and *vidas*, see A. Jeanroy, *La poésie lyrique des troubadours* (Toulouse: E. Privat, and Paris: H. Didier, 1934), 1:101 ff. The influence of these upon *The New Life* has been explored by P. Rajna, *Lo schema della Vita Nuova* (Verona, 1890), and by V. Crescini, "Les razos provenzali e le prose della *Vita Nuova*," *Giornale storico della letteratura italiana* 32 (1914): 463 ff.

the Latin tradition. In the *Banquet*, Dante mentions Boethius's *Consolation of Philosophy* and Augustine's *Confessions* as precedents for speaking of oneself when one's own life needs justification or may teach effectively;[21] formal elements of these two works can be seen throughout *The New Life*. The *Consolation* alternates prose and verse, and provides, in Lady Philosophy, a model for Dante's ladies who instruct by attracting love and admiration; the *Confessions* takes the loves and pursuits of youth as steps on the way to a mature love of God and provides a model for Dante's spiritual progress. In its explicit apologetic passages, *The New Life* claims the name of poet, with the appertaining privileges, for a vernacular writer, and implicitly validates this claim by making vernacular forms and subjects serve a Latin theme by means of an indirection pleasing in itself and effective in its results.

The *Banquet* (1307–1319) abandons this artistic subtlety to both argue and exemplify the capacity of Italian as a language of learning and culture. It explains the indirection of *The New Life* where Dante out of respect for the genius of the vernacular was forced to represent Philosophy in the form of a "noble lady" who was the poet's love; but it also teaches speculative and moral philosophy directly, and serves the vernacular poems—Dante's own *canzoni*—which embodied these philosophic themes. As a "banquet" whose "courses" are commentaries on authoritative documents, it is modeled on such works as Macrobius's *Saturnalia* or Cassian's *Collationes*, the cultural significance of which it adapts to the needs of its time.[22] Macrobius, for instance, wished to keep alive the spirit of Greek letters and recover the elements of a fading Latin piety, and does so by explaining in detail Virgil's adaptations of his Greek models to the requirements of a newly unified Augustan system of values. It seemed to Macrobius that Roman values had lost their force in the fourth century because they had been deprived of nourishment from Greek culture, but that they could be revived if the greatest work embodying them, Virgil's *Aeneid*, were to be reset in its proper milieu. Dante,

---

21. See *Banquet* 1.2.12–17.

22. On the cultural significance of these "banquets" in late antiquity, see P. Courcelle, *Late Latin Writers and Their Greek Sources*, trans. H. Wedeck (Cambridge: Harvard University Press, 1969).

by the same token, wished to keep alive the spirit of Latin letters by showing that it had been embodied in vernacular poetry where it would remain a cultural force for those whose business and lack of opportunity had prevented them from acquiring the language of learning. The *canzoni* of the *Banquet* are to be understood by the principles of poetic allegory; like the epics of Virgil, Statius, Ovid, and Lucan, they teach the virtues appropriate to each stage of life. But it is not essential to the understanding of the *canzoni* that they be derived from Latin culture. Rather they themselves, by so perfectly embodying Latin culture, bring to light aspects of that culture whose present relevance might otherwise have been overlooked. Where Macrobius regretted the passing of an old culture and its values, Dante is confident that the new culture has the capacity to keep the essence of the old alive.

This confidence is supremely manifested in the ambitions of the treatise *On Eloquence in the Vernacular* (1304–1309), which was to have explained how all forms of discourse, from the most exalted poetry to the humblest domestic conversation, could be derived from principles suited to common speech. Dante's ambition, as he remarks, was unprecedented. The nearest thing to a model for Dante's work, Quintilian's *Institutes*, which purports to give a citizen mastery of all forms of speech required in the exercise of his duties, bases the rules of eloquence upon the uniformities of a language, or "grammar," set apart from common speech, and finds examples of its forms in those poets and orators who wrote in this grammar. To claim as Dante does that there can be rules of eloquence for a changing and varied medium is to set for oneself an almost paradoxical task: to prescribe rules would seem in itself to destroy the unique character of the vernacular, and put eloquence out of the reach of the unlearned. To get around this paradox, Dante seeks to discover in the purposes of human speech the principles which have made necessary the rules of grammar and eloquence, and to use these principles to evade the rules themselves. It is to this end that he discusses in Book One the origin of language, finding perfect eloquence in Adam's praise of God, and uniformity of speech in human communication such as prevailed before the building of the tower of Babel, not directed to the purposes of human pride. Rules of grammar and eloquence are attempts to compensate for the effects of human sin; but it is human nature, and not these rules, which produces works of eloquence. Thus, in Book Two, he finds that the experts in eloquence who used common speech could, and did, discover by intuition uniformities different in detail, but not in kind, from those prescribed by the grammarians and rhetoricians. It happens, therefore, that the great Italian poets had written without knowing it in an "Italian" language, not in their native dialects, and that they had followed rules of form which were equal in rigor and rationality with those of Latin prosody. These rules, the products and not the instruments of eloquence, were based upon qualities inherent in vernaculars, and made possible the fulfillment of Dante's ambitions.

Rules of eloquence, however, cannot make a culture, and Dante's larger ambitions put a stop to both this treatise and the *Banquet* before either was carried very far. When Dante saw in the accession of Henry VII as Emperor the opportunity to unify Italy and revive Augustan glories, and when he conceived a poem of heroic stature equal to his political vision, he chose to devote his energies to politics and poetry, and to leave his lesser cultural works unfinished. But although the *Banquet* ends when only three of the proposed fourteen *canzoni* have been explicated, and although the treatise breaks off near the end of its discussion of the first and highest vernacular form, "tragic poetry," both works are long enough to establish the feasibility of their objectives. Dante must have been confident that, with the simultaneous creation of a new poem and a new society of equal magnitude and sublimity, there would be others to do the lesser work of cultural consolidation.

Though Dante's political hopes were never fulfilled, his confidence was not misplaced; his new poem, the *Divine Comedy* (1314–1321), attracted a host of commentators and was the object of emulation for many generations of Italian poets. Italian culture became a reality even when the political unity he desired had to wait five hundred years. In the meantime, however, the poem itself served as a guide to the development of Italian culture which never completely lost its force. The *Comedy*, by calling attention to its roots in vernacular style, through the speeches of Buonagiunta Orbicciani, Guido Guinizelli, and Arnault Daniel, and its roots in the vernacular tradition of poetic political satire, through the speeches of Sordello, asserts the continuity of vernacular culture which is at any rate most fully represented in the figure of Beatrice, the apotheosis of those noble ladies to whom vernacular poetry, Dante's own earlier efforts included, had been addressed. By giving Virgil the functions of guide, stylistic model, and precedent for an underworld journey, and by letting Statius explain the natural mode of transition between ancient and medieval culture, it makes ancient poetry the model and source of the excellence of a new poem, as if the epic scope and allusions of the *Comedy* itself had not demonstrated this point. By means of such explicit and implicit statements of intention, Dante required of his commentators and followers that they find in his subject and technique a synthesis which adapted classical Latin culture to new conditions and expanded the scope and potential functions of the vernacular.

The *Comedy* was thus by intention and subsequent treatment a classic from the beginning; if one accepts Dante's authorship of the *Letter to Can Grande*, he claimed such status for the work as early as 1317.[23] The letter, a presentation and dedication of the *Paradise* to his patron and political ally, contains a specimen commentary which is in the form of an *accessus*, an introduction of the sort attached to the

23. The letter was formerly often considered a forgery because it was not alluded to until the sixteenth century and not published until 1700; because its phrasing seems derivative from other, later documents, especially the early commentaries (compare, for instance, the passages from Boccaccio's *Life of Dante* translated in I. Brandeis, *Discussions of the Divine Comedy* [Boston: D. C. Heath, 1961], pp. 1 ff., with the text of the *Letter* below); and because it seems to differ in important theoretical ways from Dante's known opinions, particularly in ignoring the distinction between the allegory of the poets and of the theologians expressed in *Banquet* 2.1 (see below, n. 31). This view has been supported most recently by Colin Hardie, "The Epistle to Cangrande Again," *Deutsches Dante-Jahrbuch* 38 (1960): 51–74. Its authenticity has generally been assumed in more recent criticism, however, since it is not in the least implausible that the *Letter*, though not widely circulated, was available to Boccaccio and other early commentators, and was considered so consistent with Dante's principles and practice that its publication was not thought important.

school texts of established, usually ancient, authors.[24] When Dante identifies the author, lists the characteristics of the form, outlines the subject matter, and suggests the purposes and effects of his work (these constituting its four causes—efficient, formal, material, and final—according to Aristotelian logic), and as well explains its title and places it in its proper philosophic category, he makes his poem, like all other classics, available to an overall program of studies. Not only the form, but some of the content, such as the definition of "comedy" and the terms for the treatment of a treatise, are borrowed from other *accessus*; but otherwise the letter summarizes what Dante had said in earlier works about the allegorical meanings and rhetorical techniques of poetry, applying these ideas to a detailed interpretation of the proem of *Paradise*. He concludes the letter by wishing for the opportunity to complete his useful work of commentary. He need not have worried that otherwise the job would never be done; there were many commentators who set forth, without his help, the cultural significance of the poem.

Though such significance is clearly dependent upon its having been written in Italian, there is an early tradition, reported by Boccaccio, that Dante began the composition of the *Divine Comedy* in Latin.[25] And indeed, the relative status of the vernacular and classical Latin in Dante's earlier writing would make it plausible that he would have thought of Latin as appropriate to a work of high ambition. At any rate, one of his humanistic friends, Giovanni del Virgilio, wrote him a Latin verse epistle, urging him to abandon the limited and transitory reward of the vernacular poet in order to gain the immortality and learned regard which could be conferred on a Latin poem. In reply, Dante wrote his *Eclogue* (1319), justifying his choice of the vernacular, and implicitly acknowledging that he could have taken the path suggested by Giovanni's letter. The

24. See Bruno Nardi, "Osservazioni sul medievale 'accessus ad auctores' in rapporto all'epistola à Cangrande," *Studi e problemi di critica testuale*, Collezione di opere inedite o rare pubblicate dalle Commissione per i Testi di Lingua, vol. 123 (Bologna, 1961).

25. See *Tutte le Opere di Giovanni Boccaccio*, vol. 6, *Esposizioni Sopra la "Comedia" di Dante*, ed. G. Padoan (Milan: A. Mondadori, 1965), pp. 17–18.

shepherd who stands for Dante expresses his confidence that, when his correspondent receives ten pails of milk from a prize ewe (representing ten cantos of the *Paradise*), he will recognize the full potential of the vernacular, and applaud Dante's choice. At the same time, the *Eclogue* is in elegant Latin, and employs the Virgilian technique of representing real people and events through shepherds and pastoral activities; it thus gives evidence of Dante's mastery of the standard Latin forms and techniques. Had Dante's political and cultural ambitions not taken precedence over any purely personal aims, he might well have written the *Comedy* in sublime Latin just as he wrote the Eclogue in elegant Latin. Certainly his rejection of Giovanni's specific exhortation was no rejection of poetic immortality; his own efforts, he believed, would result in the transfer of greatness from the Latin to the vernacular tradition.

An English translation can neither confirm nor deny Dante's implicit claim to mastery of Latin style, and neither prove nor disprove his contention that Italian was capable of expressing learned ideas. A reader who is skeptical on these points must consult the originals; but these issues are hardly live ones in the present day. The implicit arguments which are validated by Dante's abilities as a stylist are at any rate not so interesting as the explicit ways in which he met the perennial problems of the artist and those problems which he shared with his contemporaries. With the aid of a few original texts, this translation attempts to reproduce clearly and exactly the rather complex artistic principles which give Dante's criticism its lasting value. It should be useful, therefore, to examine these principles briefly to establish the precise nature of the larger problems they were meant to solve and of the criteria they had to meet in order to constitute a satisfactory solution. For the purposes of this examination, the problems may be reduced to two: how to make poetry artistic and how to give it meaning; and the criteria should be those two qualities of classical culture which Dante most admired and most desired to emulate, rigor and universality.

THE PROBLEM OF VERNACULAR POETIC ART

Since Dante assumed, quite plausibly, that the art of classical poetry was based upon a grammar, a secondary language derived from the vernacular and given regularity and stability by the common agreement of the learned, he might reasonably have been expected to construct an Italian grammar as the basis of his own vernacular art. He was quite aware that one relatively early Latin writer, namely Cicero,[26] felt the necessity of arguing the merits of a newly established Latin grammar against the claims of Greek, and he could have undertaken to set forth similar arguments for Italian. He also knew, from his reading of Priscian and Donatus, that Latin grammar was understood as a derivation of and a variation on the Greek. Greek grammar was, to the grammarians, the model of rationality and consistency in inflections, syntactic ordering, and word formation; Latin grammar, therefore, had either to be identical with Greek in these matters, or to be derivable from the Greek by consistent rules. By the same token, Italian grammar might have been fashioned after the Latin model, for Italian, as Dante proudly points out, has more traces of "grammar" than any other medieval vernacular. Dante could have undertaken the laborious task of constructing such a grammar, and perhaps the more difficult task of securing the agreement of the learned Italian world.

This reasonable procedure, of course, would not have worked, for there is no evidence that the learned world was dissatisfied with the grammar it had been using, and no indication that it was willing to adopt a grammar which would have isolated Italy from the rest of Europe. But more importantly this procedure would not have served Dante's larger cultural purposes. He needed the stability and uniformity of a grammar as the basis for rules of art, and he needed an art in order to make vernacular poetry a useful instrument of learning and culture. But he could not, in securing this art, exclude from "the culture" all poets who wrote before the grammar, nor cut off from the culture those users of common speech which the culture was to serve. Rather than to devise a grammar, therefore, he sought only to discover in the practice of vernacular "experts in eloquence" principles of uniformity operating on vernacular speech itself which would satisfy the cultural requirement of universality and the artistic requirement of rigor. He had, for instance, to dispute claims of various Italian dialects to cultural primacy, for in rejecting

26. *Banquet* 1.11.14, alluding to Cicero *De finibus* 1.8.

the prescriptive rigidity of grammar he could not accept instead the infinite diversity of dialects. He had also to refute the contentions of various vernacular poets that, being without artistic precedents, they could invent their techniques as they composed, and use any resources which their language made available.

The treatise *On Eloquence in the Vernacular* records his search for these principles of universality and rigor in the eloquent Italian poetry available to him, and his discovery of several happy coincidences which seemed to confirm the rightness of his procedure. Writers in various dialects, it happened, had departed from their native speech in a common direction. They had excluded from their poetry words and phrases peculiar to their dialects and of native, usually plebeian or peasant, origin, and used instead only those words, and in only those forms, which were clearly derivable from Latin grammar, and which were common, at least as variants, to all the dialects. They presumably made these choices for the sake of euphony, but in so doing they followed intuitively the process whereby grammars had been devised. It happened, furthermore, that these poetic words, suitable to vernacular meters and phonetically pleasing in themselves, also included the semantic counters of the highest or "tragic" style. For instance, the words for "love," "lady," "virtue," "joy," and "safety," which belong conceptually to the world of refinement and moral excellence where tragic poets dwell, seemed to be precisely the ones which escaped from any unpleasant vulgar qualities, such as oiliness or harshness, in the process of linguistic change which produced modern Italian. This fact made high-style diction distinguishable in Italian as it had been in Latin, and not offensive to those who had been raised on Virgil.

Certain other linguistic changes, however, made it impossible for an Italian poem to be composed entirely in high-style diction. Thus for the principle of dictional uniformity which determined the level of style in Latin, Dante substitutes a principle of harmony by contrast. Latin meters were based on quantity: they were patterns of long and short syllables. A long syllable is one with a diphthong, or long vowel, or one followed by two consonants; all other syllables are short. A word may have all long syllables or none; and, with the flexibility of Latin syntax, any word could be fit somewhere into the pattern of the meter. Italian and other Romance languages have stress as well as quantity; and any word of two syllables or more, or any noun, verb, or adjective, will have a single dominant stress. Words of three syllables or less, where the dominant stress falls on a long syllable, could form the basis of a euphonious prosody of the Latin sort. Dante calls such words, for this reason, "excellent." No line which makes sense could be composed of these words alone, however, though no line without these words will be euphonious at all. These words may be set off by prepositions, pronouns, and articles—one-syllable, unstressed words, necessary to the sense. They will stand out when combined with words of more than three syllables, including the technical language of science and philosophy, where the succession of unstressed syllables would not be euphonious in itself. They will contrast with such vulgar words as *pizza* and *allegro* (to use modern instances) where the unstressed syllables are long. The Italian poetic line will not be a pattern of long and short, or stressed and unstressed syllables; it will be merely a certain (odd) number of syllables. The "excellent" words in a line will suggest a pattern, however, and the contrasting words will accommodate themselves to the pattern imperfectly, but sufficiently for a sense of harmony. Thus Dante's prosody makes a virtue of necessity. No interesting or even grammatical Italian sentence could be composed of "excellent" words alone; but no euphonious prosody could be devised in a language of stress rather than quantity without a principle of harmony by contrast which makes the euphonious words stand out.

This harmony, of course, cannot come from the simple fact of combination, but only from the manner in which the combining is done. For the Latin poet, there were three distinct sets of rules, or arts, which specified and classified the desirable modes of combination. The first was prosody, which created metrical feet based upon syllabic quantity, classified poetic lines according to the number and kinds of feet they contained, and gave names to stanzas and larger units of poetry as these were made up of various kinds of lines. The presence of meter made a discourse poetry rather than prose, but there were also varying degrees of skill and accomplishment in the use of meters.

The second art, rhetoric, had two branches. The one created schemes or colors based upon syntactic features in either clauses or sentences; it classified clauses according to their moods or inflections, and sentences according to the manner of their subordination and coordination. The other branch created figures or tropes based upon the semantic features of comparisons; it classified them according to the categories (animate or inanimate, abstract or concrete) of the terms involved, or according to the grammatical means, such as direct address or exclamation, which introduced them into the discourse. Figures and colors made a discourse moving or charming, rather than simply expository, and could be used with varying degrees of skill and self-consciousness. The third art, the art of poetry itself, created stylistic levels requiring different degrees of skill and self-consciousness in the exercise of the first two arts; it matched these levels to the status of persons and activities as determined by the values of Roman society. It made possible distinctions of genre, and determined the relative verisimilitude and decorum of a poem.

An art, in other words, puts recognizable features of its medium into systematic classes for the sake of distinguishing artistic from other uses of the medium, and for the sake of determining the relative worth and ambition of works done according to art. Few learned men before Dante would have claimed, or even thought, that art in this sense had any relation to vernacular poetic practice. Written rules for the vernacular, insofar as they existed at all,[27] were too fragmentary and unsystematic to have produced artistic poetry, while the vernacular forms themselves, the *canzone*, sestina, sonnet, rondel, and ballade, among others, seemed so much alike that they could not have been distinguished from each other by means of the application of rigorous and universal rules. In the art of prosody, as we have seen, vernacular poets could not have followed the rules of Latin. Similarly, the rules for rhetorical schemes could have been followed only in part in an uninflected language which restricted the number of possible variations in the word order of clauses. In

27. See the introduction by Aristide Marigo to this third edition of Dante's *De Vulgari Eloquentia* (Florence: Felice le Monnier, 1957), pp. xxx–xl, for a listing and discussion of the treatises on vernacular composition which preceded Dante's.

other areas the Italian poets did not in fact follow the classical rules where they could have. The figures of speech in the stilnovistic poems (e.g., Cavalcanti's *Donna mi prega*) were based upon a complex epistemology of love unknown in the pre-Christian world, and they could not usefully be explained by referring to such simple classical semantic categories as "animate" or "inanimate." Again, the varieties of vernacular forms could not usefully be distinguished by referring to the social level of the persons and activities they portrayed. When Dante claimed, nevertheless, that vernacular poetry was artistic, he did so on the basis of three principles—comparability, analogy of procedure, and incorporation—which not only made his case, but also accounted for the seeming lack of art and left open the possibility of further development.

The principle of comparability is the most obvious and the simplest one. It states that, wherever there is an element of art in Latin poetry, there must be one also in vernacular poetry; and it must be of comparable rigor. Thus if meter is the characteristic which distinguishes classical poetry from prose, there must be such a characteristic in vernacular poetry. In *The New Life*, Dante asserts that rhyme is this characteristic, and with this assertion claims to refute that learned snobbery which did not allow the title of "poet" to those who wrote in the vernacular. If in classical poetry, lines were defined by the number and kind of feet, meters by the manner of combining lines, and the forms by the meter, then the vernacular must have a comparable system. In *On Eloquence in the Vernacular*, Dante sets up such a system, wherein lines are defined by the number of syllables, stanzas by the "arrangement" of different lines in a set order, and forms by the nature of their stanzas. He emphasizes the comparability by remarking, in an aside, that, whereas in Latin a "line" is defined by the number and kind of its "feet," in the vernacular what he calls a "foot" is defined by the number and kind of its "lines." And he further emphasizes the comparability by demonstrating that the term "music," which implied both a melody and a mathematical ratio, and which was the technical term for Latin prosody, was basic to the vernacular as well. A vernacular stanza has not only a melodic line which it follows, but also a consonance with mathematical principles, so that, for instance, the

number of its syllables will always be odd, and so that the hendecasyllable, by the principle of divisibility,[28] will be the longest possible
line. Thus vernacular prosody is as rigorous as classical prosody,
and, incidentally, uniquely suited to the Italian language and
tradition.

Dante can compare Italian with Latin prosody because meters
are based on sound patterns which can be considered in the abstract
apart from the meanings and effects of poetry. But he could compare
Italian poetic figures with their Latin equivalents, as he does in *The
New Life* (chapter 25) when he talks about his personifying of Love,
only on a level which ignores the stylistic niceties of both languages.
He is more successful in explaining the rigors of art when he posits,
in both languages, an analogous procedure of composition as the
means for introducing into discourse the subtle beauties of figurative
language and rhetorical schemes. In this analysis, a rhetorical
characteristic such as the high style would be produced, in both
Latin and the vernacular, by following in rigorous order the same
steps of composition. The writer first determines that the parts of
the sentence agree grammatically and are in a proper order. He
then makes sure that the sentence conveys a meaning, that is, may
be given a single semantic interpretation, even though, having as
yet no art, it is flavorless. He may then introduce a scheme or color,
a variation from normal word order, which will give the sentence
what Dante calls the "flavor" of art. If he wishes to go beyond the
severity of the "flavorful" style, he will add a figure or trope to give
it the "charm" of a pleasing sound, tone of voice, or apt comparison.
If he adds some further complexity or profundity of thought, his
style will be "elevated." It is the combination of these distinct levels
of art in the construction of sentences which makes the style of the
Latin epic or history, and in the same manner produces the difficult
beauties of the *trobar clus* and *dolce stil nuove* in the vernacular.[29]

28. This principle of divisibility (implied in *On Eloquence* 2.5.6) would state that
all lines longer than eleven syllables would sound like several shorter lines. In
English, for instance, "fourteeners" and "alexandrines" will always sound as if
made up of a tetrameter and a trimeter, or two trimeter, lines.

29. *Trobar clus*, the "closed mode of composition," was presumably the highest
mode among Provençal poets; it was deliberately obscure and deliberately complex
in its phrasing and vocabulary. Dante defines the *dolce stil nuove* as deriving from a

The *canzone*, however elevated its style, did not as a genre seem, like the epic, to possess a dignity appropriate to such a style. The subject matter of *canzoni* would seem to the classical scholar no different from the subject matter of lesser vernacular genres, or of the middle- and low-style elegies and epodes of Ovid and Horace. To explain this seeming indecorousness, Dante again appeals to the principle of comparability. In Latin poetry, the level of persons or activities had been determined by the hierarchy of the social world rather than by the comparable, but much more basic, hierarchy of the human soul. Man is made up of vegetable, animal, and rational souls, which dispose him to stay alive, reproduce, and live purposefully. It follows that self-preservation, the pleasures of love, and the exercise of virtue are the primary ends of man. Arms, love, and virtue are therefore the noble activities, and those who pursue them, the noblest persons. *Canzoni* treat these activities exclusively, seriously, and without the introduction of any lesser, or more vulgar, activities; they do so in the most elevated style; and they therefore may be called "tragic." Presumably the other vernacular forms would have taken their places under the *canzone* and would have been defined by their departure from the highest form just as the other classical genres fall into place under the epic and tragedy; but we do not know how Dante would have completed his theory of vernacular genres.

It is perhaps fortunate that Dante never finished writing the rules of vernacular poetry as he had planned to do in the rest of the treatise; his more interesting, if less systematic, characterizations of the rules for the vernacular expounded in his later works follow the principle of incorporation rather than that of comparability. According to these characterizations, features of vernacular poetry are doubly artistic, since they are produced by two sets of rules. The first set is that worked out by an early vernacular poet who invented the feature in response to some accidental necessity of his situation. The second set is that worked out by a later poet as a deliberate strategy for incorporating existing features of the vernac-

certain kind of inspiration (*Purgatory* 24.52–62); but in general the term applies to those poets who, according to Dante's principles of construction, rendered their poetry as artistically complex as was possible.

ular into the classical system of rules. Early poets wrote in the vernacular because they had to: the noble ladies they addressed and attempted to persuade could not read Latin. The consequence was, as Dante says in *The New Life* (chapter 25), that love has priority among the subjects of vernacular poetry. So when Dante wished to write philosophic poetry, for which there was Latin but not vernacular precedent, he found (as he says in *Banquet* 2.12) that he could use a feature of the vernacular, the noble lady who was the object of the poet's praise and devotion, as a figure for Philosophy itself. And finally, in the *Divine Comedy*, he could give an even nobler lady the function of a goddess in the classical epic, praise her in the terms of the vernacular tradition, and have her understood in the terms of the highest genre of classical poetry. By the time of the *Comedy*, Dante had abandoned his constraints against the writing of discursive philosophy in the vernacular; but he did not abandon thereby the principle of incorporation which insured the recognition that his art was rooted in both the vernacular and the classic tradition.

The *Comedy*, furthermore, gets both its title and its generic classification by the same strategy of incorporation. A comedy, according to Latin rules, is written in the low style, and has a plot which begins with adversity and ends with prosperity. The vernacular is, by definition, colloquial, and it is regularly used by the unlearned, even by women; it therefore fits all the criteria of classical low-style diction. There is no greater adversity than Hell, and no greater prosperity than Heaven; a journey from Hell to Heaven, therefore, is the comic plot par excellence. This justification of his title, which appears in the *Letter to Can Grande*, is of course both disingenuous and over-ingenious. It was most certainly a gesture of modesty, for Dante was quite aware, as is every reader, that the real classical precedent for his work is the epic, not the comedy.[30]

But it should not be dismissed as a gesture of modesty alone. For one thing, considering comedy a mode rather than a form, Dante's generic attribution is clearly correct, and his attempt to show that the rules of the form do, in some degree, also apply emphasizes his

---

30. See Boccaccio's remarks on the inappropriateness of the term "comedy" in his *Life of Dante* (translated in Brandeis, *Discussions* [above, n. 23], pp. 2–3).

modal correctness. For another thing, the attribution serves a real cultural purpose. It is clearly preferable to fulfill perfectly the specifications of one set of rules, those for comedy, than to depart in some ways from another and more ambitious set, those for epic, and thus produce a poem which appears defective. Dante's practice in this regard, his claiming to follow the rules of one genre (comedy) while in part emulating another (epic), suggests that he believed that rule-following and imitation were two distinct ways of deriving vernacular works from the classical tradition. His claims never caused anyone to regard his poem as an imitation of Terence or Plautus, but they also never allowed a critic to find the poem deficient in Virgilian tragic grandeur. Vernacular works which attempt to follow all the original rules of the classical poems they imitate have not usually been regarded as either decent copies or respectable realizations of the rules. Vernacular culture, therefore, is better served by the sort of ingenuity which lets it develop in its own way than by the wooden application of the classical rules.

A work of the magnitude of the *Comedy* renders the question of rules versus imitation irrelevant, and, indeed, renders much of Dante's earlier critical speculation obsolete. The completion of that poem made it no longer necessary to prove that vernacular works could be artistic. Indeed, the rules in his early criticism do not account very fully for the *Comedy*'s technique, form, or subject matter. Yet, given the example of the earlier rules, and following the same principles, rules could easily be devised to fit the practice of the *Comedy*. *Terza rima*, for instance, uses only that line of eleven syllables considered by Dante the most excellent in Italian; it makes rhyme, instead of meter, the basis for continuous poetic discourse comparable to Latin hexameters; and it makes rhyme, as in shorter poems, the means of joining together the units of the poem. And love, virtue, and, to a lesser extent, arms, are, in a most basic way, still the subjects of the *Comedy* as they had been the subjects of *canzoni*, even if their scope has been extended in this poem to subsume all of the possible activities of the human soul. The purpose of Dante's earlier rules was to demonstrate that there were already works of art in the vernacular, not to prevent the writing of works in the future which might follow different rules. He wished to establish for vernacular culture the principle that its works must follow rules which were systematic, suited to the medium, and capable of producing effects which could not be obtained without them. This principle, for certain, was put into practice in the composition of the *Comedy*.

THE MEANING AND THE JUSTIFICATION OF POETRY

If the technical arts of poetry must be rigorous and universal in their application, so, too, must the strategies and devices which determine its meaning. From this point of view, a poem may be defined as a meaning made into a unity ("sentential ad unam"), with the further specification that this meaning will be a proposition whose truth and validity could have been established apart from the poem itself. Poetry teaches, and it teaches nothing which contradicts the rational conclusions of other sciences, including ethics, physics, or theology. It follows that the meaning of each part or division will contribute to this single meaning, and be necessary to it. If the poem uses the methods of rhetoric or dialectic, it must also conform to the rules of those disciplines, rules which, for instance, designate the parts of an argument and its ordering, or specify legitimate and illegitimate appeals. When the subject of an argument is that of a particular science, then the methods of that science will be employed in the argument. Similarly, if a poem uses the methods peculiar to poetry, its meaning must still be independently valid. Dante strikes from the company of poets those who use figures whose meaning they could not paraphrase in completely unpoetic language. When a poem is allegorical, and therefore has more than one level of meaning, it must be capable of a systematic explication, beginning with the establishment of its literal or historical meaning, and proceeding by degrees to the meanings of its other levels. A poem, in other words, is rationally ordered to allow, or indeed require, the discovery of a meaning which will then be applicable to practical behavior.

Thus the reader's interest in the speaker of a poem, whose character constitutes its ethical argument, will be calculated to enhance the meaning of the whole. The speaker and usually the principal character in all of Dante's works is Dante himself, but not because he believed in the legitimacy and authority of private experiences and feelings as the motive for poetic expression. Rather he wrote in the first person to make his speaker and protagonist the unquestioned authority for ethical distinctions which confirmed and supported the central purposes of his poems. Dante's explanation of the identity of the "noble lady" of *The New Life* not only removes from himself the shame of an improper love but also sets out the attractions of philosophic study. Cacciaguida's charge to Dante, that he must write without sparing those great men who might be offended to read of their sins, not only removes from Dante the attribution of envy and presumption, or cowardice, but also establishes the prophetic and moral function of the examples of famous men. These exculpations, then, are strategic, and point to strategies beyond themselves. In other cases, personal references serve as particularizations of the general human condition. In the proem to *Paradise*, Dante promises to recount, to the best of his ability, his vision of blessedness, and hopes by this promise, as he says in the *Letter to Can Grande*, to excite admiration and enforce attention. But he claims further that the effectiveness of the proem is dependent upon the fact that his capacity is limited in no singular or subjective way but only by the limitations inherent in the general capacities of human intelligence and speech; hence his vision is available to his readers as well.

In this same letter, as earlier in *The New Life*, Dante adheres to the principle that the meaning of a whole work is nothing other than the sum of the meanings of its parts. These parts, or "divisions," are determined by two considerations of form which Dante calls the "form of the treatise" and the "form of the treatment." The first of these forms fits the external divisions to the nature of the subject matter and art of a poem, so that the *Comedy*, for instance, is divided into canticles, in turn into cantos, and then into rhymed units, corresponding in the first instance with the three worlds visited in the vision and in the second and third to the elements of art which allow for proportion and continuity. The form of the treatment makes ever more minute divisions based upon changes in rhetorical strategy. Each new form of address, figure of speech, method of proof, scene, or event is in itself purposive and subsumes,

contributes to, or augments the effects of smaller, larger, and col-
lateral divisions. The ordering of these strategic divisions is determined not so much by the subject matter or by the rules of art as
by the nature of the human soul, which is the instrument of the
discovery of meaning. It is a requirement of human intelligence,
for instance, that the direction, interest, and usefulness of a discourse
be specified in advance, and thus a proem will always precede an
executive part. It is characteristic of men to prefer what is positive
and favorable, so a poet will dwell on these things and pass quickly
over their opposites, and even may be so dishonest as to promise
in his proem to deal with his pleasing matter first, but actually put
it last when disposing the executive part so as to end his argument
most effectively. A little lie, Dante implies in *Banquet* 4.2, may be
countenanced if it helps secure assent to the truth.

Figures of comparison, like structural divisions, will be effective
to the extent that they conform to the operations of human intelligence and feeling. Things dissimilar in themselves may be shown
to resemble each other as objects of human thought and feeling, and
thus their places in a purposive universe be made clear in their
relations to a purposive intelligence. Ladies and disciplines, for
instance, may both be pursued; they may both attract a man with
the promise of granting happiness; they may both at times put
difficulties in the way of their pursuers; but they will both reward a
persistent effort by granting knowledge of the inner sources of their
attractive appearances. A noble lady is thus an appropriate figure
for the noble discipline of philosophy, and, through the comparison,
the purposes of human love may be manifested. God and the sun
belong to the dissimilar categories of intelligible and sensible objects
respectively; but a being which has both intellect and sense, namely
man, will understand the operation of the intelligible world on the
analogy of the sensible, thus fulfilling the intentions of the Creator
of both worlds. A friend is a human being, while a language is the
product of a human competence. But human products share in the
purposiveness of human beings, so that the relationship of a man
with his language may be described as friendship; they may work
together for goods, such as stability and honor, which will be of
mutual benefit. Dante's explanations of such poetic figures seem at

times farfetched, but they all manifest his desire for rigor and his belief in the unitive efficacy of poetic figures. Whereas the scientific disciplines are most precise when they treat different categories of things by different methods, poetic figures, insofar as they accurately reflect the operations of human thought and feeling, bring to light the purposive unity of all things.

Poetic allegory complements poetic figures in this respect by making possible the discovery of the interconnections between the findings of various independent disciplines. An historical or fictive narrative, which is the literal level of a poem, is true or plausible to the extent that the details of its plot or circumstances correspond to acknowledged fact or to acknowledged psychological principles. As a particular configuration of human possibility, it cannot make the claim that the choices manifested within it will have the same value or the same consequences in other circumstances. A narrative may be plausible, but not meaningful in a general way. On the other hand, there are disciplines which claim universal validity apart from circumstances by showing that their conclusions are inferences in a chain of reasoning which starts from fixed and true premises (and also in some instances, by allowing these conclusions to be tested under rigorously controlled circumstances). These disciplines include physics, metaphysics, and ethics, which in varying degrees allow of empirical confirmation, and theology, which, on the one hand, is self-confirming in the acts of faith and church discipline, and, on the other hand, awaits its confirmation at the end of time. An allegorical poem claims to confirm an ethical principle by demonstrating its dependence upon a metaphysical or theological truth; it claims to do so not by inferring the one from the other in a chain of reasoning, but by embodying them both in the same chain of circumstances. In an allegorical poem, the details, besides being elements in a plausible configuration, will be meaningful in themselves. Consequently, the whole poem will be both a convincing representation of a possible human action and a figurative manifestation of conceptual truths.

In practice, the interpretation of an allegorical poem begins with the identification of some person or thing in the poem with a doctrinal or ethical concept. This identification may be arbitrary insofar as it need not be required either for the plausibility of the narrative or by the independent nature of the thing, but it will turn out not to have been arbitrary insofar as it allows the narrative itself to be drawn into a conceptual scheme which makes sense of its other details as well. This practice is illustrated by two examples from the *Banquet*, Book Two. In scriptural exegesis, the identification of Egypt with the unredeemed state of the sinful soul in the world has nothing to do with the political or geographical conditions of that country, nor does it explain why a tribe of people would wish to escape from bondage there, such a wish being always plausible. This identification having been made, however, the Exodus in all its details will conform to the doctrine of the redemption through Christ, to the ethical concept of release from the bondage of sin, and to the eschatological settlement of souls in their promised land. In poetic exegesis, the identification of Orpheus's music with the eloquence of the wise man gives an ethical plausibility to a narrative whose surface motives are those of myth; it encourages the elaboration of the effects of one art, rhetoric, in terms suggested by the hyperbolic effects of another, music; and it thus justifies the poetic fiction itself by showing its capacity for exemplifying an underlying conceptual truth.

In neither of these cases, it should be noted—that of Egypt considered as the state of bondage to sin or that of Orpheus considered as the manifestation of wise eloquence—is the allegorical meaning a simple generalization of the elements in the narrative which has been turned into a lesson to be applied in similar circumstances. The tradition of allegorical interpretation extending from Saint Paul through Saint Augustine to Dante would call such generalization a carnal reading, in contrast to a spiritual reading. The flesh is bound to its own desires in apprehending things of the world and the literal level of a text; it assumes that the uses and pleasures of things are exhausted in the causal nexus of the world. The spirit, on the other hand, is free to apprehend the deeper intentions in things and in texts. It can view its own life, no matter what its particular outward circumstances, as a journey from Egypt to the Promised Land and interpret the events of the journey in the terms provided by Scripture; it can see in the myth of Orpheus not just a pathetic fable but a live scheme of spiritual operation manifested whenever a wise man speaks well. This freedom of the spirit, not to read into a text anything which pleases it but to find intentions which transcend worldly causality, is elicited by the allegorical poet on a level just slightly below that of Scripture itself.

In the *Banquet*, Dante distinguishes the allegory of the poets from the allegory of the theologians, recognizing that it makes some difference in the interpretation of a text that poets wrote acknowledged fictions to fit the underlying concept, while the writers of Scripture wrote history which came only later to embody a concept. In the *Letter to Can Grande*, he does not refer to this distinction and, in his explanation of the allegorical technique, he uses scriptural examples exclusively. It does not follow, however, that he employed the allegory of the theologians in the *Comedy*.[31] In the *Banquet*, he derives from scriptural texts meanings which are not specifically doctrines of the faith: Christ's taking two disciples to the Transfiguration illustrates the principle that in important matters, we should have few companions. By the same token, a poetic text could be written so as to embody doctrines of the faith, as was the case with Lucan, according to Book Four of *The Banquet*, when he described the return of Marcia to Cato. The two sorts of allegory differ, not in the kinds of meaning they convey, but in the historical truth of the letter. And the *Comedy*, for the purposes of this distinction, is clearly a fiction. In both the *Banquet* and the *Letter to Can Grande*, Dante distinguishes three levels of allegorical meaning, the one dealing with doctrine, the second with morals, and the third, or anagogical, with the mysteries of the end of time, such as the Last Judgment and the final disposition of souls. To conclude, however, that the story contained in the *Comedy* is anagogical because it

31. Whether Dante intended the *Comedy* to be understood as representing the allegory of the poets as against the allegory of the theologians has been the subject of much recent dispute. Charles Singleton's assertion in his chapter on "Allegory" (*Dante Studies I: "Commedia": Elements of Structure* [Cambridge: Harvard University Press, 1954]), that Dante wrote the allegory of the theologians, was answered by R. H. Green, "Dante's 'Allegory of the Poets' and the Mediaeval Theory of Poetic Fiction," *Comparative Literature* 9 (1957): 118–28, and was followed by Professor Singleton's rejoinder. The dispute has been recently and intelligently summarized by Aleramo P. Lanopoppi, "La *Divina Commedia*: allegoria 'dei poeti' o allegoria 'dei teologi'?" *Dante Studies* 86 (1968): 17–39.

describes the state of souls after death is to confuse the surface fiction of the poem with the levels on which it can be interpreted. The journey through the three worlds of death is a fiction which makes plausible Dante's "meetings" with persons long dead (and some even fictive to begin with), and makes credible the prophetic content of some of the speeches. The anagogical meaning of this fiction, like any other, must be derived by the prescribed method of interpretation; it may be useful to note that Dante's medieval commentators found anagogical meaning in the *Comedy* far less often than they found moral and doctrinal meaning.

In observing so carefully these traditional distinctions, Dante avoided making any unusual claims for his own poetry. But in fact the very rigor of Dante's synthesis of traditional poetic theory caused certain themes to appear as particularly suited to the practice of this theory, and Dante developed these in an original way. The rigorous exposition of the theory made it clear that the discovery of meaning in poetry depended upon and required the simultaneous discovery of the purpose and nature of the human soul. Therefore Dante made the progress of these parallel discoveries one of his principal themes, as reflected in, for instance, the development of greater scope and depth in the meaning of his love for Beatrice. These discoveries were made possible by the process of giving poetic form to the medium of language. Language is common to all men, and the means by which they communicate with each other. Poetry is the product of calculation and therefore a manifestation of the purposiveness which all men share; and the calculations of poetry were intended for the advancement of the purpose of language. The discoveries made possible by poetry, therefore, were not just personal, but also universal. To discover one's own spiritual nature is to be regenerated, but this regeneration is potentially universal. The theme of a new age, therefore, may be expressed with particular aptness according to the method prescribed by traditional poetic theory. When this method has been fitted to the particular language and poetry of Italy, the new age will be given a local habitation and a name. Dante's poetic themes of individual spiritual discovery and of European political regeneration, in other words, were almost required by his poetic theory.

In this sense, Dante's criticism is most useful as a gloss on his own poetry: it explains his intentions, and even accounts for his survival as a great poet of the Western world despite his failure as a political prophet. If poetry could not bring in a new Empire, it could hold up the ideal of regeneration itself, and embody this ideal in a new culture suitable for that Empire. In another sense, of course, the usefulness of Dante's criticism extends much beyond his own poetry, or even the poetry of Italy. The desire for a vernacular humanism was not confined to fourteenth-century Italy, but rather determined the direction of poetic development in all the European countries from the thirteenth through the seventeenth centuries. Dante's criticism is full enough and early enough to be of use in varying degrees for the understanding of all stages of this development. In the earlier stages, poets and theorists were almost certain to use some aspects of Dante's theory, though all did not use the theory with equal rigor; in the fourteenth century, at least, most humanists conceived of the problem of vernacular art essentially as Dante did. In the later stages, when poets had before them examples in the vernacular of attempts to imitate and equal the ancients, they might reject earlier theories, like Dante's, at least in part, and seek new rules of art by means of which they could improve upon their vernacular predecessors. But even if such were the case, their aims would still be those expressed in Dante's works. When the virtual founder of an art is also its most excellent practitioner, the principles of his art cannot be dismissed until they are surpassed in practice, or until the art itself is put to new uses. Dante's criticism is perhaps not so great in its kind as is his poetry, but it still explains in large part the nature of the art which can produce poetic greatness.

A Note on the Translation

I have used the following texts as the basis for my translations; any departure from them have been indicated in the notes.

Vita Nuova. Ed. M. Barbi, in *Le Opere di Dante: Testo Critico della Società Dantesca Italiana.* Florence: R. Bemporad and figlio, 1921.
De Vulgari Eloquentia. Ed. Aristide Marigo. 3rd ed. Florence: Felice le Monnier, 1957.

Convivio. Ed. G. Busnelli and G. Vandelli. Florence: Felice le Monnier. Vol. 1, 2nd ed., 1957; vol. 2, 1937.

La Divina Commedia. Ed. C. Grandgent. Rev. ed. Boston: D. C. Heath, 1933.

Epistola ad Canem Grandem. In *Dantis Alagherii Epistolae*, ed. Paget Toynbee. 2nd ed. Oxford: Clarendon Press, 1966.

Ecloga. In *La corrispondenza poetica di Dante Alighieri e Giovanni del Virgilio*, ed. E. Bolisani and M. Valgimigli. Florence: L. S. Olschki, 1963.

I have consulted, and found most useful, the translation of Dante's *Convivio* by W. W. Jackson (Oxford: Clarendon Press, 1909), of Dante's letters by Paget Toynbee in the edition cited, of the *De Vulgari Eloquentia* by A. G. Ferrers Howell (Temple Classics: London, 1904), of the *Commedia* by Dorothy Sayers (Penguin Books, 1949–1962), and of the *Vita Nuova* by William Anderson (Penguin Books, 1958).

My effort has been to produce a readable text which is also accurate in all technical matters of literary criticism. My translation is therefore rather free except in the case of the technical vocabulary of literary criticism. I have tried to translate each appearance of a technical word with the same English word, even at the expense of the smoothness of the English. The Glossary at the back of the book defines the technical terms and refers the reader to the passages, if any, where Dante himself has explained them. Where there is no English equivalent of a word which would not be misleading to a reader of English I have left the word in its original Latin or Italian. Brackets are used to supply words necessary to the sense but not directly in the original.

Explanatory notes have been kept to a minimum. I have filled out Dante's explicit references to other works, but have not indicated the sources of his ideas or phrasings where he does not tell them. Dante's ideas of construction, prosody, and form are illustrated in the *canzoni* quoted and translated in Appendix A, and certain texts which are the subjects of Dante's commentary have been translated at the appropriate place in the book. Appendix B contains an index of the poets and works cited by Dante, giving, wherever possible, the bibliographic information about any translations into English.

The headings and sections of this translation are numbered as they are in the principal editions consulted. This numbering in turn is based on the authority of the manuscripts or earliest editions. Numbers of books and chapters are found in the headings of the treatise *On Eloquence* and at the end of shorter passages from other works. Numbers of sections within chapters are bracketed. In all cases, the numbering of this translation follows the standard practice of Dante scholarship, and may be used for cross-reference to the original editions or in citing Dante's works.

ROBERT S. HALLER

University of Nebraska–Lincoln

Selected Bibliography

The list of books and articles below is limited to works in English. For a fuller listing, and for works in other languages, see Umberto Cosmo, *A Handbook to Dante Studies*, trans. David Moore (Oxford: Clarendon Press, 1950), and consult the annual bibliographies in *PMLA*, *Dante Studies*, *Studi Danteschi*, and *Deutsches Dante Jahrbuch*.

AUERBACH, ERICH. "Figura," in his *Scenes from the Drama of European Literature*. Trans. R. Manheim. New York: Meridian Books, 1959.

————. "The Western Public and Its Language," in his *Literary Language and Its Public in Late Latin Antiquity and in the Middle Ages*. Trans. R. Manheim. New York: Random House, Pantheon Books, Bollingen Series no. 74, 1965.

COLISH, MARCIA. "Dante: Poet of Rectitude," in her *The Mirror of Language: A Study in the Mediaeval Theory of Knowledge*. New Haven: Yale University Press, 1968.

CREMONA, J. "Dante's Views on Language." In U. Limentani, ed., *The Mind of Dante*. Cambridge: At the University Press, 1965.

DAMON, P. "The Two Modes of Allegory in the *Convivio*." *Philological Quarterly* 40 (1961): 144–49.

EWERT, A. "Dante's Theory of Diction." *Annual Bulletin of the Modern Humanities Research Association* 31 (1959): 15–30.

FOSTER, K., and P. BOYDE. "Introduction" and "Note on Dante's Metric and Versification" in *Dante's Lyric Poetry*, vol. 1. Oxford: Clarendon Press, 1967.

GRAYSON, CECIL. "'Nobilior est vulgaris': Latin and Vernacular in Dante's Thought." In *Centenary Essays on Dante by Members of the Oxford Dante Society*. Oxford: Clarendon Press, 1965.

GREEN, RICHARD H. "Dante's 'Allegory of the Poets' and the Mediaeval Theory of Poetic Fiction." *Comparative Literature* 9 (1957): 118–28.

MAZZEO, JOSEPH. *Structure and Thought in the "Paradiso."* Ithaca: Cornell University Press, 1958.

SINGLETON, CHARLES. *Dante Studies I: "Commedia": Elements of Structure*. Cambridge: Harvard University Press, 1954.

————. *An Essay on the "Vita Nuova."* Cambridge: Harvard University Press, 1958.

DICTION AND PROSODY

On Eloquence in the Vernacular

(De Vulgari Eloquentia—Latin)

BOOK 1

CHAPTER 1

[1] Since I find that no one, before me, has treated systematically the doctrines of eloquence in the vernacular, and since I see that such eloquence is unquestionably needed by almost everyone, for not only men, but even women and children (to the extent that nature allows) strive for it, I shall try, with the inspiration from heaven of the Word, to enhance the speech of vernacular speakers, wishing in some manner to enlighten the discernment of those who, like the blind, roam the streets thinking for the most part that what is really behind is in front; and not only drawing upon the waters of my own natural talent to fill this large vessel, but mixing in the best of what I can extract or compile from others, in order to offer for drinking a most sweet honey-water.

[2] But because it is required of any field of study not that it prove, but that it delineate its subject so that what it is concerned with may be known, I say (quickly coming to the point) that what I call "vernacular speech" is that which babies become accustomed to from those around them when they first begin to articulate speech; or, as it could be put more succinctly, I would claim as vernacular speech that which we learn without any rules in imitating our nurse.

[3] We can also acquire another speech which is dependent on this one called by the Romans "grammar." The Greeks and other peoples, but not all peoples, have this sort of secondary speech; and furthermore, very few people attain fluency in this speech because we do not adapt ourselves to its rules and teachings without concentrated attention over a long period of time.

3

[4] Of these two [kinds of speech], then, the vernacular is the nobler; both because it is enjoyed by the whole world (though it has been divided into [languages with] differing words and paradigms), and because it is natural to us, while the other is more an artificial product.

And my purpose is to treat systematically this more noble kind of speech.

CHAPTER 2

[1] This is, in our case, the true original speech. But I do not say "in our case" meaning thereby that there are other than human languages, for man alone among all existing things was given the capacity for speech, since he alone needed it. [2] Neither angels nor lower animals have any need for speech; rather, to have given speech to them would have been a purposeless act, and, as we know, nature refuses to act purposelessly.

[3] Indeed, if we consider carefully what it is we intend when we speak, it becomes clear that we intend nothing other than to express to others the thoughts in our minds. Therefore, since angels have a most immediate and ineffable capacity of the intellect for the purpose of setting forth their glorious thoughts, by means of which each one makes himself known to the others either within himself, or in that most brilliant mirror in which all things are most beautifully reflected and most eagerly contemplated, they would seem not to require any outward sign in speech. [4] And if the case of the spirits who fell be put forth as an objection, it can be answered in two ways: first, since I am writing about those things which are necessary to perfect being, I ought to ignore those who perversely refused to wait for divine care; or, a second and better answer, these demons, to make known among themselves their treachery, needed only to know, each about the other, his existence and his capacity [for evil]; and this they must have known in some way, because they identified each other before their fall.

[5] And it would not have been right for lower animals to be provided with speech, since they are led by natural instinct alone. For all [animals] of the same species are the same in their actions and passions, and thus can know others by themselves; while

between those of different species, not only is speech not necessary, it would have been absolutely reprehensible, since there could have been no friendly interchange in it.

[6] And if it be objected that the serpent who spoke to the first woman and Balaam's ass both had the capacity for speech,[1] I would reply to this that an angel in the one case, a devil in the other, operated in such a way that the animals themselves moved their organs, so that an articulate voice would result resembling true speech, and not that the ass did anything else but bray, nor the serpent but hiss. [7] And if it should be argued to the contrary what Ovid says in the fifth book of the *Metamorphoses*[2] about the speaking magpies, I would reply that this is said figuratively, meaning something else. And if it is said that even in the present magpies and other birds speak, I would reply that this is false, because these acts are not speech, but rather a certain imitation of the sound of our voices; which is to say that they succeed in imitating us insofar as we make sounds, not insofar as we speak. Thus if someone enunciates distinctly "magpie" to one of them, and he answers "magpie," this would be nothing but a reproduction or imitation of the sound made by the person enunciating.

[8] And thus it is evident that only to man was speech given. Now I shall try to explain briefly why he should need this capacity.

CHAPTER 3

[1] Now, since man is moved, not by natural instinct, but by reason, and since reason itself may vary with each individual and on the levels of discernment, or judgment, or will, so that it would seem that almost everyone takes pleasure in being a species to himself, I am of the opinion that no man understands another by his own actions and passions, as does a brute animal. Nor does it happen that, like an angel, one man enters into another by spiritual reflection, since the human spirit is impeded by the grossness and opacity of its mortal body. [2] Thus, human beings, for the communicating of their thoughts among each other, required some sign which was both

1. Genesis 3:1–5; Numbers 22:28–30.
2. Lines 294 ff.

rational and sensible. For, since the sign's function is to carry something from the reason and bring it to the reason, it had to be rational; and since nothing can be transferred from one reason to another except through a sensible medium, it had to be sensible. If it had been only rational, it could not have been transported; if it had been only sensible, it could not have either carried something from the reason, or brought something to the reason.

[3] And thus this sign is itself that noble subject of which I shall speak; for it is something sensible insofar as it is sound, but something rational insofar as it means something at the pleasure of a speaker.

CHAPTER 4

[1] As should be evident from the reasons given, to man alone was it granted that he might speak. Now I think it should be established who gave speech to the first man; what was the first thing said, and to whom, and where, and when; and also in what language the first speech flowed out.

[2] To be sure, according to what Genesis says in the beginning, where the most holy Scriptures treat of the origin of the world, a woman, that is, the most presumptuous Eve, is found to have spoken before all others, when to the devil's question she responded: "Of the fruit of the trees that are in Paradise we do eat; but of the fruit of the tree which is in the midst of Paradise, God hath commanded us that we should not eat; and that we should not touch it, lest perhaps we die." [3] [3] But although in Scripture woman is found to have spoken first, it is nevertheless more reasonable for us to believe that man spoke first; for it is against what is fitting to think that such a noble act of the human race did not flow from the lips of man before woman. It is in accord with reason, therefore, for us to believe that Adam himself was first granted speech by him who had just formed him.

[4] But I do not hesitate to affirm what occurs immediately to any man in his right mind, that what the voice of the first speaker first sounded was the word for "God," which is to say "El," either in the

3. Genesis 3:2–3.

form of a question, or in the form of a response. It would seem absurd and repugnant to reason for man to have said the name of anything else before that of God, since man had been created by him and in him. For just as after the transgression of the human race, anyone's first venture in speech is a cry of woe, it is reasonable that whoever existed before this transgression would have started out in joy. And since outside of God there is no joy, since all joy is with God, and since God himself is all joy, it follows that the first speaker said first and before anything else, "God."

[5] What I said above, that man's first speech was in the form of a response, would seem here to raise the question of whether this response was to God. For if it had been to God, then it would seem that God had spoken first, which would appear to contradict what I touched on above. [6] To this I can answer that he could very well have responded to God's asking without God's thereby having spoken what I would call speech. For who has any doubt that whatever exists is able to move at the will of God by whom surely all things were made, preserved, and, as well, governed? Then since the air is moved to such great alterations at the command of inferior nature, which is God's minister and creature, as when it makes the thunder roar, the lightning flash, the waters shake, the snow fall, or the hailstones lacerate, could it not at the command of God be moved to make the sounds of certain words rendered distinguishable by Him who made distinct greater things? And why not?

I believe this is enough to clear up this and certain other doubts.

CHAPTER 5

[1] Since it is my opinion, then (for reasons based upon the nature of higher as well as of lower things), that the first man directed his speech on the first occasion to God himself, I may say with reason that this first speaker was no sooner breathed into by the animating Power than he spoke without delay. For I believe it more in the nature of man to make himself felt rather than to receive sensations, insofar as he does either in accord with his nature. If therefore he who is the Creator and Beginning of perfection and the Lover filled

our progenitor by breathing on him with all perfections, it would appear to me reasonable that the most noble animal would no sooner have begun to receive sensations than to make himself felt.

[2] To anyone who would speak to the contrary, objecting that the first man had no need to speak, because up to this point he was the only man in existence, and because God discerns all our secrets without words even before we do, I would reply (with that reverence which I ought to use when making any judgment about the eternal Will) that, granting that God knew, or rather foreknew (which is the same thing in God's case) without there being any speech the thoughts of the first speaker, he still wished as well that man should speak, so that he who had given so generously this capacity could glory in the orderly display of so great a gift. And thus it is that the joy which we feel in the actualizing of our capacities to the ends for which they were ordained must be considered of divine origin in us.

[3] And from what has been said we can clearly derive that place in which the first speech was emitted; for I have given evidence to show that the location of the first speech was outside Paradise if man was breathed into outside Paradise, but within Paradise if within.

CHAPTER 6

[1] Since human commerce is carried on in so many and such different languages that people in many instances cannot make themselves understood to others, with or without words, we must hunt down that language which a man would use had he neither mother nor nursing, had he gone through neither schoolboy stage nor adolescence.

[2] In this, as well as in many other cases, Petramala[4] is the most important city and the "home town" of the greater part of the children of Adam. For whoever is so beneath contempt in his reasoning as to believe the place of his birth to be the most delightful under the sun attributes this same preeminence as well to his own vernacular, that is, his mother tongue, against all others, and consequently believes that his own native language was the same as

4. Ironic, meaning literally any city of which one happens to be native. Petramala was a small town in the Apennines between Florence and Bologna.

Adam's. [3] I, on the other hand, have the world as my native land, as a fish has the sea; and although I drank of the Arno before I had teeth, and although I have loved Florence so much that I have suffered exile unjustly for my love, I support the shoulders of my judgment on reason rather than on sense impressions. And even if there exists no place in the world more in accord with my delight or with the repose of my senses than Florence, in reading over the volumes of the poets and of other writers in which the world is described totally and in its parts, and in considering within myself the situations of the various places in the world and their arrangement in relation to either pole and to the equator, I have decided and firmly believe that there are many regions as well as cities both more noble and more delightful than Tuscany and Florence where I was born and a citizen, and that there are many nations and peoples who use a language more delightful and more useful than the Latins.

[4] Returning, then, to my subject, I say that a certain form of speech was created by God along with the first soul (meaning by "form" the words for things, the constructions made from words, and the agreement of paradigms in the constructions). And this form would be used by all the tongues of those who speak had it not been dissipated by the sin of human presumption, as will be shown below.

[5] In this form of speech Adam spoke; in this form of speech all his posterity spoke up to the time of the building of the tower of Babel, which is interpreted, the tower of confusion; this form of speech was inherited by the sons of Heber, who are called Hebrews after him. [6] In them alone it remained after the confusion, so that our Redeemer, who was born out of them insofar as he was human, could enjoy the language, not of confusion, but of grace. [7] The Hebrew language, therefore, was that formed by the lips of the first speaker.

CHAPTER 7

[1] Oh! what feelings of shame it brings to repeat the ignominy of the human race! But since I can go no further without passing through it, I shall hasten through it, though a blush rise to my face and my spirit take flight. [2] You! our nature, always prone to sin;

you! an evildoer from the beginning and without respite: did it not suffice for your chastisement that, deprived of light by your first transgression, you were exiled from your delightful native land? Or was it not enough that whatever was yours to control perished in a cataclysm because of the universal lechery and irascibility of your whole society, one family excepted, and that for what you had committed the animals of both the sky and the earth suffered punishment? Surely this was enough. But, as the proverb says, "Not before the third time will you ride the horse," so you chose to approach in your misery the miserable horse.[5] [3] See, reader, how man, either forgetful or contemptuous of the earlier discipline, and averting his eyes from the stripes still remaining, stood up a third time for a beating, presuming with foolish pride.

[4] For incurable man, at the instigation of the giant Nimrod,[6] presumed in his heart that he could not only outdo nature, but even the creator of nature himself, who is God, through his own art; and he began the building of a tower in Sennear, which was afterwards called Babel, that is, "confusion," by means of which he hoped to ascend into the heavens, intending unperceived not just to reach a level equal to, but even above, his own creator. [5] But what limitless mercy there is in the rule of heaven! for what father would tolerate such an insult from his own son? Yet he rose up with the weapon of a father, not of an enemy, already inured to the giving of blows, and punished his rebelling son with a merciful, but still memorable, corrective.

[6] Almost the whole human race, indeed, had come together for this work of iniquity. Some were giving orders, some acting as architects, some forming the walls, some making them straight with levels, some laying on mortar with trowels, some quarrying stone, some transporting it on land, some on the sea, and various other groups were engaged in various other occupations, when they were

5. Apparently a reference to a mode of punishment in schools, involving a particularly brutal beating administered on horseback. This punishment was reserved for a third offense, the order of punishment being discipline, whipping, and beating, which Dante, in the next sentence, makes parallel to the Fall, the Deluge, and the Confusion of Tongues.

6. Compare here the account in Genesis 10:8–10 and 11:1–9; and in St. Augustine *City of God* 16.4.

struck with such confusion from heaven that, where all had been served in the work with one and the same language, they, having been divided among many languages, ceased their labors, and never again found themselves able to cooperate in a common medium of exchange. [7] For the same language remained only to those who worked together in the same action; that is, all the architects had one language, all those rolling the stones, one, all those preparing them, one; and so forth with each group of workers. And thus to the extent that there had been varieties of skills contributing to the labor, to that extent the human race was now divided into language groups; and to the extent that their skills were more noble, to that same extent their language was now more crude and barbaric. [8] But those to whom the sacred language remained were neither there nor approved of the labor; but hating it deeply, they mocked the folly of the laborers. And this group, a small minority in their numbers, were, as I conjecture, of the seed of Shem, who was Noah's third son, from whom, indeed, the people of Israel had their origin, who used the most ancient language up to the time of their dispersion.

CHAPTER 8

[1] It is for no slight reason that I am of the opinion that, following the confusion of languages recalled above, men were then, for the first time, dispersed throughout the climatic zones of the world,[7] both in the habitable regions of these zones, and in their outward reaches. And since the original root of the human progeny had been planted on Eastern shores, and from there our progeny had spread out in either direction by means of the multiple branching of shoots, finally extending to the borders of the West, it was probably then, for the first time, that rational mouths drank from the rivers of all Europe, or at least from some of them. [2] But whether they were natives making their way back at this time to Europe, or foreigners coming for the first time, they brought with them a language having three forms; and some of those bearing this language came to dwell in the southern part of Europe, others in the northern, while a third group, whom we now call Greeks, settled partly in Europe, partly in Asia.

7. The "no slight reason" for this statement is the authority of Genesis 11:9.

[3] Later on, different vernaculars branched off from one and the same language received at the time of the punishing confusion, as I will show below. [4] For in that whole territory from the mouth of the Danube, or rather from the marshes of Maeotis, to the western border of England, which is bounded by the borders of France and Italy and by the Ocean,[8] one language alone prevailed, although later it branched out into different vernaculars among the Slavs, the Hungarians, the Teutons, the Saxons, the English, and a large number of other peoples, with this alone remaining to all of them as a sign of their common origin, that almost every people named above answers, in the affirmative, *jo*. [5] Starting at the borders of this language-group, that is, at the border of Hungary, another [language] prevails in all that territory between it and the East which belongs to what is called Europe, and it extends even beyond this [into Asia].

[6] Then a third language-group took over all the territory of Europe which is left outside of these two, though it now seems to have three forms. For some of them say *oc* by way of affirmation, others *oïl* and others *si*, that is, the Spanish, the French, and the Latins. But the fact that the vernaculars of all three of these peoples were derived from one and the same language is quite clear, in that it can be noted that they name many things with the same word, such as "God," "heaven," "love," "the sea," "the earth," "to be," "to live," "to die," "to love," and almost all other things. [7] Of these three groups, those who speak in the language of *oc* occupy the western part of southern Europe, beginning at the border of Genoa. [8] At the same time, those who speak the language of *si* occupy the area east of this border, which is to say as far as the promontory of Italy which extends into the head of the Adriatic sea, and including Sicily. [9] And then those who speak the language of *oïl* are to be found more or less north of the other two. For they have the Germans to the east of them, and are surrounded on the north and west by the English or French seas, and bounded by the mountains of Aragon, while to the south they are closed in by the peoples of Provençe and by the curving slopes of the Pennine Alps.

---

8. Dante of course knew only one ocean, the Atlantic.

CHAPTER 9

[1] Now I must put to the test all the powers of reasoning I have, since I propose to investigate a subject in which authority can give me no support: the successive divisions of what was in the beginning one and the same language. And since the better known a route is, the more safely and more quickly it may be traveled, I shall proceed only along that language which is my own, leaving aside the others. For what is the cause in the one case should logically be so in the others as well.

[2] The language-group over which my treatise is making its way is, then, of three forms, as I said above; for some say *oc*, others *sì*, and still others *oïl*. And that it was one language at the beginning of the confusion (which has been demonstrated earlier) is apparent in the fact that we are in agreement about many words, as the experts in eloquence show, which agreement contrasts with that confusion which fell down from heaven during the building of Babel. [3] Thus, the experts in the three languages are in agreement on many words, and particularly on the word for "love." Take this poem by Girautz de Borneilh:

> Sim sentis fezelz amics,
> per ver encusera *amor* . . . .[9]

And this of the King of Navarre [Thibaut de Champagne]:

> De fin'*amor* si vient sen et bonté . . . .[10]

And this of the honorable Guido Guinizelli:

> Nè fe'*amor* prima che gentil core,
> nè gentil cor prima che *amor*, natura . . . .[11]

[4] But now let us investigate why it was differentiated primarily into three forms, and why each of these different forms are differentiated within themselves, as is true, for example, of the speech of the right side of Italy as against that of the left side, for the Paduans

9. "If a faithful friend were to hear me, / I would make an accusation against love."

10. "From fine love comes wisdom and goodness."

11. "Nature did not make love before the noble heart, / nor the noble heart before love."

speak one way, the Pisans another; and why those living even closer to each other still have dissimilarities in their speech, as is true of the Milanese and the Veronese, or of the Romans and the Florentines, not to speak of those who have a common national descent, such as the Neapolitans and the Gaetani, or the people of Ravenna and Faentine; or what is even more remarkable, those residing in the same city, like the Bolognese of the Borgo di San Felice as against the Bolognese of the Strada Maggiore. [5] Why all of these differences and variations in speech have occurred can be explained through one and the same cause.

[6] Now I take as a premise that no effect may exceed its cause, at least insofar as it is an effect, because nothing is able to produce as an effect that which it is not itself. Thus, since all of our dialects (with the exception of that one created by God along with the first man) were refashioned according to our pleasure after that confusion, which was nothing other than forgetfulness of the former language, and since man is the most unstable and variable animal, the language could not either endure or be uniform, but, like other of our characteristics, such as manners and fashions, it necessarily differs with the change of time or place. [7] Nor do I myself think I am wrong in saying "change of time": rather I think the phrase has strong justification. For if we look closely at our other activities, we would seem to be more at variance from our fellow-countrymen of very ancient times than from our contemporaries a great distance from us. Thus I would venture to say that if the most ancient Pavese were to come back now, they would speak to the modern Pavese in a different or variant language. [8] And what I assert does not seem to be more remarkable than our observing a young man grown up whom we had not seen growing; for the motion of a thing which moves very slowly is hardly noticed, and the longer the time it takes to notice a difference in a thing, the more stable we think that thing to be. [9] And for this reason it does not surprise me that men whose perceptions hardly differ from those of brute beasts think that in a single city the public interchange has always been carried on in an unchanging language, since differences in language (in the same city) occur slowly (and gradually) over a long period of time, and since the life of man itself is, by its very nature, extremely short.

[10] If, then, a language changes gradually over a long period of time, as has been said, among a single people, and since it can by no means remain stable, it follows of necessity that it will be changed in different ways among peoples living separately and some distance from each other, just as manners and fashions change in different ways, since they are not kept stable either by nature or by public agreement, but rather are born of the pleasure of man and of appropriateness to place.

[11] The inventors of the art of grammar were moved by this consideration, grammar being indeed nothing other than a certain uniformity of language which does not change in different times and places. Since its rules have been established by the common consent of many peoples, it would not seem to be subject to the will of any individual and consequently it cannot be changed. They invented it, then, out of a fear that, because of the change in language which issues from the will of individuals, we would be able to understand either not at all or at least imperfectly the authoritative ideas and histories of the ancients or of peoples whom the difference of place makes different from us.

CHAPTER 10

[1] In making comparisons within our language group among the three forms (described above) which have become three systems of sounds, I am apprehensive and hesitate to weigh them against each other, not daring in the comparison to give precedence to this, that, or the other division (unless I were to do so on the basis of finding that the compilers of grammar have taken *sic* to be the adverb of affirmation, which fact would seem to grant a certain priority to the Italians, who say *si*).

[2] But each division could defend its claims with abundant evidence. The language of *oïl* could maintain on its part that, because it is the vernacular language read with the most facility and most pleasure, whatever is translated or invented for the general public is its alone, such things as the Bible or the histories of the Trojans or Romans, or the most attractive wandering adventures of King Arthur, or any number of other historical and doctrinal works.

[3] But the partisans of the second, the language of *oc*, would argue that those with eloquence in the vernacular first wrote poetry in it as though in the more perfect and sweeter language, as for example Peire d'Alvernhe and the other older experts. [4] But then the third, that of the Latins, would claim preeminence on the basis of two prerogatives: that is, first of all, the fact that those who have written the most subtle and sweetest poetry in the vernacular are of its society and household, as, for example, Cino di Pistoia and his friend [Dante]; and secondly, because it would seem to be based more on grammar than on common speech, which, in looking at the matter rationally, appears the stronger argument.

[5] But leaving aside a decision on this question, and returning the treatise to the subject of the Latin vernacular, I shall try to describe what variants it has undergone in itself, as well as to contrast these variants with each other. [6] I say first of all that Latium is divided into two parts, left and right. If someone should ask what the line of division is, I would answer, in a word, the ridge of the Apennines, which, in the manner of a tile roof which lets the water run down this way and that in separate streams, releases its waters to one and the other side toward the shores through long gutters, as Lucan describes it in the second book of the *Pharsalia*; [12] and the right side drains in the Tyrrhenian Sea, while the left falls into the Adriatic. [7] The regions on the right are the following: Apulia (though not the whole of it), Rome, the Duchy [of Spoleto], Tuscany, and the March of Genoa; and those on the left: the rest of Apulia, the March of Ancona, Romagna, Lombardy, and the March of Treviso with Venetia. Friuli and Istria could belong only to the left side, while the Islands of the Tyrrhenian Sea, that is Sicily and Sardinia, could belong only on the right side of Italy, or at least are associated with the right side. [13] [8] Now in each of these two sides, and in the regions accounted to each, the languages of men are different, which is to say that the language of the Sicilians differs

12. Lines 396–413.

13. Dante's division of Italy into regions does not correspond exactly to the actual political divisions of Italy in his own time, or to the ancient Imperial regions, or to the present Italian provinces; his attempt is to make linguistic distinctions which correspond approximately to ethnic groups.

from that of the Apulians, that of the Apulians from that of the
Romans, that of the Romans from that of the Spoletans, theirs from
that of the Tuscans, that of the Tuscans from that of the Genoese,
that of the Genoese from that of the Sardinians, and, as well, that of
the Calabrians [14] from that of the people of Ancona, theirs from that
of the people of Romagna, that of the people of Romagna from that
of the Lombards, that of the Lombards from that of the Trevisians
and Venetians, theirs from that of the Aquileians, [15] and theirs from
that of the Istrians. On this matter I do not think any of the Latins
will disagree with me.

[9] From this it appears that Italy alone is divided into at least
fourteen vernaculars. And all of these vernaculars are further
divided within themselves, so that in Tuscany, for instance, the
language of the Sienese differs from that of the Arezzi, and in
Lombardy, that of Ferrara from that of Piacentia. And we may even
observe certain differences within a single city, as I remarked above
in the last chapter. And so if I were to add up the primary, secondary,
and subsidiary differences in the vernaculars of Italy, I would not
just approach a figure like one thousand different dialects in this,
the smallest corner of the world, but would even exceed this figure.

CHAPTER 11

[1] There being so many variants, discordant in sound, of the
Latian vernacular, let us track down the more suitable one, the
illustrious speech of Italy. And so as to have a clear path for our
tracking, let us first clear away from the grove the tangled shrubs
and the briars.

[2] And since the Romans think they have priority over all other
peoples, it is not without merit that I grant them priority in this
eradication or pruning by claiming that they should not even be
touched on in any rational consideration of eloquence in the
vernacular. For I assert that the Roman "vernacular"—or rather
foul speech—is the ugliest of all the vernaculars of Italy, which is no
surprise, since they appear also to stink, in comparison with all

14. "Calabrians," apparently, refers to the Apulians of the left side.
15. Aquileia is a major city in Friuli; the term here stands for that region.

others, in the deformity of their manners and fashions. They even say, "Messure, quinto dici?"[16]

[3] After them, let us rip out the inhabitants of the March of Ancona who say, "Chignamente scate, siate";[17] and along with them, I can throw out the Spoletans. And it is worth mentioning that a great many *canzoni* have been composed in scorn of these three peoples. I have seen one of these, tied together perfectly, and according to the rules of [poetic] art, which a certain Florentine named Castra composed. And it begins:

> Una fermana scopai da Cascioli,
> cita, cita sen gia 'n grande aina.[18]

[4] After them, let us tear out the people of Milan and Bergamo,[19] along with their neighbors, about whom I also remember a *canzone* written in contempt, which goes,

> Enter l'ora del vesper
> ciò fu del mes d'occhiover.[20]

[5] After them, let us eliminate the Aquileians and the Istrians, who belch out, "Ces fas tu?"[21] in a crude accent. [6] And along with them I would eject all the dialects of mountain and rural areas, such as those of Casentine and Fratta,[22] which always seem dissonant to city dwellers because of the ugly irregularity of the accents.

16. "Sir, what did you say?" As against what he would consider a proper expression ("Messere, come dici?"), Dante finds the expression here vulgar (addressing a titled person in the familiar second person singular), crude to pronounce (especially the *u* in *Messure*), and without justification in Latin grammar, since it is impossible to see how *quinto* could be derived from a Latin original.

17. Apparently, "However you are, may you remain so" ("come state, siatelo"), but the meaning is obscure: Dante objects, apparently, to its distance from Latin, and to its palatalization.

18. "I met a peasant-girl of Cascioli, / She ran away in a hurry." Nothing is known of the "Castra" to whom the poem is attributed.

19. Major cities in Lombardy; other cities in the region are treated in chapter 14.

20. "Toward the time of evening, / this happened in the month of October."

21. "What are you doing?" As against the more standard form ("Che fai tu?"), this form is over-sibilant.

22. Mountain and rural cities respectively (Fratta is modern-day Umbertide), the one in Tuscany, the other in the Duchy of Spoleto.

[7] And then let us eject the Sardinians, who are not Latians, though it appears they should be associated with the Latians, because they alone seem to be without their own vernacular, and rather imitate grammar, like apes imitating men, for they say such things as "dominus nova" and "domus novus." [23]

CHAPTER 12

[1] Having, in a manner of speaking, sifted out the chaff among the Italian vernaculars, let us now quickly select the one most honorable and honorific by making comparison among those which remain in the sieve.

[2] And first let us put the natural talent of the Sicilians to the test. For evidently the Sicilian vernacular claims for itself greater renown than any of the others, both because of the fact that whatever poetry has been written by Italians has been called Sicilian, and because of the fact that we find a great many of its native experts have written poetry in a grand manner, as, for example, in these *canzoni* [of Guido delle Colonne]:

> Anchor che l'aigua per lo foco lassi,[24]

and

> Amor che lungiamente m'ai menata.[25]

[3] But, if we carefully examine the direction of its significance, we discover that this renown of the Trinacrian land [26] has survived primarily as a reproach to the present princes of Italy, who devote themselves to pride in the plebian, not the heroic, manner. [4] In contrast, those illustrious heroes, the Emperor Frederick and

23. Dante assumes they try to speak Latin, but are totally ignorant of Latin case endings: they modify a masculine noun (*dominus*) with a feminine adjective (*nova*) and a feminine noun (*domus*) with a masculine adjective (*novus*). The expressions would mean "new lord" and "new house." There were, apparently, many places in Sardinia called "*domus novas*," an expression in perfect agreement in the Sardinian dialect, of which Dante was obviously ignorant. His phrases closely resemble the textbook definitions of solecism.

24. "Just as the water melted in the fire."

25. "Love, which long has led me."

26. Another name for Sicily, arising from its three promontories (from the Greek for "triangle").

Manfred,[27] a son well-born of him, were devoted to what is human, and disdained what is bestial, displaying, while fortune allowed, the nobility and uprightness of their souls. For this reason, those of noble heart and endowed with the gifts of divine grace strove to attach themselves to the majesty of these great princes, with the result that, in their time, every product of the efforts of the noblest Latin spirits first came to light in the throne room of these great sovereigns. And ·because Sicily was then the royal throne, it happened that whatever writings our predecessors published in the vernacular were called Sicilian; we still hold to this practice, and it is unlikely that our posterity will change it.

[5] Racha, racha.[28] What is the rallying cry sounded by the trumpet of the most recent Frederick, or by the bell of Charles the Second, or by the horn of those powerful Marquises, John and Azzo,[29] or by the cornets of other magnates, except, "Come, you murderers. You deceivers, come. Come, you who are devoted to avarice?"

[6] But to return to my subject, where I am less likely to speak in vain. Now if we would choose to consider as the Sicilian vernacular that which prevails among the native common people, for the speech coming from their lips should serve as the basis of our judgment, I would say that it is by no means worthy of the honor of being preferred because it cannot be spoken except in a drawl, as in this case:

Tragemi d'este focora, se t' este a boluntate.[30]

27. The Emperor Frederick I (1194–1250), was crowned in 1220 and deposed by the Pope in 1245. (On this passage, cf. *Banq.* 4.10.6 and *Inf.* 10.) Manfred, his successor, was an illegitimate son, who, Dante proceeds to claim, was legitimized ("well-born") by his being worthy, in character, of his father; cf. *Purg.* 3.103–45.

28. Matthew 5:22 is Dante's source for these words of contempt.

29. Frederick II of Sicily, king from 1296 to 1337, grandson of Manfred and son of Peter III of Aragon (cf. *Banq.* 4.6.182; *Purg.* 7.115–20; *Parad.* 19.130, 20.63); Charles II, king of Naples, d. 1309 (cf. *Purg.* 7.124–29); John I, Marquis of Monferrat, came to rule 1292, d. 1305; Azzo VIII, Marquis of Este, accused by Dante of parracide (*Inf.* 12.111) and murder (*Purg.* 5.77). (These passages are not to be found in this volume.)

30. "Pull me from this fire, if such is your will." The third line of a *contrasto*, "Rosa fresca aulentissima." The drawling of which he speaks would be produced by the ending of *focora* (which should be *foco* or *fochi*), by the verb *este*, used instead of *è*, and by the *boluntate*, which should be *voluntà*; he doubtless was also offended

But if we choose to consider it in the form in which it issues from the lips of Sicilians of the highest class, which can be observed in the two *canzoni* cited above, it differs in no way from the vernacular most worthy of praise, as I will show below.

[7] The Apulians also make use of the most appalling barbarisms, either because of their native harshness of speech, or because of their closeness to their neighbors, the Romans and the people of the March of Ancona. For they write such things as:

Volzera che chiangesse lo quatraro.[31]

[8] But although the native-born Apulians speak, as a rule, in the most disgusting manner, some of the more brilliant men among them express themselves with elegance, selecting for their *canzoni* more curial words, as is clearly apparent to those who look closely at their writings. Take, for example [this poem by Jacopo da Lentino, known as "Il Notario"]:

Madonna dire vi volglio,[32]

and [this by Rinaldo d'Aquino]:

Per fino amore vo si letamente.[33]

[9] And thus whoever considers what I have said above must realize that neither the Sicilian nor the Apulian is that vernacular which is the most beautiful in Italy, since I have shown that the natives who have eloquence depart from their own native vernacular.

CHAPTER 13

[1] Let us pass on from these peoples to the Tuscans who, infatuated in their madness, seem to want to claim for themselves the title of having the most illustrious vernacular. Not only does this

---

by the repetition of *este* (where he would think that the first *este* should be *questo*), and by the failure to balance words of different poetic value, a four-syllable word not being proper in a line with two three-syllable words, and the whole exceeding eleven syllables.

31. "I would like the boy to cry." Dante is offended by the letter *z* in *volzera*, where he would say *vorrei*; by the palatal *chi* in *chiangesse*, and by its departure from grammar (he would say *piangesse*, more closely related to the Latin *plangere*); and by the harshness and vulgarity of *quatraro*, a peasant word with no Latin equivalent.

32. "Lady, I wish to say to you."

33. "Because of fine love I go so joyfully."

pretension drive the common people mad; I have also known several famous men who have maintained it, such as Guittone d'Arezzo, who has never aimed at the curial vernacular, Buonagiunta of Lucca, Gallo of Pisa, Mino Mocati of Siena, and Brunetto of Florence, whose writings, if there were time to examine them closely, would be found to be not curial, but rather municipal. And since the Tuscans surpass all others in this drunken frenzy, it would be worthwhile and useful to deflate them somewhat by citing individual examples of Tuscan municipal vernaculars. [2] The Florentines both speak and write things like:

> Manchiamo introque / che noi non facciamo altro.34

The Pisans, things like,

> Bene andonno li fanti / de Fiorensa per Pisa.35

The people of Lucca, things like,

> Fo voto a dio, ke in grassarra
> eie lo comuno de Lucca.36

The Sienese, things like,

> Onche renegata avesse io Siena.
> Ch'ee chesto?37

34. "Let us eat right away / for we have nothing else to do." *Manchiamo* (as against *mangiamo*) and *introque* (as against *intanto*) are Florentine "municipal" words, crude departures from the sound of the true Italian vernacular, and from Latin. Dante, however, uses both words in the *Comedy* (*Inf.* 32.60 and 20.130—not in this volume) which, generically, allows for low-style words. Dante also objects to the vulgar inclusion of modality in the indicative form of *facciamo*; he would say "null'altro abbiamo da fare."

35. "Surely the soldiers of Florence are going through Pisa." Dante objects to the improper third-person plural ending of the verb (*andonno* should be *andarono*) and to the *s* in *Fiorensa*.

36. "I thank God that the commonwealth of Lucca is in abundance." Dante objects to the vulgar oath (where he would say *Giuradicco*), to the crude sound of *grassarra* (instead of *abbondanza*), and to the endings of *eie* and *comuno*, which should be *è* and *comune*.

37. "If I had only renounced Siena in good time! What is that?" (the last phrase, apparently, with the force of "What are you saying?"); Dante apparently objects to *onche*, *ee*, and *chesto* as departures from *anche*, *è*, and *questo*, and therefore departures from "grammar."

The Aretines, things like,

> Vuo' tu venire ovelle?[38]

(I have no intention of discussing the vernaculars of Perugia, Orvieto, Viterbo, not to speak of Città di Castella, because of their affinity with the Romans and the Spoletans.) [3] But although almost all Tuscans are inured to their foul speech, I know of several who recognize [what constitutes] excellence in the vernacular, such as Guido [Cavalcanti], Lapo [Gianni], and one other [Dante himself], all Florentines, and Cino, of Pistoia, whom I undeservedly put last on the list, though forced to do so for a good reason.[39] [4] Thus, if we look closely at the Tuscan dialects, and consider in what manner its most honored men depart from their own [vernacular], there will be no remaining doubts that the vernacular we are looking for is something other than the one which the Tuscan people employ.

[5] But if anyone thinks that what we have said about the Tuscans ought not to be said about the Genoese, let him bear this in mind, that if the Genoese should lose the letter *z* through forgetfulness, they would either become mutes or would have to discover a new dialect. For *z* is the greater part of their speech, and this letter cannot be enunciated without great harshness.

CHAPTER 14

[1] Now, crossing over the leafy shoulders of the Apennines, let us search in a leisurely fashion, the left side of Italy, proceeding as is the custom, toward the East.

[2] Entering, then, into Romagna, I say that I have found two vernaculars in Latium which differ from each other in having certain corresponding features in which they are exact opposites. One of them is so feminine, because of the soft sounds of its words

38. "Will you come somewhere?" To Dante *vuo'* (for *vuoi*) and *ovelle* (for *qualche luoga*) are vulgarisms. This passage, unlike the others cited, seems to be quoted from common speech and not from a song or poem.

39. His "good reason" may be the necessity of rhetorical balance: were he ranking the poets in order of excellence, he would have to interrupt his list of Florentine poets (putting Cino after Guido); or perhaps his reason is the inferiority of Pistoia, as a city, to Florence.

and pronunciations,[40] that it causes a man, even one with a manly voice, to be taken for a woman. [3] This [vernacular] prevails among the people of Romagna, and especially of Forlì, a city which, although very new,[41] would seem to be the center of the whole province. They use *deusci*[42] as an affirmative answer, and say, caressingly, *oclo meo* and *corada mea*.[43] But I have noted in listening that certain among them, such as the Faentines, Tomasso and Ugolino Buccioli, have departed from their own [vernacular] in the writing of poetry. [4] The other of these vernaculars I mentioned above is so shaggy and bristly in its words and accents that, because of its crude harshness, a woman speaking it does not just go beyond the bounds [of womanhood], but you, reader, might even suspect she was a man. [5] This [vernacular] prevails among all those who say *magara*,[44] which is to say, the Brescians, the Vernonese, and the Vicentines, not to speak of the Paduans, who syncopate the participles ending in -*tus* and the nouns ending in -*tas*, as in *mercò* and *bontè*.[45] To these I would add the Trevisans, who, after the fashion of the Brescians and their neighbors, say *f* for consonantial *u*, and cut the word short. They say, for example, *nof* for *nove* and *vif* for *vivo*,[46] a barbarism which I condemn.

40. The word Dante uses here (*prolatio*) I have elsewhere translated as "paradigm"; but, as Marigo (see above, p. xlv) points out in his edition, it seems to mean "pronunciation" in this case, just as the verb from which it is formed (*profero*) is usually used in this treatise to mean "to pronounce."

41. The meaning of *novissima* here is unclear. The city itself is very ancient, so Dante must be referring either to its recent release from French tyranny, or to its recent constitution. He may also mean that it is "the least" of cities.

42. This word seems to be an intensive form of *si*, which has become *sei*. Dante is offended at the "cute" amplification of the word, and by the extension of *s* to *sc* (*sk* in English).

43. For *occhio mio* ("my eye") and *cuor mio* ("my heart"), terms of endearment. Dante objects to the lilting cadence (it can be pronounced "caressingly"), as well as to the liquidization (and perhaps, unrepresented in the spelling, the palatization of *oclo* and the non-Latin ending of *corada* (from late Latin *coratum*).

44. An affirmative answer, indicating strong assent ("would it were so"), but, to Dante's taste, too rough. The cities mentioned belong to the region of Lombardy.

45. "Market" and "goodness." The proper forms (as Dante sees it) would be *mercato* and *bonità*, both closer to the Latin. He assumes that *mercato* is derived from the past participle of the verb.

46. "Nine" and "alive."

[6] The Venetians would not by any means think themselves worthy of the honor of being said to have that vernacular which we seek; but if someone among them, transfixed by error, should have delusions on this point, let him recall whether he has ever sung,

Per le plaghe de Dio, tu no verras.[47]

[7] Among all the Venetians I have heard only one who has made an effort to separate himself from his mother [tongue] and to strive for the curial vernacular, and that is Aldobrandino of Padua.

[8] And thus, all these [vernaculars] having presented their cases before the review board, I hand down the decision that neither the vernacular of Romagna nor that of what I have called its opposite, nor that of Venice, is the illustrious vernacular we are searching for.

CHAPTER 15

[1] And now let us attempt to investigate expeditiously that [vernacular] which still remains in the Italian woods.

[2] I say, then, that those who assert that the Bolognese speak the most beautiful of speeches hold an opinion which is by no means false; for the Bolognese have absorbed into their own vernacular certain elements from the vernaculars of Imola, Ferrara, and Modena, those cities which surround it, as, I conjecture, each city does from its neighbors. Sordello has demonstrated this with respect to his native Mantua, which borders on Cremona, Brescia, and Verona; for he, a man of great eloquence, not only in the writing of poetry, but also in any number of other forms, deserted the vernacular of his fatherland.[48] [3] And so the citizens [of Bologna] mentioned above have adapted the smoothness and softness of the citizens of Imola, and, as well, from the citizens of Ferrara and Modena, some of the gutturalness which is characteristic of Lombards, left over,

47. "By the wounds of God, you shall not come." Besides the bad taste of the oath, Dante objects to the irregularity of *de* (for *di*) and *no* (for *non*), and to the *l* in *plaghe* and *s* in *verras*, which, although closer to Latin than the more usual *piaghe* and *verrà*, make the sound too consonantial.

48. The point of the passage seems to be that, while Bologna absorbed a nicely balanced set of elements from its neighbors, Mantua got a set totally unsuited to each other, with the result that Sordello, if he was to write eloquently at all, had to write in a totally foreign language (in this case, Provençal).

I believe, from the mingling of the natives with the foreign Lango-bards. [4] And this is the reason we find no poets from Ferrara, Modena, or Reggio: they have become so accustomed to their own gutturalness that they can by no means approach the courtly vernacular without [retaining] a certain amount of harshness. And this explanation applies with even greater force to the people of Parma, who say such things as *monto* instead of *molto*.

[5] If then the Bolognese have adopted elements from either side, as I have said, it would be reasonable to expect that their speech, because of the combining of what I have called "opposites," [49] would be left tempered to an admirable sweetness; and, in my judgment, this is certainly the case. [6] And therefore I readily agree with those who place the Bolognese first among vernacular languages, considering them only in relation to the other municipal vernaculars of Italy. But if they, on the other hand, think that the vernacular of Bologna is to be preferred in an absolute sense, I disagree with them strongly. For it is certainly not the vernacular I would call "courtly" and "illustrious"; since, if it had been so, the poets of Bologna, such as the superlative Guido Guinizelli, or Guido Ghisilieri, or Fabruzzo, or Onesto, or the others, would never have departed from their own vernacular. And they were illustrious experts, filled with discernment in matters relating to vernaculars. The superlative Guido wrote:

Madonna, lo fino amor ch'a vui porto.[50]

Guido Ghisilieri has written:

Donna, lo fermo core.[51]

Fabruzzo has written:

Lo meo lontano gire.[52]

Onesto [degli Onesti] has written:

Più non actendo il tuo secorso, Amore.[53]

49. See above, 1.14.2.
50. "My Lady, the fine love which I bear for you."
51. "Lady, the constant heart."
52. "My distant travel."
53. "No longer do I expect your aid, Love."

These words are absolutely different from those of the inhabitants of the center of Bologna.[54]

[7] Since I do not think that anyone is uncertain about the remaining cities located at the edge of Italy (and whoever might be uncertain I would think unworthy of any resolution on my part), very little remains to be said in my discussion. [8] Wishing to empty my sieve so that I can immediately see what remains, I say that Trento, Torino, and, in addition, Allessandrio, lie so near the border of Italy that they could not have pure dialects, so near, in fact, that even if they, who have the most disgusting vernaculars, had the most beautiful, I would deny that they were truly Italian because of their mixture with other [languages]. And so, if we are tracking down the illustrious Italian [vernacular], what we are tracking cannot be found among them.

CHAPTER 16

[1] Since we have hunted through the rugged mountains and green pastures of Italy without finding the panther we have been trailing, let us track it down in a more rational manner, so that we can discover it, and with skillful diligence bring wholly within our trap her who leaves her perfume everywhere yet appears nowhere.

[2] Taking up the weapons of the hunt again, then, I say that in all categories of things there must be one thing to which everything in the category is related and by which everything is weighed, from which we take the measure of all the others. Thus among numbers all are measured against one, and are considered to be larger or smaller as they are farther from, or nearer to, one; and among colors, all are measured against white, for they are considered more or less visible to the degree that they approach or depart from white. And I assume that the same method ought to be used for things with other attributes, and even for substances: that is, each individual thing, insofar as it belongs to a category of things, can be measured against the simplest thing in that category. [3] For this reason, that standard

54. Apparently Dante does not, as in earlier cases, mean to refer to any specific crudities of Bolognese speech; rather he seems to refer only to the general purity of the language in these passages, and to the transformation it undergoes in becoming part of a high-style poem.

should be found against which our actions, according to the types into which they have been divided, can themselves be measured. For insofar as we act as human beings in the simplest sense, we are virtuous (as this term is generally used); for we judge men as good or bad according to this. When we act as men who are citizens, we have the law, according to which a citizen is called good or bad; when we act as men who are Latins, we have certain standards, the simplest [in the categories] of custom, fashion, and speech, against which the actions of Latins are weighed and measured. [4] And surely these, the most noble standards against which the actions of Latins are measured, do not belong to any particular Italian cities, and are common to them all; and among these we can now discern that vernacular we have been tracking above, which suffuses its perfume in every city, but has its lair in none. [5] It could, however, be stronger in one than in another, just as the most simple substance, which is God, is more perceptible in man than in brute animals, in brute animals than in plants, in these more than in minerals, in these more than in elements; in fire more than in the earth, and just as the most simple quantity, which is one, is more perceptible in odd numbers than in even; or just as the most simple color, which is white, is more perceptible in yellow than in green.

[6] Having thus found what I have been searching for, I declare that the illustrious, cardinal, courtly, and curial vernacular of Latium is that which belongs to all the Latian cities and seems to belong to none, against which all the Latin municipal vernaculars are measured, weighed, and compared.

CHAPTER 17

[1] Now I should explain for what reasons I use the terms "illustrious," "cardinal," "courtly," and "curial" to describe this [vernacular] which I have found, and, in so doing, I will make more clear the nature of this [vernacular] itself. [2] First, then, I will lay bare what I mean by the term "illustrious" and why I apply it to this vernacular. In using the term "illustrious," I understand something which is illuminated, and, being illuminated, spreads its light. And for this reason we call men illustrious either because illuminated with power, they illuminate others with justice and charity, or

because, excellently instructed, they instruct excellently, like Seneca and Numa Pompilius.[55] And the vernacular of which I am speaking is exalted both in instruction and power, and itself exalts its followers with honor and glory.

[3] It surely would seem to have been exalted by instruction, since we see that its nobility, clarity, perfection, and elegance, as demonstrated in the *canzoni* of Cino di Pistoia and his friend,[56] have been distilled from the coarse words, tangled constructions, defective paradigms,[57] and rustic accents of the Latins.

[4] And that it is exalted by power is evident. For what has greater power than something which can change the human heart, making the unwilling willing and the willing unwilling, as this vernacular has done and continues to do?

[5] Then, that it exalts in honor is quite clear. For do not those of its household surpass in fame kings, marquises, counts, and magnates? This is not difficult to prove. [6] For, indeed, I myself know how acclaimed it makes its followers, I, who pay no attention to my exile because of the sweetness of such acclaim.

[7] For these reasons we ought rightly to call it illustrious.

CHAPTER 18

[1] Nor is it without reason that I honor the illustrious vernacular with a second epithet, calling it also "cardinal." For just as the whole door follows the pivot (*cardo*),[58] so that whichever way the pivot turns, the door also turns, moved either outward or inward, so also the whole company of municipal vernaculars turns and turns back, moves and stands, in the same manner as this vernacular does;

55. Numa Pompilius was the legendary successor to Romulus and therefore the second king of Rome. He is alleged to have founded Roman civil and religious law, and to have tamed and civilized a barbaric populace.

56. Note that Dante usually refers to himself in this treatise as either "Cino's friend" or "one other."

57. Or "pronunciations." See above, n. 40.

58. This passage depends on the derivation of the word "cardinal" from the Latin for "hinge" or "pivot" (*cardo*). The *cardo* was not our present-day hinge, but was a sort of pivot in a socket, or a wedge, by means of which a large door would be moved. In directing the door, it is like the legal head of household. The agricultural extension of this comparison is derived from Horace *Art of Poetry* 60–72.

this [vernacular] might indeed appear to be the head of the household. Does not a head of household every day pluck up the thorny bushes from the Italian woods? Does he not every day insert grafts and plant seedlings? And what else keeps the cultivators of this vernacular busy except these very tasks of rooting out and planting? And therefore it surely deserves to be honored by such a term.

[2] And my reason for calling it courtly [59] is this, that if we Italians had a royal court, this vernacular would be spoken in the palace. For if a court is the common house for the whole kingdom and the august ruler of each part of the kingdom, it is right that everything common to the whole and not peculiar to any part should frequent it and reside in it. There is no other dwelling worthy of so great a resident, so great, that is, as the vernacular to which I refer would certainly seem to be. [3] And this is the reason that those who frequent all royal courts speak in the illustrious vernacular; and also the reason our illustrious vernacular wanders like a stranger and finds hospitality in lowly refuges: for we have no royal court.

[4] It is also deservedly called curial because "curiality" is nothing other than a balanced rule for things which must be done. And because the scales for this sort of balancing are usually found in the highest courts (*curiae*), we have come to call all of our actions which are well-balanced, curial. And so, since this vernacular has been balanced in the very highest Italian court, it deserves to be called curial.

[5] But my statement that it has been balanced in the very highest Italian court (*curia*) would seem to be frivolous, since we have no such court. But it is easy to answer such an allegation. For even though there is no court in Italy, if the court is to be understood as a single entity, such as the court of the King of Germany, still there are the potential members of an Italian court; and just as members of a court are unified by a single sovereign, so the members of this vernacular are unified by the grace of a divine intellectual light. For this reason, although we lack a single sovereign, it would be false to

59. The word translated "courtly" (*aulicus*) refers, specifically, to the royal palace, our "court." The *curia* was also a court, but the term usually refers to administrative or judicial bodies, as against the company of courtiers and others who would participate in the ceremonial and private life of a royal court.

say that we lack an Italian court: we do have such a court, although the members of its body are scattered around.

CHAPTER 19

[1] This vernacular, then, which has been shown to be illustrious, cardinal, courtly, and curial, is the one which I say should be called the Latian vernacular. [2] For just as it is possible to find a particular vernacular which belongs to Cremona, so it is possible to find one which belongs to Lombardy. And as it is possible to find one belonging to Lombardy, so it is possible to find one which belongs to the whole left side of Italy; and as it is possible to find a vernacular for each successively larger area, it is also possible for the whole of Italy to do so. And just as the first would be called Cremonese, the second Lombard, and the third half-Italian, so that one which belongs to the whole of Italy would be called the Latian vernacular. And it has, in fact, been the one used by all of the illustrious experts who have written poetry in the vernacular tongue in Italy, including the Sicilians, the Apulians, the Tuscans, the Romagnoli, the Lombards, and the men of either of the Marches.

[3] And because it is my object, as I promised at the beginning of this work, to give instruction in the doctrines of vernacular eloquence, I will begin with this illustrious Italian since it is the most excellent, and discuss in the following books what persons I consider worthy of using it, for what subjects and in what forms, as well as where, and when, and to whom it should be directed. [4] Having clarified these matters, I shall try to throw light on the lesser vernaculars, descending by steps to that which belongs to one household alone.

BOOK 2

CHAPTER 1

[1] Calling once again upon the quickness of my natural talent, and taking my pen up again for beneficial works, I first declare that the illustrious Latian vernacular is suitable for use in both prose and verse. But because the prose writers mostly pick up this vernacular

from those who have knit it in verse, and because what is knit in verse seems to have remained the model for prose writers, and not the reverse (which facts would seem to confer a certain superiority on verse), let us first purify [60] the form [of this vernacular] which is put into meter, ordering our discussion as we promised at the end of the first book.

[2] Let us inquire first whether all verse writers in the vernacular ought to use this vernacular. It would seem so on the surface, because it is required of all verse writers that they embellish their verses to the extent that they are able. And since nothing more embellishes than the illustrious vernacular, it would seem that every verse writer ought to make use of it. [3] Furthermore, if something which is the best of its kind is mixed with something inferior to it, the superior thing does not simply not detract from the inferior, it actually improves it. Therefore any verse writer, even though he might write very crudely, who mixes this vernacular with his crudity would seem to do not just a good thing, but even the required thing: those with little ability can use much more assistance than those with much. And thus it appears that all writers of verse should be allowed to make use of it.

[4] But this conclusion is absolutely false: even the most excellent poets should not use [61] it all the time, as can be gathered from my discussion below. [5] Such a vernacular demands men of its own level, just like our other customs and fashions: magnificence demands men of great power; the purple, noble men; and, by the same token, this vernacular seeks out those with the greatest natural talent and learning, as will be made clear later. [6] For what is appropriate to us is so because of the qualities of either our genus, or species, or individual natures, such as the capacities for feeling, or laughing, or making war. But this vernacular is not appropriate to us because of

60. This verb (*carminare*), translated "purify," literally refers to that process by which wool is cleansed and separated into strands. The weaving or knitting of a fabric is one of the two principal metaphors for the making of poetry in this treatise, the other being the tying together of a bundle of sticks.

61. The verb *induere* translated here as "use" means, literally, "to put on clothes"; it thus makes more compelling the comparison between the suitability of a man and his clothing and the suitability of a thought to the language in which it is expressed.

our genus, since it is not appropriate to animals; nor because of our species, since it is not appropriate to all men, as there can be no doubt no one would claim that it is appropriate to mountaineers with their rustic pursuits—so it must be appropriate to individual natures. [7] Now things are appropriate to an individual as they suit his particular level of dignity, as is true of trading, fighting, and ruling. Thus, if things are appropriate to a level of dignity, which is to say, to those who are worthy (and some men may be worthy, others worthier, and still others worthiest), then clearly good things are appropriate to the worthy, better to the worthier, and the best to the worthiest. [8] And since a dialect is no less a necessary instrument for [the expression of] our thoughts than a horse is to a soldier, and since the best horse is appropriate to the best soldier, the best dialect is appropriate to the best thoughts. But the best thoughts can exist only where there is learning and natural talent. Therefore the best dialect is appropriate only to those who have the greatest learning and talent. So the best dialect is not appropriate to every writer of verse (as so many of them write verse without having either learning or talent), and therefore neither is the best vernacular. It follows that if it does not fit everybody's capacities, it should not be made use of by everybody, on the grounds that no one should act with impropriety.

[9] And as for the statement that everyone ought to embellish his verses to the extent of his ability, I affirm its truth. But we do not say that a decked-out cow or a garlanded pig have been embellished: we rather laugh at them, considering them vulgarized; for embellishment is the addition of something appropriate. [10] Concerning the statement that a superior thing mixed with an inferior brings it assistance, I say that it is true whenever the distinction between the two is broken down, as when we melt gold and silver together. But if the two remain distinct, the inferior will be made more contemptible, as when beautiful women are mixed with ugly ones. And therefore since the verse-writer's meanings always remain distinct from the words with which they are mixed, they will appear not better, but worse, when accompanied with the best vernacular, for the same reason that an ugly woman looks worse when she is dressed in gold or silk.

CHAPTER 2

[1] Now that I have established that not all verse writers, but only the most excellent, should make use of the illustrious vernacular, my next step is to establish whether all subjects should or should not be treated in it, and, if not, to separate out those which are worthy of it.

[2] For this task it must first be discovered what we mean by the word "worthy." And we call something worthy which has dignity, just as we call something noble which has nobility. And just as we know what someone is by his clothing, insofar as the clothing identifies him, by knowing what the clothing means, so we know what is worthy by knowing what dignity is. [3] And dignity, then, is the effect or the end of desert: we say that someone has achieved dignity for a good when he has deserved well, and for an evil when he has deserved evil. Someone who has fought well as a knight has the dignity appropriate to victory, someone who has ruled well, the dignity appropriate to sovereignty, and, as well, a liar has the dignity appropriate to disgrace, and a murderer, the dignity appropriate to that which causes death. [4] But since there are degrees among those who deserve well, and among their opposites as well, some deserving well, some better, and some the best, some evil, some worse, and some the worst; and since these degrees are distinguished by the end of the deserts, which, as I said, we call dignity, it follows that there will be degrees of greater or lesser among dignities, some being great, some greater, and some the greatest; and consequently it is evident that some things will be worthy, some worthier, and some the worthiest. [5] And since these degrees of dignity are not applied to the same, but to different objects, so that we would say that something was more worthy when it was worthy of a greater object, most worthy when of the greatest object (since nothing can be more worthy of the same object), it is clear that, in the nature of things, the best things are worthy of the best. And so since that vernacular which I call illustrious is the best of all of them, it follows that only the best subjects should be treated in it, which we would then call "the worthiest" among possible subjects.

[6] I will now therefore search out what these worthiest subjects

might be. To see clearly which they are, it should be noted that man travels a threefold road according as he has been granted three souls, the vegetable, the animal, and the rational. For he seeks what is useful insofar as his nature is vegetative, and in this respect shares his nature with plants; he seeks what is delightful insofar as his nature is animate, and in this respect shares his nature with the beasts; and seeks what is honest, insofar as his nature is rational, and in this respect he is alone or is perhaps of the same nature with the angels. It is evident that in all of our actions, we act for these three ends. [7] And because in all three of these cases, certain ends are greater, others the greatest, it is clear that those ends which are the greatest in their kind should be written about with the best available means, and consequently in the best vernacular.

[8] But it should be explained what these greatest ends are. First, if we consider carefully the intention of all things which seek usefulness, we would find among those things sought for their usefulness that the best end is nothing other than self-preservation.[62] Secondly, we would say in considering those things sought for the sake of delight, that that thing is most delightful which gives delight as the most precious object of the appetite: and this is the enjoyment of love.[63] Third, in considering those things which are sought for their honesty, no one may doubt that the best end is virtue. For this reason, these three (that is, self-preservation, the enjoyment of love, and virtue), are certainly those "splendidly great things" which should be written about using the best available means; or rather, the things which to the greatest extent tend toward them, which are prowess in arms, the flames of love, and the direction of the will. [9] I have found, if I can trust my memory, that the illustrious men have written poetry in the vernacular on these subjects alone: Bertran de Born, on arms; Arnault Daniel, on love; Girautz de Borneilh, on rectitude; Cino di Pistoia, on love; his friend, on rectitude. Bertran, for example, has written the poem,

62. The word *salus* has the primary meaning of "health" or "well-being," but it is used by Dante here in one of its secondary senses to mean "self-preservation" or "safety."

63. Dante's word is *venus*, derived of course from the name of the goddess of love, and meaning here, as in classical writings, the enjoyment of the act of love.

> No posc mudar c'un cantar no exparja [64]

Arnault, the poem,

> L'aura amara fa·l bruol brancuz
> clarzir [65]

Girautz, the poem,

> Per solaz reveillar
> che s'es trop endormitz. [66]

Cino, the poem,

> Digno sono eo de morte. [67]

His friend, the poem,

> Doglia mi reca ne lo core ardire. [68]

[10] I myself have found no Latian poets, up to this time, who have written on the subject of arms. But having looked over these poems, it should be clear which subjects are to be written about in poems in the greatest vernacular.

CHAPTER 3

[1] Now I shall endeavor to establish in what sort of metrical form those subjects which are worthy of so great a vernacular should be confined.

[2] Therefore, wishing to indicate the metrical form in which they are worthy to be bound, I would first have it borne in mind that those who have written poetry in the vernacular have published their poems in many different metrical forms, some of them in

---

64. "I cannot choose but send forth a song"; a poem in honor of King Richard the Lion-Hearted, celebrating his victory over the French king Philippe II, who aided Richard's brother, John. The date of the victory was 1194.

65. "The bitter air makes the leafy trees / grow thin"; a poem on the sufferings and anxieties of love.

66. "To waken solace, which is too often asleep"; a poem on the decay of ancient gallantry and manners.

67. "I am worthy of death"; an elaborate conceit, in which the poet claims to deserve death for having "stolen" Love from his lady's eyes.

68. "Sorrow causes me to burn in my heart"; a poem in condemnation of love and in praise of virtue.

canzoni, some in ballades, some in sonnets, and others in irregular and illegitimate metrical forms, as I will demonstrate later. [3] But from among these metrical forms I would single out the *canzone* as the most excellent form; and for this reason, if the most excellent things are as I proved earlier, worthy of the most excellent, then the subjects which are worthy of the most excellent vernacular are also worthy of the most excellent metrical form, and consequently should be written about in *canzoni*.

[4] And that the metrical form of the *canzone* is such as I say it is can be established, upon investigation, in several ways. In the first place, although everything we write in verse is a song,[69] only *canzoni* happen to have this word in their name, which would never have continued to be the case had it not been planned so from the earliest times. [5] Moreover, whatever brings about by itself that for which it was made is clearly more noble than what requires help from outside itself. But *canzoni* in themselves accomplish all that they are supposed to do, which ballades do not. The latter have need of dancers to keep time, who thus bring out their form. Therefore, *canzoni* should be considered nobler than ballades, and consequently their metrical form should be considered the noblest of all, since no one may doubt that the ballade surpasses the sonnet in nobility. [6] Furthermore, something is clearly nobler when it confers greater honor on its maker. But *canzoni* confer greater honor on their makers than ballades; therefore they are nobler, and consequently their metrical form is the noblest of all. [7] Furthermore, whatever is noblest will be preserved with the greatest care. But among all the forms which are sung, *canzoni* are preserved with the greatest care, as would be clear upon the sampling of books. Therefore *canzoni* are the noblest, and consequently their metrical form is noblest. [8] To this can be added that, among the products of art, the noblest is the one which includes the whole art. Therefore, since all forms which are sung are products of art, and since the whole art is included in the *canzone* alone, *canzoni* are the noblest, and thus their metrical form is noblest of all. And that the whole art of singing in poetic style

69. The term, *canzone*, is clearly derived from the Italian word for "to sing" (*cantare*). The term itself may mean, quite simply, "a song," as well as, more particularly, a certain poetic form. See below, *On Eloquence in the Vernacular* 2.8.3.

can be found in the *canzone* is clear in this, that whatever element of art is included in other forms is included in the *canzone*, but not the reverse of this. [9] And the evidence of these things which I say is clearly available to sight, for everything coming from the very heights of those most illustrious minds writing poetry which issues at the lips can be found in the *canzone* alone. [10] Therefore, as to the question before us, it is evident that the subjects which are worthy of the highest vernacular ought to be written about in the *canzone*.

Chapter 4

[1] Having labored to set apart those poets and those subjects worthy of the courtly vernacular, as well as that metrical form which I think worthy of such honor that it alone is appropriate to the highest vernacular, I should now, before moving on to other questions, explain in detail the metrical form of the *canzone*, which many poets appear to employ more by intuition [70] than through art; and so for that form which has up to this time been adopted by intuition, let us open up the workshop of its art, putting aside any discussion of the form of the ballade or sonnet, which I intend to take up in the fourth book of this work (where I will treat the middle vernacular).

[2] Looking back over what I have already said, I note that I have often called those who write verse in the vernacular, "poets." I have presumed to do so, without reservation, and for good reason; for they are undoubtedly poets, if we consider the true definition of poetry, which is nothing other than "a fiction expressed in verse according to [the arts of] rhetoric and music." [3] These poets, however, differ from the great poets, those who follow the rules, in that the great ones have written poems in a language and with an art which follows rules, while these [vernacular poets] as I said, do so intuitively. For this reason it happens that the more closely we imitate those great poets, the more correctly we write poetry. And therefore, where we intend to write works in a learned manner, we should follow their learned poetic.

[4] So I would state first of all that everyone should make the

70. The word *casus* means "chance" or "accident," which, for the poet lacking an art to guide him, is the same as "intuition."

weight of his material equal to [the strength of] his shoulders, as it may happen otherwise that he will fall in the mud because of the excessive weight on his shoulders. This is what Horace, our master, advises when he states, at the beginning of the *Art of Poetry*, "Choose your material . . . ." [71]

[5] Next I should distinguish, among those subjects suitable for writing, which of them should be sung in the tragic, which in the comic, and which in the elegiac style. Tragedy is an example of something in the higher style, comedy of something in the lower style, and elegy is to be understood as having the style of the miserable. [6] If these subjects seem to be suitable for the tragic style, then the illustrious vernacular will also be employed, and consequently, they must be bound in the *canzone*. If, on the other hand, they seem to be suitable for the comic style, then sometimes the middle, sometimes the low vernacular is to be employed, which distinction I am saving for treatment in the fourth book. But if they are suitable for the elegiac style then we should employ only the low vernacular.

[7] But let us leave aside for the present the other styles and discuss the tragic style in its proper place. It is clear that we are using the true tragic style when the gravity of the meaning is in accord with the splendor of the lines, with the elevation of the constructions, and with the excellence of the words. [8] It is for this reason (remembering that I have already proved the highest things worthy of the highest) that the style which I call tragic is clearly the highest style. It is for this reason, too, that the subjects which I pick out as suitable for poetry in the highest style, these being self-preservation, the enjoyment of love, and virtue (along with whatever activities not trivialized by some accidental quality which we undertake in pursuit of these ends), must be sung about in this style alone.

[9] But let anyone reading this be cautious and discern what I have said; when he intends to sing about these three subjects in their essence, or about those activities which are connected directly and essentially with these subjects, having drunk from the Helicon and having tightened the strings to perfect pitch, *only then* let him begin confidently to move the plectrum. [10] But the skill in using this

71. Lines 38–39.

caution and discernment, this is the difficulty, this the labor, which he can never achieve without the exercise of his talents and the assiduous study of the art and the acquiring of facility in learning. And those who can achieve this are the ones whom the poet calls in the sixth book of the *Aeneid*[72] the "favorites of God," the ones "raised up to heaven by the ardor of their virtue," and the "sons of the gods" (though he speaks figuratively). [11] And thus those fools are refuted who, immune equally from art or learning, trusting in their native talent alone, burst into song, using the highest subjects and the highest style. Since they are geese by nature or out of laziness, they should cease from such presumption, and not try to imitate the star-seeking eagles.

Chapter 5

[1] It seems to me I have said enough about the gravity of meaning, or at least all that is relevant to my work; therefore I shall hurry on to discuss the splendor of poetic lines. [2] On this topic it may be observed that the ancients, as the moderns, have used lines of various lengths in their *canzoni*; but I have yet to find a poet who has used more than eleven or less than three syllables in a line. And although the Latian poets have themselves used the three-syllable and eleven-syllable line, and all the gradations between, their lines are most often of five, seven, or eleven syllables, with the three-syllable line, after these, more common than the others. [3] And among these the eleven-syllable line is clearly the most splendid, both because it occupies more time and because it can contain more meanings, constructions, and words. The beauty of all of these things is obviously extended in this line, for wherever weighty things are extended, their weight is also increased. [4] And all of the experts seemed to have considered this fact whenever they have begun their *canzoni* with this line. Take, for example, Girautz de Borneilh, in his poem,

Ara ausirez encabalitz cantars.[73]

72. Virgil *Aeneid* 6.126–30.

73. "Now you will hear perfect songs." In Provençal, as in other Romance languages, vowels at the end and beginning of adjoining words are elided, so that *Ara ausirez* has only four syllables.

(Although it would seem that this line has ten syllables, it in reality
has eleven, for the two final consonants do not belong to the
preceding syllable: though they do not have a vowel accompanying
them, they still have not lost their syllabic value. The evidence for
this is that the rhyme here consists of a single vowel, which could not
be unless the force of another vowel were understood here.) Or this
poem by the King of Navarre [Thibaut of Champagne]:

> De fin'amor si vient sen et bonté

(where, if the accent and its cause are considered, the line will
clearly be of eleven syllables).[74] Or this poem of Guido Guinizelli:

> Al cor gentil repara sempre amore.[75]

Or this poem by the Judge [Guido] delle Colonne of Messana:

> Amor, che lungiamente m'ai menato.[76]

Or this poem of Rinaldo d'Aquino:

> Per fino amore vo sì letamente.[77]

Or this poem of Cino da Pistoia:

> Non spero che già mai per mia salute.[78]

Or this poem of his friend:

> Amor, che movi tua vertù da cielo.[79]

[5] And although this line we are discussing would seem to be, as it
is worthy to be, the most celebrated of all the lines, it appears to
excel with a brighter and greater splendor when it is set off in
relation to lines of seven syllables, so long as it maintains its pre-
dominance. But this matter remains to be explained later. I would

74. "From fine love comes wisdom and goodness." The accent on *bonté* (a word
derived from the Latin *bonitate*) indicates according to Dante that the last syllable
has been contracted from something like *bontée*.

75. "In a noble heart Love always finds its refuge."

76. "Love, which long has led me."

77. "Because of fine love I go so joyfully." Again, the eleven syllables include
one elision (*fino amore*).

78. "I have no hope that ever for my well-being." *Mia* is one syllable.

79. "Love who sends forth our power from heaven." *Tua* is one syllable.

say, then, that the seven-syllable line ranks next after that one which is the most celebrated. [6] After it I would place the five-syllable line next in order, and then the three-syllable line. But the nine-syllable line, because it gives the impression of being three lines of three syllables, has either never been honored by use, or has fallen into disuse from contempt. [7] And then because of their crudity, we have used only rarely lines with an even number of syllables; for they retain the nature of their "numbers," [80] which underlie the odd "numbers" just as matter underlies form.

[8] And thus, to sum up what has been said, the eleven-syllable line would seem to be the most splendid, and the very one we have been seeking. Now what remains is my discussion of the elevated constructions and the excellent words; and then, having prepared the sticks and the string, I will give instructions as to the form in which someone should tie together the promised bundle, which is to say, the *canzone*.

Chapter 6

[1] I have now located the illustrious vernacular, the noblest of all vernaculars; I have picked out those subjects which are worthy of being sung in this vernacular, of which three are the noblest as I demonstrated above; I have selected for them the form of the *canzone* as the highest form of all; and, in order to make my teaching the more complete, I have just provided for it a style and a poetic line. I shall now deal with the construction [of the *canzone*.]

[2] It should be noted first that what I call a "construction" is a joining together of words according to rules, such as, for example, "Aristotiles phylosophatus est tempore Alexandri." [81] For there are five words here, joined together according to rules, and they make a

---

80. "Numbers" here refers to both rhythm and number: Dante assumes that a line with an even number of syllables will have the same rhythm (measured by accents as well as by number of syllables) as a line with one more syllable, and that this longer line is the true form of the shorter. His reasoning is based primarily upon Pythagorean theory of numbers, and (perhaps) secondarily on the nature of Romance phonology.

81. "Aristotle philosophized in the time of Alexander." The rules to which Dante refers are those which determine the agreement of words in case, number, and gender.

single construction. [3] The lowest-level consideration in the case of constructions is whether or not the parts are in [grammatical] agreement. And because, if you will recall the original principles of my digression, we are hunting only for the highest things, constructions not in agreement have no place in our hunt because they deserve to be placed low on a scale of goodness. Shame on them, then, shame on those men ignorant [of agreement] who in the future dare to burst forth with *canzoni*! I would hold them in contempt as I would the blind, trying to distinguish colors. And, as is quite clear, it is constructions in agreement which we are seeking.

[4] But before we can obtain what we are searching for, we are presented with a problem of no little difficulty, which is to distinguish the construction most filled with elegance. For there are several grades among constructions, as, for example, the flavorless, used by the unlearned, as in "Petrus amat multum dominan Bertam." [82] [5] There is also that which has flavor alone, used by the austere scholar or teacher, as in "Piget me cunctis pietate maiorem, quicunque in exilio tabescentes patriam tantum sompniando revisunt." [83] And there is that which is both flavorful and charming, which is used by those who have a superficial knowledge of rhetoric, as in "Laudabilis discretio marchionis Estensis, et sua magnificentia preparata, cunctis illum facit esse dilectum." [84] And then there is that construction which is both flavorful and charming, and, in addition, elevated, which is used by illustrious writers, as in "Eiecta maxima parte florum de sinu tuo, Florentia, nequicquam Trinacriam

82. "Peter likes Mistress Bertha very much."

83. "I, greater in pity than others, am sorry for those who, wasting away in exile, see their native land again only while dreaming." The sentence is flavorful because of its artificial grammatical order; it has an appositive (*cunctis pietate maiorem*), and two participial phrases in apparent, but not grammatical, parallelism.

84. "Laudable is the discernment of the Marquis of Este, and his generosity well calculated, who makes himself loved by all." The "flavor" comes from the artificial order, with the main clause at the end, and from the observance of the *cursus* in the members. The "charm" comes from the irony of the statement, which makes it figurative. This statement, like the others of the last four, makes specific reference to events related to Dante's exile and to the political condition of Italy: the "Marquis of Este" to whom he refers is the same "Azzo" he mentions at 1.12.5 (see n. 29 above).

Totila secundus adivit."[85] [6] This I would call the highest grade among constructions, and, since we have been hunting, as I have said, for the best, this is that construction which we seek.

It will be found that this construction alone has been woven into the illustrious *canzoni*, as in this one of Girautz de Borneilh:

> Si per mon Sobretots non fos;[86]

or in this one, by Folquetz of Marseilles:

> Tan m'abellis l'amoros pensamen;[87]

or this, by Arnault Daniel:

> Sols sui che sai lo sobraffan chem sorz;[88]

or this, by Aimeric de Belenoi:

> Nuls hom non pot complir addrechamen;[89]

or this, by Aimeric de Pegulhan:

> Si com l'arbres che per sobrecarcar;[90]

or this, by the King of Navarre [Thibaut of Champagne]:

> Ire d'amor qui en mon cor repaire;[91]

85. "The greatest part of the flower having been thrown out from your breast, Florence, in vain a second Totilla will go to Sicily." The "flavor" lies in the artificiality of the grammar: the participial clause at the beginning, and the complexity of the ordering in the main clause. The "charm" lies in the figures: the personification of, and apostrophe to, Florence; the pun of *florum* and *Florentia*; the alliteration of *Totila* and *Trinacriam* (Trinacria itself being a figure for Sicily; see above, n. 26); the allusion to Totila, presumed to have destroyed Florence during earlier barbarian invasions, and here made equivalent to Charles of Valois. It is "elevated" because of its moral gravity, and because all of these figures are carefully calculated to support that gravity.

86. "If it were not for my All-excelling one." See Appendix A, no. 1, where the first stanza of this poem is printed, translated, and analyzed. Dante's ideas about construction can be clarified by an examination of the poems printed in that Appendix.

87. "The cares of love so greatly delight me." See Appendix A, no. 2.

88. "I am the only one who knows the superfrustration of love which issues. . . ." See Appendix A, no. 3.

89. "No man can satisfactorily fulfill . . . ." See Appendix A, no. 4.

90. "Just like the tree which, from being overloaded . . . ." See Appendix A, no. 5.

91. "The disdain of love, who dwells in my heart." This poem is really by Gace Brulé. See Appendix A, no. 6.

or this one, by the Judge [Guido delle Colonne] of Messina:

> Anchor che l'aigua per lo foco lassi;[92]

or this one by Guido Guinizelli:

> Tegno de folle' impresa a lo ver dire;[93]

or this, by Guido Cavalcanti:

> Poi che de doglia cor conven ch'io porti;[94]

or this one, by Cino di Pistoia:

> Avegna che io aggia più per tempo;[95]

or this, by his friend:

> Amor che ne la mente mi ragiona.[96]

[7] You should not be surprised, reader, at the number of authors I have recalled for you; for only through such examples could I indicate to you what I call the highest construction. And, to familiarize oneself with this construction, it would perhaps be most useful to look at the poets who follow the rules [of art], meaning Virgil, Ovid in the *Metamorphoses*, Statius, and Lucan, as well as those others who have used prose of the highest style, such as Titus Livius, Pliny, Frontinus, Paulus Orosius,[97] and many others, whom loving eagerness invites me to frequent. [8] But at any rate, let the followers of ignorance cease from their praise of Guittone d'Arezzo

92. "Although some water might have lost, because of fire . . . ." See Appendix A, no. 7.

93. "I hold him of foolish daring, to tell the truth." See Appendix A, no. 8.

94. "Since it has happened that I bear a heart of sorrow." See Appendix A, no. 9.

95. "Although it has been a very long time . . . ." See Appendix A, no. 10.

96. "Love, who in my mind discourses with me." See Appendix A, no. 11.

97. Titus Livius (Livy) (59 B.C.–A.D. 17) was the writer of an enormous history of Rome, admired for its scope and accuracy as well as for its style. "Pliny" probably refers to both Pliny the Elder (A.D. 23/4–79) and his nephew Pliny the Younger (61–114). The preface to Pliny the Elder's *Natural History* was highly regarded as a stylistic model, as were the *Letters* of Pliny the Younger. Frontinus (A.D. 30–104) was the author of a treatise called *The Strategems*, which deals with the uses and qualities of military officers. Paulus Orosius (fl. A.D. 414–18) wrote a *History* of Rome which was an apology for Christianity, rebutting the charge that the new religion caused the fall of Rome.

and certain others who have never lost the habit of using the words and constructions of the common people.

CHAPTER 7

[1] The next question which presents itself to my orderly treatise demands that I explain now which are the grandiose words, those worthy of forming the basis for the highest style.

[2] I will begin by declaring that to be able to discern different kinds of words is not the least accomplishment of reason, since, as I see it, it is possible to find many different varieties among them. Some words impress one as childish, some as womanish, others as manly; among these last, some seem rustic, others urban; and of those we call urban, some seem smooth-haired or even oily, others shaggy or even bristly. It is the smooth-haired and shaggy among these which we call grandiose, while we call those oily or bristly whose sounds are excessive in some direction. By the same token, among great actions, we say that some are the works of magnanimity, others of vanity, this second term being applied where, although the action might look superficially as if it had risen higher, it had really, according to right reason, not risen higher, but fallen down the other side as soon as it had crossed the line which marks off virtue.

[3] Think carefully, then, reader, how much is required of you in the straining which separates out the outstanding words. For if you have in mind the illustrious vernacular, that which should be used, as I said earlier, for the tragic style by poets of the vernacular (and these it is my object to fashion), you will take care that only the noblest words remain in your sieve. [4] You can by no means number among those either the childish, like *mamma* and *babbo*, *mate* and *pate*,[98] because of their simplicity; or the womanish, like *dolciada* or *placevole*,[99] because of their softness; or the rustic, like

---

98. "Mama" and "papa," "mommy" and "daddy" would be the English equivalents.

99. "Sweetness" and "pleasant." Dante objects to a liquid preceded by a mute as in p*lacevole*, and also, apparently, to a liquid followed by a palatal, as in *dulciada*; to the colloquial endings of these words, in contrast to the more regular *dolcezza* and *piacente* (only the latter of which would be a "noble" word); and to the irregular derivation of *placevole* from the Latin: the usual derivation would change *pl-* to *pi-*.

greggia or *cetra*,[100] because of their harshness; or the oily and bristly, like *femina* or *corpo*.[101] You will see, then, that only the smooth-haired and shaggy among the urban words are left to you, these being the noblest and members of the illustrious vernacular. [5] And I call those words smooth-haired which are three-syllables or very near to the measure of three syllables, have no aspiration, no acute accent or circumflex, no double consonants with *x* or *z*, no doubling of two liquids or placing of one liquid after a mute—which are, as it were, polished, and are emitted by a speaker with a certain sweetness, examples of which are *amore, donna, disio, vertute, donare, letitia, salute, securtate,* and *defesa*.[102]

[6] On the other hand, I would call all other words, besides the smooth-haired, which would seem to be either necessary or ornamental to the illustrious vernacular, "shaggy." And I call those words necessary which cannot be avoided, including certain monosyllables such as *si, no, me, te, se, a, e, i', ò* and *u'*,[103] as well as interjections, and a great many others. Then I would call those words ornamental which, when mixed with the smooth-haired, produce an

100. "Herd" and "lute." Both are, as well, examples of liquids preceded by mutes (*greggia* and *cetra*), and of a doubling and syncopation which produce what Dante would call harshness.

101. "Woman" and "body." *Femina*, with the accent on the first syllable, and with long vowels in every syllable, seems to Dante too soft in pronunciation, while *corpo* not only has a grouping of a liquid and a mute, but also the repetition of an open vowel. These two words also have overtones absolutely incompatible with "elevation" since *femina*, as against *donna*, implies feminine bestiality, and *corpo*, a' against *persona*, implies a body without an animating soul.

102. The words mean, respectively, "love," "lady," "desire," "virtue," "to give," "joy," "well-being," "security," and "defended." It is no accident that these are, in meaning, some of the key words of the high style: Dante clearly thought that there was an intimate connection between sound and meaning, so that the words his theory eliminated on the grounds that their sounds were too oily or bristly would also be eliminated on the grounds that their meanings were too coarse and vulgar. At the same time he eliminates certain forms of these words themselves with his phonological rules. *Vertute* and *securtate* had variant forms, *vertù* and *securtà*, which are apparently examples of what Dante means by the "acute accent"; and *donare*, because of the long *a*, could also appear as *donar*, which is apparently what he meant by a circumflex.

103. Meaning, respectively, "so," "not," "me," "you" (sing.), "if," "to" (or "has"), "and" (or "is"), "the," "or," and "where."

attractive harmony in combination, though they themselves have some harshness because of aspiration, or accent, or double consonants or liquids or length, such words being *terra, honore, speranza, gravitate, alleviato, impossibilità, impossibilitate, benaventuratissimo, inanimatissimamente, disaventuratissimamente, sovramagnificentissimamente*,[104] this last having eleven syllables. It would be possible to find words or names with more syllables than this, but because such words would exceed the capacity of all of our poetic lines, they would not seem to be appropriate to our present discussion. An example would be *honorificabilitudinitate*,[105] which ends at the twelfth syllable in the [Italian] vernacular, but at the thirteenth in two of its case endings in [Latin] grammar.

[7] But I leave for later my instructions concerning the manner in which the smooth-haired and shaggy words of this sort should be harmonized in poetic lines. What I have already said about the sublimity of words should suffice for someone of natural discernment.

CHAPTER 8

[1] Having gotten the sticks and strings readied for the bundle, it is now time to tie it up. But because in any activity knowledge should precede the action itself—one needs a target at which to aim before releasing an arrow or javelin—let us first and most importantly see what this bundle is which we intend to tie up.

[2] This bundle, then, recalling everything touched upon earlier, is the *canzone*. Let us look now at what a *canzone* is, and at what we mean when we say *canzone*. [3] A *canzone* is, according to the plain signification of the name, singing[106] itself, either in an active or a

104. Meaning, respectively, "land," "honor," "hope," "gravity," "eased," "impossibility," "impossibly," "most fortunately," "in a most unlively manner," "in a most unfortunate manner," "in a most overmagnificent manner." They are rejected on the grounds, respectively, of the doubling of two liquids (*terra*); aspiration (*honore*); the letter *z* in a double consonant cluster (*speranza*); a liquid after a mute (*gravitate*); a double liquid (*alleviato*); an accent, and perhaps too many syllables (*impossibilità*); and, the others, too many syllables.

105. "In the manner of something having the capacity to bestow honor." The two cases in Latin are the ablative and dative plurals: *honorificabilitudinatibus*.

106. "Singing" is *canenda*, of the same root as *cantio*; and *cantio* is Dante's Latin translation of *canzone*.

passive sense, just as an "interpretation"[107] is reading in either an active or a passive sense. But let us examine what has just been said to see whether a *canzone* is so called because of the active or because of the passive sense of the term. [4] And on this question it may be observed that the term, *canzone*, is used in two ways, in one way insofar as it is the composition of its author, and this is the active sense—used so by Virgil at the opening of the *Aeneid* where he says "Arma virumque *cano*";[108] in another way insofar as, having been composed, it is performed either by the author or by anyone else, and either performed in time to music or not, and this is its passive sense. In the first case, the *canzone* is created—acted upon—while in the second, it acts upon someone, and thus in the one case it would seem to be an action of someone, but in the other, someone's passive performance. And because it must be acted upon before it can act upon another, it is therefore more the action of someone, and should certainly seem to get its name from the one who acts upon it than from the one which it acts upon. The evidence for this is that we never say "This is Peter's *canzone*," referring to the person who performs it, but rather to the person who composed it.

[5] Next it must be decided whether the word *canzone* applies to the composition of harmonized words, or to the musical setting. To this point I would say that the musical setting is called the "music" or the "tune" or the "notation" or the "melody," but never the "*canzone*." For no flutist, or organist, or lyrist ever calls his melody a *canzone*, except insofar as it is married to a *canzone*, though the harmonizers of words do call their works *canzoni*, and we even call such words, written on a page, and having no one to perform them, *canzoni*. [6] And therefore the *canzone* is clearly nothing other than the completed action of one who writes, according to art, harmonized words for a musical setting. Therefore we call "*canzoni*" not only the *canzoni* we are now discussing, but also ballades and sonnets and all metrical forms of whatever kind in which there are harmonized words, whether in the vernacular or in a language with the rules of grammar. [7] But, leaving aside the language with rules because I

107. The word is *lectio*, of the same form as *cantio* (*canzone*); there is no English word which is its equivalent in form.

108. "Arms and the man I sing"; *cano* is of the same root as *cantio*.

am concerned only with what related to the vernacular, I say that there is one poetic form in the vernacular which is the highest, which we call the *canzone* because it excels all others; and that the *canzone* does, in fact, excel has already been proved in the third chapter of this book. And because the definition given above would seem generally applicable to several forms, I shall take up the term again, already defined generically, and distinguish the particular one which we seek by giving several differentiating features. [8] I say, then, that the *canzone*, so called because it excels all others, and the one we are searching for, is the linking together in the tragic style of equal stanzas without a "reprise" with the meaning expressed as a unity, as I myself demonstrate where I write:

> Donne, che avete intellecto d'amore.[109]

I say "joined together in the tragic style" because when this joining together is done in the comic style, we call the poem by the diminutive, *canzonetta*; I intend to discuss this form in the fourth book.

[9] Thus it is clear what a *canzone* is, both when it is taken as a generic term, and when we call a poem by this name because its form excels all others. Therefore it would seem clear enough what we mean when we use the term *canzone*, and consequently clear enough what the bundle is which we are endeavoring to tie up.

CHAPTER 9

[1] The *canzone* being, as I have said, the joining together of stanzas, one will, of necessity, not know a *canzone* without knowing what a stanza is; for knowledge of a thing defined results from knowledge of the terms of the definition. It follows, therefore, that the stanza must be dealt with: that is, that we establish what it is and what we would wish to mean by the term.

[2] And on this subject it must be understood that the term was invented for the sake of the whole art, that is, so that what the whole art of the *canzone* was to be contained within would be called a "stanza," which is to say, a room, or receptacle, with a capacity for the whole art; and no stanza which follows another is allowed to

109. "Ladies who have understanding in love" (*New Life* 19).

introduce any new element of the art, but must use only those elements of the art to be found in those which precede it. [3] For this reason it is obvious that what I am now talking about is the embracement or combination of all those elements which the *canzone* draws from art, and that, having explained it, the description of what we are searching for will become clear.

[4] The whole of the art of the *canzone* would seem to consist in three things: first, in the melodic division; second, in the arrangement of the parts; third, in the number of lines and syllables. [5] I do not include rhyme because it does not belong to the particular art of the *canzone*. One may introduce new rhymes or repeat old ones freely in any stanza, which would never have been allowed if rhyme belonged to the particular art of the *canzone*, as I have defined this art. And insofar as certain things which must be observed about rhyme pertain to art, they are included where I discuss "the arrangement of parts."

[6] But I can gather together these terms of definition from what I have already said, and say that a stanza is the combination of lines and syllables within the limits of a determined melody and in harmonic arrangement.

CHAPTER 10

[1] Knowing that man is a rational animal and that an animal consists of a sensible soul and a body, one still does not have complete knowledge of man without knowing what the soul is and what the body, because complete knowledge of a thing is brought to an end at the basic elements, as the Master of the Wise asserts at the beginning of the *Physics*.[110] Therefore, to obtain that knowledge of the *canzone* which we yearn for, we must now consider in outline those terms which define its terms of definition, first investigating the melody, then the arrangement, and finally lines and syllables.

First I would assert that every stanza is harmonized so as to fit a certain melodic line. [2] But stanzas would seem to be quite diverse in their metrical forms; for some remain under the same melodic line all the way to the end, which is to say that they neither repeat

110. Aristotle *Physics* 1.1.

the melodic line nor have a "diesis," by "diesis" meaning what I would call the *volta* in addressing the unlearned: a transition from one melodic line to another. And Arnault Daniel used such a stanza in almost all of his *canzoni*, and I myself was his follower when I wrote:

> Al poco giorno e al gran cerchio d'ombra.[111]

[3] But there are certain stanzas which contain a diesis; and a diesis, in the sense in which I use the word, cannot exist except where a melodic line is repeated, either before the diesis, or after it, or both. [4] If the repetition comes before the diesis, we say that the stanza has "feet." As a rule, there will be two feet in a stanza; some poets have used three, though very rarely. If the repetition comes after the diesis, then we say that the stanza has "verses."[112] If there is no repetition before the diesis, we say the stanza has a *fronte*; if there is none after it, we say it has a *sirma* or "coda."[113]

[5] Notice, then, reader, how much freedom has been given to poets who write *canzoni*, and try to think what has caused custom to

111. "To the short day, and to the great circle of shadow." Dante's poem is a sestina, a *canzone* in which each stanza has the same six rhyme words in a different order; its complexity and art is different in kind from that obtained through the use of a diesis.

112. The Latin *versus* is probably Dante's translation of the Italian *volta*; see above, 2.10.2.

113. Examples of these stanza forms can be found in Appendix A, where the arrangement of each poem quoted is described. The stanza forms possible are as follows:

1	2	3	4
Continuous	Foot	Foot	*Fronte*
Melodic	Foot	Foot	(diesis)
Line	(diesis)	(diesis)	Verse
	Verse	*Sirma*	Verse
	Verse		Verse
	Verse		

Each "foot" or "verse" would consist of the same number of lines as the first, and each corresponding line would have the same number of syllables, so that they could in fact be sung to the same tune. Note that the continuous melodic line could be considered the combination of a *fronte* and a *sirma*, in the sense that two continuous melodic lines, one after the other, would be the same as one; it would make no sense to speak of a transition between them.

claim for itself such a large range of choice; and if reason guides you on the right path, you will see that this license of which I speak has been granted by the dignity of authority alone.

[6] This should be enough to make clear how the art of the *canzone* depends upon the division of the melody, and therefore let us proceed to the subject of arrangement.

CHAPTER 11

[1] It seems to me that what I call arrangement constitutes the greatest part of what pertains to art, because the division of the melody as well as the weaving together of the lines and the setting in relation of the rhymes are based on it. For this reason it should clearly be discussed most diligently.

[2] I begin, then, by saying that the combinations of *fronte* and verses, of feet and coda (or *sirma*), as well as of feet with verses, can be arranged in different ways in a stanza. [3] For sometimes the *fronte* will, or can, have more syllables and more lines than the verse; I say "can" because I have never seen, up to this time, such an arrangement. [4] Sometimes it can have more lines but fewer syllables, as when the *fronte* has five lines and each verse has two,[114] while the lines[115] in the *fronte* have seven syllables and in the verses, eleven. [5] Sometimes the verses have both more syllables and more lines than the *fronte*, as in that poem where I say:

> Tragemi de la mente Amor la stiva.[116]

The *fronte* in this poem had four lines, woven of three lines of eleven syllables and one of seven. It could not therefore be divided into feet, since it is required of feet, and of verses as well, that they be equal to each other in the number of lines and the number of

114. Dante calls the *fronte* "pentameter" and the verses "dimeter." To avoid confusion with the same terms as used in English prosody, I have not translated these terms literally. See below, 2.11.12.

115. Dante uses the term *metrum* to refer to lines insofar as they are made up of syllables, and calls these lines *hendecasyllable*, *heptasyllable*, and so forth. I have not translated these terms with their cognates, which look so much alike that they could be confused with each other.

116. "Love draws the plow-pole of my mind." This poem has not survived to our time.

syllables. [6] And what I say about the *fronte* I say also about the verse; for the verses can have more lines than the *fronte*, but fewer syllables, as when there are two verses, each with three lines of seven syllables, and a *fronte* with five lines woven from two lines of eleven syllables and three of seven syllables.

[7] And then sometimes the feet have more lines and syllables than the coda, as in that poem where I say:

Amor, che movi tua vertù da cielo.[117]

[8] Sometimes the feet are exceeded in every way by the *sirma*, as in that poem where I say:

Donna pietosa e di novella etate.[118]

[9] And what I have said about the *fronte*, that it can have more lines and fewer syllables, and the reverse, I would also say about the *sirma*.

[10] In addition feet can exceed verses in number and be exceeded by them: there can be three feet in a stanza and two verses, or three verses and two feet, and we are not limited to this number, but rather have equal license to weave together a greater number of both feet and verses. [11] And what I have said about superiority in the number of lines and syllables among the other combinations applies also between feet and verses: they can in the same way exceed or be exceeded.

[12] Nor should I go on without mentioning that I use the word "foot" in the opposite sense from poets in languages with rules: they say that a line is made up of feet, while I say, as appears quite evident, that a foot is made up of lines. [13] And I should not leave out the observation that feet must correspond to each other in the arrangement of lines and syllables, and have an equal number of each, or else the melody could not be repeated. And I would add that this same correspondence must be observed among verses.

CHAPTER 12

[1] There is, then, as I said earlier, a determined arrangement which we ought to have in mind in weaving lines together, so let us

117. "Love, you who send forth your power from heaven."
118. "A lady piteous and of young age" (*New Life* 23).

give an account of it, recalling for this purpose what I said earlier about lines.

[2] It is clear that in our practice three lines in particular, those of eleven, seven, and five syllables, have the privilege of more frequent use, while that of three syllables, as I have demonstrated, comes ahead of all others, following them. [3] Of these, the eleven-syllable line, when we are attempting poetry in the high style, deserves, because of a certain excellence it has in being woven together, the absolute privilege over the others. There is, indeed, a stanza which rejoices in being woven of eleven-syllable lines alone, as in this poem by Guido [Cavalcanti] of Florence:

Donna me prega, perch'io voglio dire.[119]

And I also have written the poem,

Donne, ch'avete intellecto d'amore.[120]

The Spanish have also used this stanza; and I mean by the Spanish those who have written in Provençal. Aimeric de Belenoi, for instance, has written:

Nuls hom non pot complir addrechamen.[121]

[4] There is also a certain stanza into which one line of seven syllables is woven, which can be only where the stanza has a *fronte* or a coda because, as I said earlier, care must be taken to make the lines and syllables equal in feet or verses. [5] For the same reason, a stanza without a *fronte* or a coda cannot have an odd number of lines, but in one with both or either, there can be either an odd or an even number of lines at will. [6] And just as there is a certain stanza formed with a single seven-syllable line, so it would seem that there can be those into which two, three, four or five have been woven, although for the tragic style, the first line and the majority of lines will be of eleven syllables. I have, nevertheless, found some poets whose poems in the tragic style begin with a line of seven syllables, including [Guido Guinizelli], Guido Ghisilieri, and Fabruzzo, all of Bologna, who wrote, respectively,

De fermo sofferire,

119. "A lady asks me, therefore I wish to say."
120. "Ladies who have understanding in love."
121. "No man can fulfill satisfactorily."

and

> Donna, lo fermo core,

and

> Lo meo lontano gire,[122]

as well as certain other poets. But if we were to try to penetrate deeply into the sense of these poems, we would see that this tragic poetry proceeds with a slight shading of elegy. [7] I would not grant so much to the five-syllable line, however, for in a high-style writing, one five-syllable line, or at most two in the feet, woven into the whole stanza is enough; and I say "in the feet" referring to what is required of feet and verses because of their being sung. But it is clear that a line of three syllables standing by itself may on no account be used in the tragic style; [8] and I say "standing by itself" because certain resonances of rhyme make it seem to be present, as can be found in that poem of Guido [Cavalcanti] of Florence:

> Donna me prega,[123]

and in that poem where I wrote,

> Poscia ch'Amor del tutto m'à lasciato.[124]

But it is not in these cases a whole line in itself, but rather part of an eleven-syllable line, responding like an echo to the rhyme word of the previous line.

[9] To this above all attention must be given in the arrangement of lines, that if there is a line of seven syllables woven into the first foot, there must be one in the second foot taking the same position it has there. For example, if a foot of three lines has first and last

122. Respectively, "Of steadfast endurance"; "Lady, the steadfast heart"; "My long wandering."

123. "A lady asks me." What Dante is referring to are such lines as "e qual è sua vertute e sua potenza, / l'essenza, poi chiascun suo movimento . . ." where the trisyllable, *l'essenza*, echoes the rhyme-word of the previous line. The internal rhymes of this poem come at various places; but Dante is interested here in demonstrating how short the part of the line before the internal rhyme can be.

124. "After Love has entirely left me." Dante refers to such lines as "non per mio grato / chè stato non avea tanto gioioso . . ." where the *chè stato* echoes the *grato* of the previous line.

lines of eleven syllables and the middle, or the second, of seven syllables, the second foot must also have a seven-syllable second line and the other two eleven syllables. Otherwise the repetition of the melody, for which, as I said, a foot is constructed, could not take place; consequently, they could not be feet. [10] And I would say the same things about verses which I do about feet; indeed, I do not see that feet and verses differ in any respect except in their positions, the first getting their name from coming before, the other from coming after, the diesis in a stanza. Also, what I have said about a foot of three lines should be observed in all other kinds of feet, and what I have said about a single line of seven syllables applies also to more than one, or to a line of five syllables, or to all other possible lines.

You should be able to gather, reader, from what I have said up to this point, with what sorts of lines a stanza should be arranged, and to see the arrangement which must be observed with respect to lines.

CHAPTER 13

[1] Let us now spend some time on the relationships among rhymes, not discussing for the present rhyme as a thing in itself. Let us put off a particular treatment of it until later, when I intend to deal with poetry of the middle style.

[2] At the beginning of this chapter, certain forms ought to be quickly disposed of. One is the stanza without rhyme, in which no attention can be paid to the arrangement of the rhymes. This sort of stanza has been used by Arnault Daniel with great frequency, as in this poem:

> Sem fos Amor de joi donar;[125]

and I have written,

> Al poco giorno . . . .[126]

125. "If I were to be given [so much] of joy by Love." Each stanza in this poem uses the same eight rhymes in the same order (rhyme scheme *a b c d e f g h*).

126. "To the short day . . . ." This poem is a sestina, where all six stanzas have the same six rhyme words, though in a different order (rhyme scheme *a b c d e f, f a e b d c, c f d a b e, e c b f a d, d e a c f b, b d f e c a*).

Another is the stanza in which every line repeats the same rhyme, where it would obviously be superfluous to inquire into the arrangement. Thus it remains only to dwell on stanzas with mixed rhymes.

[3] And in this matter [of rhyme] it should first of all be noted that almost all poets have taken for themselves the widest license, and that they have tried to obtain from [the use of rhyme] above all the sweetness of a whole unit in harmony. [4] There are, on the one hand, certain poets who, in some cases, do not make all the line endings rhyme within the same stanza, but rather repeat the same endings, or make rhymes with them, in the other stanzas. This was Gotto of Mantua's practice, who recited for me many of his good *canzoni*. He always wove into a stanza one line without a match, which he called a "key." And if one such line may be allowed, so may two and perhaps even more.

[5] There are certain other poets, including almost all the makers of the *canzone*, who let no unmatched line stand in a stanza, but rather give it one or more correspondences in rhyme. [6] And some poets make the rhymes in the lines coming after the diesis different from those which come before, while others do not do so, but instead carry over the endings of the first part of the stanza by weaving them into the last part. This happens most often with the ending of the first line of the last part which several poets rhyme with the last line of the first part, which is clearly a certain rather beautiful concatenation of the stanza itself. [7] Then there must obviously be granted complete freedom of choice in the arrangement of rhymes as they appear in a *fronte* or a coda, although the endings of the last lines will be arranged more beautifully if they fall into silence with a rhyme.[127]

[8] But caution must be exercised in regard to the foot: I find that a set arrangement must be kept to in this case. I would say, making a distinction, that a foot may be made up of either an even or an odd number of lines, and that in either case, the endings can be

127. This is what Dante calls, at the end of the next paragraph, "coupling" (*combinatio*). He means that the last verse of a stanza does not have to follow the rhyme scheme of the earlier verses (e.g., *a b b a*); if the poet is using "coupling," he may have the rhyme scheme *a b a a* in the last verse (though number and length of lines will remain constant).

either matched or unmatched. No one will question this in the case
of an even number of lines, and if anyone would question it in the
other case, let him recall what I said in the next-to-last chapter
about the three-syllable line which, when it is part of an eleven-
syllable line, echoes a rhyme word.[128] [9] If it happens that in one
foot an ending is without a rhyme, this rhyme must in all cases be
picked up in the second foot. But if every ending within the first foot
has a rhyme associated with it, it is allowed, in the next foot, to
either repeat the endings or to introduce new ones, and either all of
them or only some, so long as the order of the previous foot is
preserved in all respects. For example, if the outer, that is the first
and last, endings of a three-line first foot are rhymed, then in the
second foot the outer endings must rhyme; and in whatever state,
matched or unmatched, the middle line of the first foot finds itself,
the same state will be repeated in the second foot, and the same
principles must be observed with other kinds of feet. [10] We should
as well apply the same law most of the time to verses; I say "most of
the time" because sometimes it will happen that the "concatenation"
I mentioned and the "coupling" of the last endings will upset the
order I have described.

[11] It seems to me quite appropriate that I append to this
chapter a few cautions beyond what I have already said on the
subject of rhyme, since I do not intend to give any further principles
of rhyme within Book Two. [12] There are three things having to
do with the possible placement of rhymes which are unsuitable for a
poet of the courtly style. The first is excessive repetition of the same
rhyme, except perhaps when he means to claim by it the honor of
doing something new and untried in the art, just like a knight who,
on his initiation day, thinks it unworthy that his rule of life go by
without some honorable action. I myself would never have done it
unless I were one such, as when I wrote,

Amore, tu vedi ben che questa donna.[129]

128. Dante means that where there is a foot with an odd number of lines, its
match may appear as an internal rhyme; he does not, of course, mean to say that
all such internal rhymes come in the third syllable. See 2.12.8.

129. "Love, you see clearly that this lady . . ."; a poem of sixty-six lines—six
stanzas and a *tornata*—employing only five rhyme words: *donna, tempo, luce, freddo,*

The second is an ambiguity, of no use in itself, which always seems to detract somewhat from the meaning. And the third is harshness in the rhymes, or at least harshness which is not mixed with softness; for from the mixture of harsh and soft rhymes, tragic poetry itself gains in splendor.

[13] And this is enough about the art which has to do with arrangement.

Chapter 14

[1] Having discussed at sufficient length two matters which, in the *canzone*, belong to art, I should obviously now discuss the third, which is the number of lines and syllables. And first I must look at this subject in relation to the whole stanza; then I will look at it with relation to the parts of the stanza.

[2] I must first make an important distinction among the subjects which present themselves for poetic treatment, between those which seek for a long stanza and those which do not. For, since everything we write is sung towards the right or toward the left—poems are either persuasive or dissuasive, either congratulatory or ironic, either in praise or in contempt—the words tending to the left will hurry toward the end, while their opposites will take due time with each part in coming to the end . . .[130]

---

and *petra* (meaning "lady," "time," "light," "cold," and "stone"). *Freddo* appears as a rhyme word fourteen times, the others, thirteen, which is what Dante means by "excessive"; the verse form was, however, "new and untried."

130. The manuscript breaks off here, abruptly, in mid-sentence. It would seem that Dante was about to say that poems with rhetoric of the "right hand" would require the longer stanzas; but, considering the surprising turns which Dante's thought sometimes takes in going from theory to practice, even this conclusion is not a certainty.

Italian Compared with Other
Literary Languages

The Banquet *shares many concerns with the treatise* On Eloquence in the Vernacular *which Dante was writing at the same time. As an intellectual feast prepared and served to those whose station kept them from a Latin education or whose worldly occupations took precedence over learning, it had to be written in Italian. But the learned tradition did not include examples of commentary in the vernacular, and learned opinion in particular did not admit of the possibility that Italian (in comparison with Provençal) was a proper medium for intellectual discourse. In the examples below, Dante, justifying his Italian commentary, rejects the alternative of Latin on the grounds of propriety: since the* canzoni *upon which he is commenting are Italian, the commentary which serves them must be suited to their master. He then dismisses the detractors of Italian by claiming that a prose work, lacking the artificial adornment of poetry, will show the natural beauty of the tongue he loves; that the artistry of Italian discourse will expose the malice of those who use the vernacular as an excuse for their own lack of art; and that the natural "friendship" of a speaker and his native language is manifested in the "mutual benefits" conferred when the poet and his vernacular produce the stability and harmony of art.*

A. ITALIAN COMPARED WITH LATIN

[1] Now that the superficial stains have been cleaned off this bread of mine,[1] it remains for me to make excuses for one which is engrained in its substance: its having been written in the vernacular and not in Latin, or, metaphorically, its having been made of rye and not of wheat. [2] And, to be short, the excuses for this are identical with the three causes which moved me to choose the

1. The "bread" to which Dante refers is the commentary on his own *canzoni* which will constitute the principal "food" at the Banquet he is serving.

vernacular in preference to Latin. My first motive was caution about inappropriate matching; my second was spontaneous generosity; and my third was natural love of my native dialect. [3] I shall now explain in order these three motives and the reasoning which lies behind them in such a way as to answer those who could object on the grounds I have stated.

[4] That which most adorns and commends a human activity, and carries it most directly to a good end, is the possession of those dispositions which are convenient to the proposed end, as boldness of spirit and strength of body are convenient to the end of knighthood. [5] In the same manner whoever is ordained for the service of another ought to have those dispositions which are matched with this end—submissiveness, knowledge, and obedience—without which one is not prepared to serve well. If he is not submissive in all circumstances, he will always work wearily and slowly, and seldom persevere in his service; and if he is not knowledgeable about the needs of his lord nor obedient to him, he will serve only after his own fashion and at his own convenience, which is more the service of a friend than of a servant. [6] Therefore, in order to avoid such a mismatching, this commentary, whose rôle in relation to the *canzoni* contained within it is that of servant, must be submissive to the poems in all circumstances, knowledgeable about the needs of its lord, and obedient to him. [7] All of these dispositions it would have lacked had it been written in Latin and not in the vernacular, since the *canzoni* are in the vernacular. It would have been not submissive, but sovereign, because of its nobility, virtue, and beauty. It would have been nobler because Latin is perpetual and not corruptible, while the vernacular is both unstable and corruptible. [8] Thus we perceive that the language of ancient writings, both comedies and tragedies, is the same Latin we have today: no writer can modify it on his own. This is not true of the vernacular, which can be modified at will by every writer who uses it. [9] Thus in the cities of Italy we see, if we look closely, that over a period of fifty years a great many words have died out or been born, or become different; and if such a short time has made so many changes, a longer will make many more. For this reason I would claim that were those who departed this life a thousand years ago to return to their native cities, they

would believe them occupied by a foreign people, so different would be the language from their own. [10] This matter will be more thoroughly treated in a little book I intend to write, God willing, *On Eloquence in the Vernacular.*

[11] Then again, [a commentary in Latin] would not be submissive, but sovereign, in virtue. Each thing is virtuous to the extent that it does, by its very nature, that for which it is intended, and the better it does it, the more virtuous it is. Thus we say that a man is virtuous if he lives either the contemplative or the active life for which he is by nature intended. We call a horse virtuous who runs fast and a long distance, for which things a horse is intended; and a sword virtuous which cuts hard things well, for which it is intended. [12] So speech, which is intended for the expression of human thought, is virtuous when it does so, and more virtuous when it does so to a greater extent. Thus, since it is a fact that Latin can express many things conceived by the human mind which the vernacular cannot, as anyone knows who has facility in both [languages], its virtue is greater than that of the vernacular.

[13] Furthermore, [a commentary in Latin] would not be submissive, but rather sovereign, because of its beauty. Men say that a thing is beautiful when its parts are related to each other as they ought to be, because pleasure results from their harmony. Thus a man looks beautiful when his members are related to each other as they ought to be, and we say that a song is beautiful when its words are related to each other according to the requirements of art. [14] That language is more beautiful, then, in which the words are to a greater extent related to each other as they ought to be; and they are so to a greater extent in Latin than in the vernacular, since the vernacular follows usage, while Latin follows [rules of] art. Thus it is granted that Latin is more beautiful, more virtuous, and more noble. [15] This settles my first contention, that [a Latin commentary] would not be submissive to the *canzoni*, but rather their sovereign. *Banquet* 1.5.

B. ITALIAN AND OTHER VERNACULARS

[11] [The natural love of my own dialect] moves me also to defend it against the many detractors who disparage it and commend

other dialects, most particularly against those who say that Provençal[2] is more beautiful and better than [Italian] and so depart from the truth. [12] For this commentary will demonstrate the great excellence of the Italian[3] vernacular: its virtue, its capacity for expressing ideas from the highest to the lowest suitably, adequately, and gracefully (as in Latin itself) will become apparent. This could not have been so well exemplified in rhymed compositions because of the incidental adornments, such as rhyme, rhythm, and regular meter, which are attached to them. By the same token, the beauty of a woman is not rightly exemplified when the adornments of jewelry and clothes attract more admiration than does she herself. [13] So whoever wishes to judge rightly the beauty of a woman will look at her when she has with her only her natural beauty, unaccompanied by an incidental adornment. This commentary will be in such a state, and in it may be observed the easy flowing of its syllables and the propriety of its constructions, as well as the pleasing discourse which may be composed from these. Whoever looks closely at these will see that they are filled with the sweetest and loveliest beauty. [14] But because the most effective way to expose the inadequacy and malice of a detractor is to show his motives, I will dispose of those who bring charges against the Italian dialect by telling why they have been moved to do so; and I will now devote a special chapter to this so that their infamy will be more widely known.
Banquet 1.10.11–14

[11] . . . The second faction [of detractors] employs against our vernacular a vicious excuse. There are many people who would rather be thought experts than actually to be so; and to avoid the contrary, that is, the imputation that they are not experts, they always blame either the material or the tools of the art which they practice; thus the bad smith blames the iron he has available, and the bad lutanist blames his lute, thinking thereby to put the responsibility for a bad knife or for bad music on the iron and the lute, thus removing it from themselves. [12] So there are some, and

2. Dante uses the term *lingua d'oco.*
3. Dante uses the term *volgare di si.*

their number is not small, who wish men to consider them fine writers; and as an excuse for their not writing, or for their writing poorly, they lay the blame and responsibility on their material which is to say, on their own vernacular, at the same time commending another vernacular which it has not been granted them to work with. [13] But whoever wishes to see whether this iron is to blame will look at the products made from it by good workmen, and will know the viciousness of those who think to excuse themselves by blaming it. [14] Cicero voices his opposition to such people at the beginning of one of his books called *Concerning the Ends of Goods*[4] because in his time they disparaged Roman Latin and praised Greek grammar on much the same grounds that these men vilify Italian speech while extolling Provençal.

Banquet 1.11.11–14

[4] According to the Philosopher, it is not impossible for a thing to have more than one efficient cause, although one will be greater than the others, as he says in Book 2 of the *Physics*.[5] Thus fire and the hammer are efficient causes of the knife, though the smith is the greater cause. This vernacular of mine joined together my parents, since they spoke to each other in it, in the same manner that the fire disposes the iron for the use of the smith who makes a knife. For this reason it is clear that my vernacular had a part in my generation, and so was one of the causes of my coming into being. [5] Furthermore, this vernacular of mine introduced me on the path of learning, which is the ultimate perfection, inasmuch as I entered into Latin, and learned it, with the aid of the vernacular, Latin becoming then the way by which I could proceed further. And thus it is clear, and acknowledged by me, that it has been for me the greatest of benefactors.

[6] Besides, it has shared with me an identity of desire, as I can demonstrate in this manner. Each thing naturally desires its own self-preservation; so if the vernacular could have any desires of its own, it would desire to be preserved. It will be so when it is given a

4. Cicero *De finibus* 1.8
5. Aristotle *Physics* 2.

form of greater stability, and it could gain no greater stability than by being tied together in meter and rhyme. [7] And this same desire has been mine, which is so obvious as to require no evidence. So a single desire has been both its and mine; and through this agreement our friendship has been confirmed and increased.
Banquet 1.13.4–7

Style and Decorum

Having established the qualities of the highest vernacular style, Dante wishes also to demonstrate the stylistic flexibility of his native tongue. It was a requirement of the classical rules that the styles change according to the age of the speaker or the difficulty of the subject; and Dante, in his commentary on the Third Canzone *of the* Banquet, *claims that the same changes can be made in the vernacular as well.*

[16] And if in this present work, which is called the *Banquet* and which I mean to be one in truth, I treat the subject in a more virile style than in *The New Life*, I do not intend thereby to detract in the least from my earlier work, but rather to enhance it the more by means of this new work, seeing that it is reasonable that the earlier work should be ardent and empassioned, the later, temperate and virile. [17] It is right to speak and act differently at one age than at another, since certain customs are appropriate and praiseworthy at one age which are unbecoming and blameworthy at another, as I will demonstrate with appropriate arguments later, in the fourth treatise of this book. I wrote the earlier work when I was at the threshold of my young manhood, and the later when I had crossed over it. [18] And since it is true that my real intention in the earlier *canzoni* was otherwise than what they showed openly, it is my purpose to show what this intention was by adding an allegorical exposition to my discussion of the literal story; both discussions should flavor the meal for those who have gathered for this banquet.
Banquet 1.1.16–18

> [The sweet rhymes of love which I used
> to seek within my thoughts,
> I now must leave; not because I do not hope
> to return to them,

67

> but because the scornful and fierce acts
> which in my lady
> are displayed have blocked for me the way
> to my accustomed speech.
> And since it seems to me time to pause,
> I will lay aside my smooth style,
> to which I have held in discourse of love;
> and I will write of the worth,
> through which a man is noble,
> with rhymes harsh and subtle;
> refuting the false and base judgment
> of those who believe that nobility
> has its beginning in riches.
> And at the beginning I call on that lord
> who dwells with my lady in her eyes,
> through whom she is in love with herself.][1]

[11] I say "since it seems to me time to pause, I will lay aside," that is, leave behind, "my smooth style," that is, the manner to which I have held in speaking of love; and I say that I will now speak of that "worth" whereby a man is truly noble. And although "worth"[2] can be understood in several senses, here it is to be taken as a natural faculty, or rather as an excellence conferred by nature, as I will show later. [12] And I promise to discuss this subject "with rhymes harsh and subtle." Here it must be understood that "rhyme" may be construed in two senses, one broad and the other narrow. In the narrow sense, it refers only to the agreement which is usually observed between the last and next-to-last syllables of lines; when it is used in the broad sense, it refers to all the discourse which in following the rules of meters and length, falls within rhymed consonances,[3] and here in this proem it is meant and should be

1. This is the first stanza of the Third *Canzone*, commented on in the Fourth Treatise of the *Banquet*.

2. The word in Italian is *valore*, which can be translated as "value, worth, price; valour; might, force." The word has many more meanings than the English "worth."

3. The phrasing here is ". . . che'n numeri e tempo regolato in rimate consonanze cade." It is not absolutely certain that *numeri* and *tempo* should be translated "meters" and "length"; Dante's concern in general for the numbers of lines in a

taken in the broad sense. [13] And in this proem therefore the term "harsh" refers to the sound of the words, which should not be soft with such material, while the term "subtle" refers to the meaning of the words, which go on subtly arguing and disputing. [14] I add to this, "refuting the false and base judgment," thus promising further to refute the judgment of people filled with error: "false" because removed from the truth, "base" because confirmed and fortified in baseness of spirit. [15] And it ought to be noted here that in this proem I promise first to discuss what is true and then to refute what is false, while in the discussion, I do the contrary, because I first refute what is false and then discuss what is true, which would seem not to correspond to the promise. But it should be understood that anything which has either the one or the other purpose has as its principal purpose to discuss what is true; refuting what is false has this purpose insofar as it makes what is true stand out the better. [16] And so here I promise to discuss what is true first, since it is my principal purpose, which will bring to the minds of the hearers the desire to listen; but in the discussion itself I first refute what is false, in order that what is true, the evil opinions having been dispersed, will then be welcomed more freely. The master of human reason, Aristotle, follows the same procedure, always combating the enemies of truth first, and then, having overcome them, displaying the truth.

Banquet 4.2.11–16

---

stanza, or numbers of syllables in a line or a word, makes it possible that *numeri* refers to these things, in which case *tempo* would probably refer to what we presently mean in English by "meter."

Style and Meaning

Dante recognizes a break between the beauty of a poem and its meaning, though not an absolute break. Any poem should have both excellences, of style and meaning, but he suggests, in commenting on the First Canzone *of the* Banquet, *that difficulty and novelty in meaning should not have to cut a reader off from the appreciation of stylistic beauty. Furthermore, he felt it unseemly that the goodness of a poem, residing in its meaning, be appreciated where the beauty could not be; and he thus resists explaining the meaning of a poem to those who could not read it in its original language. Finally, in a selection from* Purgatory, *he acknowledges a level of inspiration, not captured through analysis, which distinguishes the great poets from the merely good.*

> [I believe, *Canzone*, that they will be rare,
> those who understand your argument clearly,
> so fatiguing and hard is your speech.
> Therefore, if by chance it should happen
> that you come before some people
> who do not seem to you to have perceived it clearly,
> then I ask you to take comfort for yourself,
> saying to them, my beloved new song,
> "Take note at least how beautiful I am."][1]

[1] Finally, following what the letter of this commentary said earlier where I divided this *canzone* into its principal parts, I turn the face of my words towards the *canzone* itself, and address it. [2] And in order that this section may be more clearly understood, I say that this section of a poem is generally called the *tornada* of a particular *canzone*, and derives from the practice of early writers who composed the *tornada* so that, having sung the *canzone* through, they

1. These are lines 53–61 of the last stanza of the First *Canzone* commented on in the Second Treatise of the *Banquet*.

70

could sing the *tornada* to the melody of a part of the *canzone* itself. [3] But I rarely compose one with this intention, and, so that others will perceive this, I give the *tornada* a different form from that of the *canzone* itself so that its meter does not fit the musical notation of the rest of the poem. Rather I compose one when I need to say something which is an adornment to the *canzone* and separate from its meaning, as can be seen in this and other cases. [4] Then for my present purposes I say that the goodness and the beauty of any discourse are separate and distinct from each other, because the goodness lies in the meaning while the beauty lies in the adornment of the language; and while both the one and the other are accompanied by delight, it is the goodness which is to the greatest degree delightful. [5] Therefore, since, in fact, the goodness of this *canzone* is not at all easy to perceive because of the many persons who are brought in to speak in it, and because of the many distinctions which arise from this, whereas its beauty is quite easy to see, it seemed to me necessary in reading this *canzone* that people in general fix their attention on the beauty rather than on the goodness. And this is the content of what I say in this part.

[6] And because it so often happens that giving advice seems presumptuous, it is a practice of an orator in certain situations to address someone indirectly, directing his words not at the person for whom they are intended, but rather towards another. And this method is what is really used here, because the words are directed at the *canzone*, but the meaning to men. [7] I say, then, "I believe, *canzone*, that they will be rare," that is, few in number, those who will understand you clearly. And I give the cause, which is twofold. First, because the discourse is fatiguing—I say "fatiguing" referring to the cause I have mentioned [that is, the number of speakers and the number of distinctions]; second, because the discourse is hard—I say "hard" referring to the novelty of the meaning. [8] Then afterwards I warn the *canzone*, saying, if by any unfortunate chance you should come where people suspect that you are lacking in sense, do not be distressed, but say to them: Although you do not see my goodness, at least fix your attention on my beauty. [9] And, as I said earlier, I do not mean to say anything else here than this: O men, you who are not able to perceive the argument of this

canzone, do not for this reason scorn it; rather fix your attention on its beauty, which is extensive in the constructions which are the concern of grammarians, in the ordering of the discourse, which is the concern of rhetoricians, and in the meter of its divisions, which is the concern of musicians. These things can be clearly perceived in it by anyone who looks at it closely.
Banquet 2.11.1–9

[13] Furthermore, had the commentary been in Latin, the *canzoni* would have been expounded for peoples of other tongues, such as the Germans and English and others, and in this case Latin would have gone beyond the commands of the *canzoni,* for it would have been against their will (I say this speaking broadly) to have their meaning expounded in any place where their beauty could not be carried with them. [14] But anyone knows that no discourse harmonized with the Muses' bonds can be translated from its own dialect into another without the destruction of all its sweetness and harmony. [15] And this is the cause of Homer's never having been translated from Greek into Latin like the other Greek writings we possess. This is the cause, too, for the absence of the sweetness of music and harmony in the lines of the Psalter; for they were translated from Hebrew into Greek and from Greek into Latin, and even in the first translation this sweetness diminished.
Banquet 1.7.13–15

The speaker here is Buonagiunto of Lucca, a poet of the earlier "Sicilian" generation in Italy.

"But tell me if I see here he who wove
the new rhymes which begin:
'Ladies who have understanding of love.'"
And I [Dante] to him, "I am one who, when
   Love breathes in me, give attention, and in that manner
   In which he dictates within me, signify outwardly."
"O brother, now I see," he said, "the knot
   Which held back the Notary and Guittone[2] and me
   From the achievement of that sweet new style which I hear.

2. Jacopo da Lentino, called "Il Notario"; Guittone d'Arezzo, usually considered the leader of the older "Sicilian" school of poets.

I see clearly how your pens
   Follow closely he who dictates
   Which was certainly not the case with ours.
And however one tried to look beyond this distinction,
   One would see no other difference between your style and ours."
   And as if contented, he fell silent.

Purgatory 24.49–62

THE RHETORICAL STRATEGIES
OF POETRY

Devices of Persuasion

In the selection below from the Banquet, *Dante takes pains to point out the extent to which he has observed in his poetry the proper manners of a rhetorician. He explains that he would violate the rule which forbids speaking of oneself only for the strongest reasons and with the most authoritative precedents. He orders his poems so that the most important points and those he wishes to have his readers take away come last. And he takes care not to offend his readers by seeming to give them advice when he is not in a position to do so. The fact that he wishes his readers to know how sensitive he has been to such considerations is an indication of his desire to justify poetry on the same grounds that any other form of discourse would be justified.*

[12] However, returning to my principal contention, I say that speaking of oneself is allowed for reasons of necessity. Among these reasons of necessity two in particular stand out. [13] The first is when one could not put a stop to great infamy or danger without discoursing of oneself, which in this case is allowed for the reason that to choose the least guilty of two paths is equivalent to choosing a good one. It was this necessity which moved Boethius to speak of himself in order that, under the pretext of finding consolation, he could defend himself against the perpetual disgrace of his exile, demonstrating its injustice, since no other defender had risen up.[1] [14] The second is when great usefulness to others in the way of doctrine would follow from discourse of oneself. This reason moved Saint Augustine to speak of himself in his *Confessions*, because by the process of his own life, which was from bad to good, from good to better, and from better to best, he gave us example and teaching which could not have been accepted on more truthful evidence. [15] Thus if either one of these reasons will justify me, my rye-bread

---

1. *Consolation of Philosophy*, Bk. 1, prose 4.

is sufficiently purged of its first stain. Fear of disgrace moves me, and the desire of putting forth teachings which no one else could put forth so truthfully. [16] I fear the disgrace which would come to me were it believed that I had actually followed such a passion as he who reads my earlier *canzoni* may posit for me as my ruler. This disgrace will be completely dispelled by my present discourse about myself, which will show that not passion but virtue was the moving force. [17] My purpose is also to show the real meaning of these *canzoni* which no one would have been able to perceive without my telling it because it is hidden under the figure of allegory. My telling it will not only give great pleasure in the hearing, but also will give subtle instruction in how to speak in this manner and in how to understand the writings of others.
Banquet 1.2.12–17

But since in every type of discourse the writer must aim above all at the persuasion, which is to say, the charming, of his audience, this being, as orators know, the beginning of all other forms of persuasion; and since the most effective form of persuasion is to render the audience attentive in promising to tell them new and most splendid things, I follow this form of persuasion which I call "charming" in the prayer I make to my audience, announcing to them my purpose, which is to tell them new things, namely, the division which I find in my mind; and splendid things, namely, the force of their own stars. This is the content of the last words of the first part of the *canzone*:

> I will tell you the new state of my heart,
> How the sorrowful mind complains within it,
> And how a spirit speaks against them,
> [A spirit] which comes from the rays of your stars.[2]

Banquet 2.6.6

[2] . . . I say that I should first speak from the mind's point of view, or the older thought, and then from the spirit's, for this

2. Lines 10–13 of the first stanza of the First *Canzone* commented on in the *Banquet*. The audience here are those intelligences which move the third heaven, or heaven of Venus.

reason, that a writer should always save until the last whatever he principally intends to say because whatever is said last will remain longer in the mind of the audience. [3] And since in fact my principal intention is to tell about and discuss what the work of those beings to whom I am speaking accomplished rather than what it undid, it was reasonable to tell about and discuss the situation of that part which was being destroyed and then to do the same for that part which was being brought to birth.
Banquet 2.8.2–3

[6] A rhetorical figure of this sort is highly praiseworthy and even necessary, that is, one in which the words are addressed to one person but meant for another, because although it is always praiseworthy and necessary to give advice, it is not always appropriate that the advice come from the mouth of a particular person. [7] For example, when a son is aware of the vices of his father, or a subordinate aware of the vices of his lord; or where a friend is aware that his friend would be embarrassed by advice or by being reminded of his honor, or aware that his friend will not take advice patiently, but rather angrily; in these cases this figure is both most attractive and most useful, and can therefore be called "dissimulation." [8] It is similar to the strategy of a wise general who attacks one side of a castle in order to draw the defense away from the other, though attacking and giving assistance are not directed to the same purpose.
Banquet 3.10.6–8

On Rational Ordering

Dante claims in general that poetry is at least as rational as other forms of discourse. In the two passages from the Banquet *which follow, he demonstrates this rationality in the explication of his own poetic figures. A figure of speech, he implies, is truly pleasing when the analysis of it will reveal an underlying concept, such as generation or the Aristotelian four causes, which has ordered the figure itself.*

[1] Because I have, as was my intention, discussed the first two divisions of this *canzone*, the ordering of this present treatise requires that I proceed to the third, in which it is my purpose to clear the *canzone* of a charge which might have been harmful to it, and it is of this which I speak. [2] This charge is that, before coming to the composition of this *canzone*, it having appeared to me that this lady had become somewhat fierce and proud in her relations with me, I wrote a short ballade in which I called this lady haughty and spiteful; and this would seem to be contrary to my earlier discussion here. For this reason, I turn to the *canzone*, and under the pretext of teaching it how to justify itself, I myself justify it. And this is a figure in which one addresses an inanimate object, called "prosopoeia" by the rhetoricians, and much used by poets. [This third division is as follows:

> Canzone, it appears that you speak the contrary
>   of what one of your sisters says;
>   for this lady, whom you describe as humble,
>   your sister calls fierce and disdainful.
>   You know that the sky is always shining and clear,
>   and, in itself, is never troubled;
>   but our eyes for many reasons
>   sometimes call the star cloudy.
>   In the same manner, when [your sister] called [this lady] haughty,

she did not look at her according to the truth,
but only according to what she seemed like to her:
for my soul had fears
and still has fears, so that she seems fierce to me
whenever I look where she takes heed of me.
Justify yourself this way, if you ever have need to;
and whenever you can, present yourself to her,
say: "My lady, if it would be pleasing to you,
I shall speak of you on every side."] [1]

[3] In order to present more easily to the understanding the meaning of this section, I should divide it into three smaller parts. The first part tells what needs the justification; the second proceeds with the justification, beginning where I say, "You know that the sky . . ."; the last part addresses the *canzone* as a person uninstructed in what he should do, beginning where I say, "Justify yourself in this way, if you ever have need to."

[4] What I say, then, in the first part is this: "*Canzone*, who speak such great praise of this lady, it appears that you are contrary to one of your sisters." I use the term "sister" metaphorically; for just as a female engendered by the same parent is called a sister, so a man can use the term "sister" to refer to the products produced by a single producer, all of our production being in some sense an engendering.
Banquet 3.9.1–4

[Therefore let no one boast
saying, "By descent I am her companion,"
for they are like gods,
those who have such grace free from sin;
for God alone gives it [nobility] to the soul
which he sees in its own person
stand complete; so that to some,
it is evident that the seed of felicity is
sent from God to the soul well-placed.] [2]

1. Lines 73–90, the fifth stanza of the Second *Canzone* commented on in the *Banquet*.

2. Lines 112–20 from the sixth stanza of the Third *Canzone*. The gift of God referred to is *gentillezza* or nobility.

[9] Finally, the text draws a conclusion from what had been said earlier (that virtues are the fruit of nobility, and that God sends [nobility] to the soul which is in a good setting), and declares that "to some," that is, to those who have understanding, and they are very few, it is evident that human nobility is nothing else than "a seed of felicity . . . sent from God to the soul well-placed," that is, to one whose body is in every part perfectly adjusted. For if virtues are the fruit of nobility, and if felicity is the sweetness acquired through them, it is clear that this nobility must be the seed of felicity, as I said. [10] And whoever looks closely will see that this definition includes all four causes: the material, the formal, the efficient, and the final. It refers to the material when it says "to the soul well-placed," this being the material and the subject of nobility; it refers to the formal where it says that it is the "seed"; to the efficient where it says "sent from God to the soul"; and to the final where it says "of felicity." And in this manner that good of ours is defined, which descends to us from the high and spiritual Virtue just as the virtue of a stone descends from the noblest heavenly body.

Banquet 4.20.9–10

The Divisions of a Poem:
Two Examples

A feature of The New Life *which manifests Dante's interest in a new poetics is the "division" of his poems. As in the examples below, before each sonnet or* canzone *he explains the set of circumstances which brought it forth; and after the poem he explains what each section contributes to its total argument. In the rational structure of a poem, each part will have a different intention which contributes to the meaning of the whole and will manifest this intention by being directed to a different audience or a different question or by using a different rhetorical figure or color. Not only in the short poems, but in the* Comedy *as well (as he says in the* Letter to Can Grande*), the discovery of the meaning of the poem is to be carried out through this process of division.*

[1] After the vision I wrote down earlier, having already written the words which Love required me to say, many different thoughts began to fight within me and to try me, none of which could be defeated. Among these thoughts, four in particular seemed to disturb the tranquility of my life. [2] The first of these was: the lordship of Love is good, since it draws the minds of his followers away from all base things. [3] The second was: the lordship of Love is not good, because the more his followers are loyal to him, the more troublesome and sorrowful are the conditions they must endure. [4] The third was: the name of Love is so sweet to hear that it seems to me impossible that his workings in most instances would be other than sweet, since it is the case that names follow after the things named, as it is written: "Nomina sunt consequentia rerum."[1] [5] The fourth thought was: this lady who is the means by which Love so binds you is not like other ladies, whose hearts

1. "Names are the consequences of things."

are easily moved. [6] Each of these thoughts so fought with me that they made me stand like someone who cannot choose which road to take, who wishes to go but does not know where he is going; and if I were to seek a way which would suit them all, a way upon which all of them could agree, it would be a way to which I was strongly opposed: to call upon, and to place myself within the embrace of, Pity. [7] And while I remained in this state, there came upon me a desire to write a rhymed discourse on this subject. And at this point I set down this sonnet, which begins, "All my thoughts."

[8] All my thoughts speak of Love;
    And they have among themselves such great variety
    that one of them would have me wish him power,
    while another considers the first's force foolish,
and the third brings me the sweetness of hope,
    while the last makes me many times complain;
    and they agree only on seeking pity,
    trembling with the fear which is in my heart.
[9] Thus I do not know which subject matter to choose;
    I would like to speak, but do not know what to say:
    thus I find myself in the aimlessness of love!
And if I should wish to make them all agree,
    I must call upon my enemy,
    My Lady Pity, asking her to defend me.

[10] This sonnet can be divided into four sections. In the first I explain that all my thoughts are of Love. In the second I say that they are different, and state these differences. In the third I say in what they seem to agree. In the fourth I say that, while I wish to speak of Love, I do not know from which side to take my subject matter; but that if I were to choose all of them, I should have to call upon my enemy, My Lady Pity. I say "My Lady" as a scornful mode of address. The second part begins with the words, "and they have among themselves"; the third with the words, "and they agree only"; the fourth with the words, "Thus I do not know." *The New Life* 13

[4] Ladies, you who have understanding in love,
    I wish to speak to you about my lady,

not because I expect to exhaust her praise,
but rather by discussion to clear my mind.

[5]   I say that in thinking of her worth,
Love makes me feel so sweet,
that if I did not later lose my ardor,
by speaking I would make all people love her.

[6]   But I do not wish to speak so grandly,
since I might become base through fear;
but I will discourse on her noble station
in a manner inadequate to her
with you, loving ladies and young ladies,
because this is not a matter to speak of to others.

[7] An angel cries out in the divine intellect,
and says, "Lord, in the world there can be seen
a marvel in action which issues
from a soul which shines even up to this place."
Heaven, which has no other defect
but the lack of her, begs its lord for her,
and each saint cries for this reward.

[8]   Pity alone takes our part
when God speaks, understanding my lady:
"My beloved ones, for a while endure in peace
what is my will, that she your hope remain
there where there is one who awaits the loss of her,
one who shall say in hell, 'O ill-born ones,
I have seen the hope of the blessed.'"

[9] My lady is desired by the highest heaven:
Now I wish to make her virtue known to you.
I say, whoever wishes to appear a noble lady,
should go into her company, because when she walks along the way,
Love throws upon wicked hearts an ice,
by means of which all their thoughts freeze and perish;
and whoever can endure to stand there and look
will become a noble thing, or else die.

[10] And when she finds one who is worthy
to look at her, she demonstrates her powers,
for it happens that where she gives a salute,
he is humbled and forgets all offenses.
Furthermore God has given her greater grace
so that he who speaks to her cannot come to a bad end.

[11] Love says of her, "A mortal thing,
      how can it be so adorned and so pure?"
      Then he looks at her, and swears within himself
      that God intended here to create a new thing.
      She has almost the color of pearl, in such a form
      as a lady should have, and not beyond measure;
      she is as much of the good as nature could make;
      in comparison to her beauty is judged.

[12] From her eyes, whatever way she moves them,
      issue flaming spirits of love,
      which strike the eyes of anyone who is looking at her,
      and pass on until they find the heart:
      you see Love depicted there on her face
      where no one can gaze fixedly at her.[2]

[13] *Canzone*, I know that you will go speaking
      to several ladies when I have released you.
      But I will advise you, since I have brought you up
      to be a daughter of Love, naive and open,
      that wherever you come, you make this request:
      "Tell me where to go, for I am sent
      to her with whose praise I am adorned."

[14] But if you wish not to travel in vain,
      do not remain among base people:
      try, if you can, to be understood
      only among courteous ladies and men,
      who will direct you to the shortest route.
      You will find Love in her company;
      recommend me to him as you should.

[15] So that this *canzone* can be better understood, I will divide it
more carefully than the earlier poems. First, it is made up of three
sections. The first section is the proem for the discourse which
follows; the second is the discussion of the subject; and the third is a
sort of servant to the discourse which precedes it. The second
section begins with the line, "An angel cries out"; the third, with the
line, "*Canzone*, I know that." [16] The first section is divided into
four parts. In the first, I say to whom I wish to speak about my
lady and why I wish to speak; in the second I explain what I seem
to feel when I think of her worth, and how I would speak if I had not
lost my ardor; in the third, I state how I intend to speak of her in

2. That is, on her mouth.

order not to be impeded by baseness; and in the fourth, while repeating once more whom I intend to address, I give my reason for addressing them. The second part begins with the words, "I say"; the third with the words, "But I do not wish to speak"; and the fourth part begins with the words, "ladies and young ladies." [17] Next, where I say, "An angel cries out . . .", I begin my discussion of this lady. And this section is divided into two parts, one in which I tell what is understood about her in heaven, and another in which I tell what is understood about her on earth, beginning, "My lady is desired." [18] This second part is further divided into two parts, one in which I speak of her as she has nobility of soul, telling something about the effective powers which proceed from her soul, and another in which I speak of her as she has nobility of the body, describing some of her beauties, this part beginning with the words, "Love says of her." [19] And this second part is divided into two subsections, the first telling some of the beauties which belong to her whole person, and the second telling some of the beauties which belong to particular parts of her person, the second subsection beginning with, "From her eyes." [20] And this second subsection is itself divided into two parts, one dealing with her eyes, which are the beginning of love, and another dealing with her mouth, which is the end of love. And in order to avoid any lewd thoughts, I would have the reader remember what I wrote earlier, that it was my lady's greeting, which came from the moving of her mouth, which was the end of my desires so long as I was still able to receive it. [21] Next, where I say, "*Canzone,* I know that you . . . ," I add a stanza which plays the part of a maidservant to the others, in which I tell what I desired of my *canzone.* But because this last section is easy to understand, I will not bother with further divisions. [22] But I will say that a deeper understanding of this *canzone* would require the use of even more minute divisions. However, anyone who does not have enough intelligence to be able to understand it through those divisions I have already made will not offend me if he lets the matter rest here, since I am in fact afraid that I have already communicated too much of its meaning in making only the divisions I have, if it should happen that many people were to hear them.

The New Life 19.4–22

The Limits of Language

Poets have always claimed that the beauty of a woman or the sadness of the fall of a city exceed the capacity of language. This claim is standard poetic strategy for expressing sublime excellence or the extremes of emotion. Dante claims the same transcendence for his philosophic speculations and spiritual visions, and validates these claims to the extent that he manifests elsewhere his capacity for expressing those experiences which lie within the capabilities of human language. The Second Canzone *of the* Banquet *(the text of which may be found in Appendix A, no. 11) manifests this transcendence; Dante's commentary on it appears below. And the climax of the* Paradise *makes use of this ultimate rhetorical strategy of asserting a range of possible experience beyond rhetoric, using some of the ideas already expressed in the* Banquet.

[1] Having discussed two ways in which this material is ineffable, I must now proceed to comment on the words which tell of my inadequacy. And I say, then, that my inadequacy has a double source, just as the loftiness of my lady is in two ways transcendent, as I have already said. [2] For I had to leave behind, through the poverty of my intellect, much of what is true concerning her, which as it were radiates in my mind and is received by the mind as by a transparent body, without its being arrested. This I state in that small section which begins, "And for certain [those things] I must leave behind." [3] Then when I say, "and of those things which it does grasp," I state that not only am I inadequate to those things which my intellect could not hold on to, but even to those which I understand, since my tongue does not have the eloquence to be capable of expressing the discourse about it which is in my thoughts. For this reason it may be perceived that, in comparison to the truth, what I will say will be quite small. From this there results great praise of my lady, as can be clearly seen, which is my principal

intention; and any speech in which each part lends strength to the principal intention may well be said to come from the workshop of a master rhetorician. [4] Then where I say, "Therefore, if there is any defect in those rhymes," I offer excuses for a fault for which I should not be blamed, other people perceiving that my words fall very short of her dignity. So I declare that if there is any defect in my rhymes, which is to say, in the words which are set forth as a discussion of her, the blame for this lies in the weakness of the intellect and in the limitations of our speech, which is so outrun by thought that it can follow it only a short way, particularly where the thought is generated by love, because here the soul endeavors to go deeper than it does elsewhere.

[5] Someone might say, "You excuse yourself and accuse yourself at the same time." For I have proved, and not eliminated, the fault insofar as I have shown it to lie in my intellect or in my speech; for if I ought to receive the praise when my speech is good so ought I to receive the blame when it is defective. To this charge I will give a brief answer, showing that I really am excusing, and not accusing, myself. [6] It may be assumed, from the principle which the Philosopher expresses in the Third Book of the *Ethics*,[1] that a man deserves praise or blame only for those things which it is in his power to do or not to do. But he deserves neither praise nor blame for those things over which he has no control, since the praise or blame are attributed to someone else, even if the things are in some way a part of the man himself. [7] Thus we ought not to blame a man because he has a body which has been ugly from his birth, since it is not in his power to make it beautiful, but rather to blame the bad disposition of the material of which it is made, which is itself the source of nature's fault. By the same reasoning, we ought not to praise a man for that beauty of his body which he had from his birth, but rather ought to praise its artificer, human nature, which produces such beauty out of its material when it is not impeded by this material. [8] Thus the priest made a good answer to the emperor who laughed in scorn of the ugliness of the latter's body: "God is the Lord: he made us, and not we ourselves;" these are the words of the Prophet in a verse of the Psalter, written without a

1. Aristotle *Nichomachean Ethics* 1.3.

word more or less than the reply of the priest.[2] And of this let those ill-born wretches take note, those who pay more attention to decking out their persons than they do to adorning their actions which ought to be adorned with all honesty: what they do is to adorn another's work while neglecting their own.

[9] Then turning again to the subject, I say that our intellect, because of a defect in that faculty by means of which it draws whatever it has perceived to itself (this faculty being an organic one, the imagination) cannot rise to certain things (because the imagination, not having what is required, cannot help the intellect). These things include substances separated from their material, which we cannot understand or completely comprehend, although we can speculate about them. [10] For this man is not to be blamed, since he was not, I say, the creator of this defect, which was rather the doing of universal nature, which is God, who wishes to deprive us of this light in this life, since had he given it to us, we would have been presumptuous in our reasonings. [11] Therefore, if my speculations took me to a place where my imagination fell behind my intellect, I am not to blame for my being unable to understand. Furthermore, there is a limit on our capacity in any particular activity which has been placed on it by universal nature, not by us, and thus it should be known that the limit does not restrict the capacity for thought as much as it does the capacity for speech; which is itself less restricted than gesture. [12] Then we are not to blame when a thought exceeds the capacity of speech—whether the thought arrives at the level of complete understanding or whether it does not—because we did not create the limits [of either understanding or speech]. [13] Therefore it is clear that I truly do excuse myself when I say, "The blame belongs to the feeble intellect / and to our capacity for speech which lacks the power / to repeat all that Love says." For the good will which ought to characterize our weighing of human merit should be clearly visible in us.

Banquet 3.4.1–13

---

2. Psalm 99:3. The anecdote of the priest and the emperor is taken from Vincent of Beauvais *Speculum Historiale* 25.12.

I saw, brighter than a myriad of lamps,
　　One Sun, which lit up all other things,
　　Just as our sun does the sights of the sky;　　　30
And through the living light there shone
　　upon my sight, which could not sustain it,
　　the bright Substance, in perfect clarity.
Oh, Beatrice! sweet and dear guide!
　　She said to me, "What overmasters you　　　35
　　Is the might which no one can oppose.
Here is the Wisdom and the Power
　　Which opened the road between heaven and earth,
　　As had been for so long desired."
Just as fire will release itself from clouds　　　40
　　(Expanding to the point that it cannot be held)
　　And against its nature throws itself downward,
So my mind, in the middle of such a feast,
　　enlarged, issued from itself,
　　And what it did, I cannot remember.　　　45
"Open your eyes, and see what I am!
　　You have seen things which have made you
　　Capable of sustaining my smile."
I was like one who feels again
　　A forgotten vision, and who endeavors　　　50
　　In vain to bring it back to his mind,
When I heard this offer, worthy
　　Of such gratitude as will never be erased
　　From the book which records the past.
If through me were to sound all of those tongues　　　55
　　Which Polyhymnia and her sisters make
　　Fatter with their most sweet milk,[3]
In aid of me, not to a thousandth of the truth
　　Would they reach, in singing of this holy smile,
　　And of how brightly the holy face was lit up.　　　60
And so, in figuring forth Paradise,
　　The consecrated poem must leap up
　　Like one who finds his way blocked.
But whoever weighs the heaviness of the theme

---

3. The Muses nourish (or "make fatter") the tongues of poets, who are then capable of the highest eloquence.

Against the mortal shoulders which must carry it,   65
Will not blame me if I stagger under it.
This is not the voyage of a little ferry-boat
On which this daring prow goes, cleaving the waves,
Nor of a pilot who would spare himself.

Paradise 23.28–69

ALLEGORY AND OTHER
POETIC FIGURES

The Letter to Can Grande

(*Epistolam X ad Canem Grandem della Scala*—Latin)

The Letter to Can Grande *is a poet's explanation of how he puts his principles into practice. It also exemplifies the relation, in medieval commentary, between the general characterization and the detailed interpretation of a work. Its general format is an expansion of the kind of introduction or* accessus *which usually preceded commentaries on the ancient poets. It thus contains the kind of information thought to be important for the study of any poem. In the number of his distinctions, however, Dante goes beyond the usual commentator, though what he has to say about the difference between the form of the treatment and the form of the treatise, or between the "end" of the work considered on the literal as against the allegorical level, represent divisions implicit in early commentators rather than novelties. The commentary is an interesting complement to the introduction because it shows that specific interpretations were not expected to follow the theory of levels in a wooden and systematic way. The fact that the poem could be interpreted literally and on three allegorical levels did not imply that every section and every symbol had to have four meanings. Dante's practice in this regard is consistent with scriptural commentary, where the exegete, after acknowledging the existence of four levels, would proceed to his detailed commentary without feeling that he had to label the levels of his interpretation or find a meaning on all levels to fulfill the requirements of his system.*

To the magnificent and most victorious lord, Lord Can Grande della Scala, Vicar General for the most holy Principate of Caesar in the city of Verona and the town of Vicenza: his most devoted servant, Dante Alighieri, a Florentine by birth but not in character, prays for him a happy and long life, and the perpetual increase of his glorious name.

[1] The glorious praise of your Magnificence, which Fame, ever wakeful, spreads abroad in her flight, draws different people in different directions: some are raised up by the hope of prosperity, others cast down by the fear of destruction. I myself judged that the report of your deeds, exceeding those of our contemporaries, was somewhat exaggerated, since it went beyond the appearance of truth. Therefore, not wishing to be held in the suspense of continual uncertainty any longer, I sought Verona, as the Queen of the East sought Jerusalem,[1] or as Pallas sought Helicon,[2] so that I could examine with my own trustworthy eyes that of which I had heard. There I was witness to your splendor, there I was witness to, and, as well, recipient of, your generosity; and to the same degree as, before, I had suspected that the words were, in part, extravagant, I afterwards knew that it was the deeds themselves which were extravagant. And thus it came to pass that from hearing alone, I became, with a certain subjection of my mind, your well-wisher, but from my first sight of you, your devoted servant and your friend.

[2] Nor do I think that in assuming the name of friend I make myself liable to the charge of presumption, as perhaps some would object, since unequals are as readily united in the sacred bonds of friendship as are equals. Indeed, were one to look closely at friendships which have been both delightful and useful, one would find, upon inspection, that they have most often joined eminent men with their inferiors. And if one turns one's attention to true friendship, friendship for its own sake, would one not establish that the friends of the noblest and most illustrious princes have often been men of obscure fortune, distinguished for their honesty? And why not, since friendship between God and man is not even impeded by the great disparity between them? But if what is asserted here seems indecorous to anyone, let him hear the Holy Spirit declaring that certain men have shared friendship with Him; for in *Wisdom* he may read, concerning Wisdom, "For she is an infinite treasure to men! which they that use, become the friends of God."[3] But ignorance, judgment without discernment, prevails among the

1. See Matthew 12:42 and Luke 11:31, as well as 1 Kings 10 and 2 Chronicles 9.
2. Ovid *Metamorphoses* 5.254; Virgil *Aeneid* 12.641; 10.163.
3. *Wisdom* 7:14.

common people; and the same foolish credulity which makes them think the sun a foot wide determines their thinking on moral questions. It is not fitting, however, that we, who have been given knowledge in ourselves of what is best, follow the tracks of the herd; we are rather obligated to meet their errors head on. For those who live[4] according to intellect and reason, and who are endowed with a certain divine liberty, are not restricted by precedent. And this is not surprising, since the laws are guided by them, not they by the laws. It is evident, therefore, that what I said earlier, namely, that I am your most devoted servant and friend, is in no respect presumptuous.

[3] And so, considering your friendship a most valuable treasure, I wish to preserve it through careful planning and solicitous attention. Therefore, since it is taught as a principle of moral philosophy that friendship is preserved and equalized by reciprocity, it is my earnest desire to make reciprocal return for benefits more than once conferred upon me. On this account I have often and at length looked over the little things I have, setting them apart from each other and judging each individually, trying to decide which one would, as a gift, be most worthy of you, and most pleasing. And I could find nothing more fitting to even your great eminence than that sublime canticle of the *Comedy* which is adorned with the title of *Paradise*. And so, dedicated to your self, and with this letter serving as its introduction, I inscribe it to you, offer it to you, and, in short, commend it to you.

[4] The single-minded ardor of my affection will not allow me to pass over in silence the fact that this presentation would seem to confer greater honor and fame on the gift than on the recipient.[5] But to the contrary, the title itself will have been recognized by the careful reader to express my prediction of the growth of the glory

4. Toynbee reads here *vigentes* ("those who have vigor") for the unanimous attestation, *degentes*, of the texts.

5. Toynbee amends to "on the recipient than on the gift" in order to preserve the cursus. This passage is obscure enough without the emendation, and I have retained the original order. Dante would seem to state that certain envious people will say that he is trying to gain glory for his poem by attaching it to Can Grande, to which Dante answers that his gift is really a prediction concerning Can Grande's coming glories. It therefore does at least equal honor to the recipient.

of your name, which was my purpose. But paying no attention to envy,[6] my eagerness for your favor urges my preface toward that end which was its from the beginning. And so, having completed the formula, for a letter, I shall undertake, in my capacity as commentator, to present systematically something of an introduction to the work I have offered to you.

[5] As the Philosopher says in the second book of the *Metaphysics*, "As a thing is with respect to being, so it is with respect to truth";[7] and the reason for this is that the truth concerning a thing, which consists in the truth as its subject, is the perfect image of the thing as it is. And so, of all things which have being, some are such that they have absolute being in themselves, others such that their being is dependent upon a relationship with something else: they exist at the same time with something which is their correlative, as is the case with father and son, master and servant, double and half, the whole and the parts, and many other such things. Because such things depend for their being upon another thing, it follows that their truth would depend upon the truth of the other; not knowing the "half," its "double" could not be understood, and so with the other cases.

[6] Therefore, if one should wish to present an introduction to a part of a work, it is necessary to present some conception of the whole work of which it is a part. For this reason I, who wish to present something in the form of an introduction to the above-mentioned part of the whole *Comedy*, have decided to preface it with some discussion of the whole work, in order to make the approach to the part easier and more complete. There are six questions, then, which should be asked at the beginning about any doctrinal work: what is its subject, its form, its agent, its end, the title of the book, and its branch of philosophy. In three cases the answers to these questions will be different for the part of the work I propose to give you than for the whole, that is, in the cases of its subject, form, and title, while in the other three, as will be clear upon inspection, they will be the same. Thus these first three should

6. Accepting Toynbee's emendation of *vitam* to *invidiam*. It is impossible to see the relevance of Dante's "holding his life in contempt."

7. Aristotle *Metaphysics* 2.1.

be specifically asked in a discussion of the whole work, after which the way will be clear for an introduction to the part. Let us, then, ask the last three questions not only about the whole but also about the offered part itself.

[7] For the clarification of what I am going to say, then, it should be understood that there is not just a single sense in this work: it might rather be called *polysemous*, that is, having several senses. For the first sense is that which is contained in the letter, while there is another which is contained in what is signified by the letter. The first is called literal, while the second is called allegorical, or moral or anagogical. And in order to make this manner of treatment clear, it can be applied to the following verses: "When Israel went out of Egypt, the house of Jacob from a barbarous people, Judea was made his sanctuary, Israel his dominion." [8] Now if we look at the letter alone, what is signified to us is the departure of the sons of Israel from Egypt during the time of Moses; if at the allegory, what is signified to us is our redemption through Christ; if at the moral sense, what is signified to us is the conversion of the soul from the sorrow and misery of sin to the state of grace; if at the anagogical, what is signified to us is the departure of the sanctified soul from bondage to the corruption of this world into the freedom of eternal glory. And although these mystical senses are called by various names, they may all be called allegorical, since they are all different from the literal or historical. For allegory is derived from the Greek *alleon*, which means in Latin *alienus* ("belonging to another") or *diversus* ("different").

[8] This being established, it is clear that the subject about which these two senses play must also be twofold. And thus it should first be noted what the subject of the work is when taken according to the letter, and then what its subject is when understood allegorically. The subject of the whole work, then, taken literally, is the state of souls after death, understood in a simple sense; for the movement of the whole work turns upon this and about this. If on the other hand the work is taken allegorically, the subject is man, in the exercise of his free will, earning or becoming liable to the rewards or punishments of justice.

8. Psalm 113:1–2 (114:1–2 in the King James version).

[9] And the form is twofold: the form of the treatise and the form of the treatment. The form of the treatise is threefold, according to its three kinds of divisions. The first division is that which divides the whole work into three canticles. The second is that which divides each canticle into cantos. The third, that which divides the cantos into rhymed units. The form or manner of treatment is poetic, fictive, descriptive, digressive, and transumptive, and it as well consists in definition, division, proof, refutation, and the giving of examples.

[10] The title of the work is, "Here begins the Comedy of Dante Alighieri, a Florentine by birth but not in character." To understand the title, it must be known that comedy is derived from *comos*, "a village," and from *oda*, "a song," so that a comedy is, so to speak, "a rustic song." Comedy, then, is a certain genre of poetic narrative differing from all others. For it differs from tragedy in its matter, in that tragedy is tranquil and conducive to wonder at the beginning, but foul and conducive to horror at the end, or catastrophe, for which reason it is derived from *tragos*, meaning "goat," and *oda*, making it, as it were, a "goat song," that is, foul as a goat is foul. This is evident in Seneca's tragedies. Comedy, on the other hand, introduces a situation of adversity, but ends its matter in prosperity, as is evident in Terence's comedies. And for this reason some writers have the custom of saying in their salutations, by way of greeting, "a tragic beginning and a comic ending to you." And, as well, they differ in their manner of speaking. Tragedy uses an elevated and sublime style, while comedy uses an unstudied and low style, which is what Horace implies in the *Art of Poetry* where he allows comic writers occasionally to speak like the tragic, and also the reverse of this:

> Yet sometimes even comedy elevates its voice,
> and angry Chremes rages in swelling tones;
> and in tragedy Telephus and Peleus often lament
> in prosaic speeches . . . .[9]

So from this it should be clear why the present work is called the *Comedy*. For, if we consider the matter, it is, at the beginning, that is,

9. Horace *Art of Poetry* 93–96.

in Hell, foul and conducive to horror, but at the end, in Paradise, prosperous, conducive to pleasure, and welcome. And if we consider the manner of speaking, it is unstudied and low, since its speech is the vernacular, in which even women communicate. There are, besides these, other genres of poetic narrative, such as pastoral verse, elegy, satire, and the hymn of thanksgiving, as could also be gathered from Horace in his *Art of Poetry*. But there is no purpose to discussing these at this time.

[11] Now it can be explained in what manner the part I have offered you may be assigned a subject. For if the subject of the whole work, on the literal level, is the state of souls after death, in an absolute, not in a restricted sense, then the subject of this part is the same state, but restricted to the state of blessed souls after death. And if the subject of the whole work, considered allegorically, is man, through exercise of free will, earning or becoming liable to the rewards or punishments of justice, then it is evident that the subject in this part is restricted to man's becoming eligible, to the extent he has earned them, for the rewards of justice.

[12] And in the same manner the form of this part follows from the form ascribed to the whole. For if the form of the whole treatise is threefold, then the form in this part is twofold, that is, the division into cantos and into rhymed units. This part could not have the first division as its form, since this part itself is [a product] of the first division.

[13] The title of the book also follows; for while the title of the whole book is, as was said earlier, "Here begins the Comedy, *etc*," the title of this part is, "Here begins the third canticle of Dante's *Comedy, etc.*, which is called *Paradise*."

[14] Having settled these three questions, where the answer was different for the part than for the whole, it remains to deal with the other three, where the answers will not be different for either the part or the whole. The agent, then, in the whole and in the part, is he who has been mentioned above; and he is clearly so throughout.

[15] The end of the whole and of the part could be multiple, that is, both immediate and ultimate. But, without going into details, it can be briefly stated that the end of the whole as of the part is to

remove those living in this life from the state of misery and to lead them to the state of happiness.

[16] The branch of philosophy which determines the procedure of the work as a whole and in this part is moral philosophy, or ethics, inasmuch as the whole and this part have been conceived for the sake of practical results, not for the sake of speculation. So even if some parts or passages are treated in the manner of speculative philosophy, this is not for the sake of the theory, but for a practical purpose, following that principle which the Philosopher advances in the second book of the *Metaphysics*, that "practical men sometimes speculate about things in their particular and temporal relations." [10]

[17] Having presented these basic principles, I will now offer a sample exposition of the literal level; and I should say ahead of time that the exposition of the literal level consists in nothing else than the making explicit of the form of the work. Thus this part, or the third canticle which is called *Paradise*, is divided into two parts, that is, into a prologue and an executive part. The second part begins where it says "Through diverse outlets rises on mortals . . . ." [11]

> [The glory of him who moves all things
>> Penetrates through the universe, and shines
>> More in one part, and less in another.
> In that heaven which receives more of his light
>> I was, and I saw things which to relate
>> He who descends below neither knows how nor is able;
> Because, approaching near to its desire,
>> Our intellect goes so deeply
>> That the memory cannot follow so far.
> In truth, as much as I could make a treasure of
>> In my mind out of [what I saw] in the holy kingdom
>> Will be now the matter of my song.
> O good Apollo, for this final labor
>> Make me through your power to be made a vessel
>> As you require before you will give the beloved laurel!
> Up to this point one summit of Parnassus
>> Has been enough for me, but now with both
>> I am required to enter the remaining arena.

10. Aristotle *Metaphysics* 2.1.

11. *Paradise* 1.37. The entire passage (lines 1–38) which is the subject of Dante's exposition is printed immediately below, for the convenience of the reader.

Enter my breast, and breathe through me
  As when you drew Marsyas [12]
  From the sheath of his members!
O divine virtue, if you will grant me this,
  So that a shadow of the blessed kingdom,
  Sealed in my head, I may express,
You shall see me come to the tree of your pleasure,
  And then crown myself with those leaves
  Which my matter and you make me worthy of.
So rarely, father, it is gathered
  For the triumph of a Ceasar or a Poet
  (Because of the sin and shame of human desires)
That the Peneian leaf [13] must bear [a child/fruit] within
  Of joy to the joyous Delphic god,
  Whenever it makes anyone thirst for itself.
From a small spark a great flame follows:
  Perhaps behind me with a better voice
  Prayer will be made so that Cyrrha [14] may respond.
Through diverse outlets rises on mortals
  The light of the world . . . .]

[18] Concerning the first of these parts, it should be noted that, although in a general way it could be called an exordium, it should, in this particular case, be termed a prologue. This is what the Philosopher would seem to imply in the third book of the *Rhetoric*, where he says, "The proem is the exordium of an oration, corresponding to the prologue of a poem or to the prelude in flute-playing." [15] It should be further noted that this introductory section, which can be called in general the exordium, becomes a different thing in the hands of a poet than it is in the hands of an orator. For orators usually give some sample of what they are about to say, in order to make the minds of their listeners receptive. Poets, on the other hand, not only do this, but also follow it with some sort of invocation. And this is right for them since they require so

12. The satyr Marsyas challenged Apollo to a musical contest. Defeated, he was punished for his presumption by being flayed. See Ovid *Metamorphoses* 6.382–400.

13. Daphne, daughter of the river god Peneus, who was transformed into the laurel.

14. Seaport of Delphi, here standing for Apollo's residence.

15. Aristotle *Rhetoric* 3.14.

much more of their invocation and must therefore ask the superior powers for a thing, resembling a divine gift, beyond the ordinary capacity of man. And so the prologue under consideration is divided into two parts, the first outlining what is about to be said, the second invoking Apollo. And the second part begins with the line, "O good Apollo, for this final labor . . . ."

[19] Concerning the first of these parts, it should be noted that three things are required of a good exordium, as Cicero says in the *New Rhetoric*; it must render the listener well-disposed, attentive, and willing to learn, particularly when the matter is of a type which excites amazement, as Cicero himself says.[16] And since the matter dealt with in the treatise under consideration is of the type which excites amazement, it is the purpose of the first part of the exordium, or prologue, to bring about these three conditions of the listener with relation to the source of the amazement. For the author says that he is about to relate what he saw in the first heaven and was able to retain in his mind. This statement fulfills all three of the requirements; for the usefulness of the relation makes the listener well-disposed; its capacity to excite amazement makes him attentive; and its being possible makes him willing to learn. The author implies usefulness when he says he is about to recount that which is to the greatest extent attractive to human desire, namely, the joys of Paradise; he touches on the source of amazement when he promises to tell of things as remote as they are sublime, namely, the conditions of the kingdom of heaven; and he shows that it is within the realm of possibility when he says he will tell what he could retain in his mind; for if he could do so, others could as well. All three of these things are touched on in the passage where he says that he has been in the first heaven, and that he intends to tell, concerning the kingdom of heaven, whatever, like a treasure, he was able to retain in his mind. Having thus noted the goodness and completeness of the first part of the prologue, let us proceed to a literal exposition.

[20] The author writes that the "glory of Him who moves all things," who is God, "penetrates through the universe," but in such a manner that it is "more in one part, and less in another." Now that

16. The *New Rhetoric* is the *Rhetorica ad Herrenium*, long attributed to Cicero: see Book 1, chapter 41. Cf. the *De Inventione* 1.15.20 and 22.

it does shine everywhere, both reason and authority attest. Reason does it in this way: Everything which is, has being either from itself or from something else. But it is clear that only one thing, the first or beginning, which is God, must have being from itself, since to have being does not argue the necessity of having being through oneself, and since only one thing, namely, the first or beginning, which is the cause of all other things, has attached to it the necessity of having being through itself. Therefore all things which exist, except this one thing, have their being from another. If therefore one takes not just any thing, but rather the final thing in the universe, it would clearly have its being from something else; and this something else from which it has it will have its being either from itself or from something else. If it has it from itself, then it is the first thing; if from something else, that, too, will in the same way have its being either from itself or from something else. And since it would be so in following causal agents to infinity, as is proved in the second book of the *Metaphysics*,[17] it will be so in arriving at the first thing, which is God. Thus everything which has being, gets its being, either directly or indirectly, from Him; for it is by virtue of what it receives from the first cause that the second cause has influence over what it causes, in the manner of a body which receives and reflects a ray. And for this reason the first cause is the stronger cause. And this is the meaning of the passage in the book, *On Causes*, which says, "All primary causes have greater influence on what they cause than any second cause does."[18] So much for the question of being.

[21] As to the question of essence, I prove it in this manner: Every essence, except the first, is caused. Otherwise there would be more than one thing whose being was necessarily through itself, which is impossible. Since every essence is caused, its cause is either nature or intelligence, and, if nature, it follows that the cause is an intelligence, since nature is the product of intelligence. Therefore everything which is caused, is caused by some intelligence, either directly or indirectly. Since, then, a virtue follows from the essence of which it is a virtue, it will be entirely and solely of the intellect if the essence which caused it is so. And thus, just as earlier, in the case

17. Aristotle *Metaphysics* 2.2.
18. *On Causes*, prop. 1.

of being, the chain of causality went back to a first cause, so the
chain of causes goes in the cases of essence and virtue. For this
reason it is clear that both the essence and the virtue of any thing
proceed from the first thing, and are received by things of lesser
intelligence as if from something sending out rays; and that these
things in turn reflect the rays from the higher things, like mirrors,
to the lower things. This matter would seem to be adequately
dealt with by Dionysius in his work *On the Celestial Hierarchies*.[19]
And because of this principle, the book *On Causes* says, "Every
intelligence is filled with form."[20] And thus it should be clear how
reason would demonstrate that the divine light, which is to say, the
divine goodness, wisdom and virtue, shines everywhere.

[22] Authority also demonstrates the same thing, and with
greater knowledge. For the Holy Spirit says, through Jeremiah,
"Do not I fill heaven and earth?" and in the Psalm, "Whither shall
I go from thy spirit? or whither shall I flee from thy face? If I
ascend into heaven, thou art there: if I descend into hell, thou art
present. If I take my wings . . ." and so forth. And Wisdom says
that "The spirit of the Lord hath filled the whole world." And
Ecclesiasticus, in the forty-second chapter, "Full of the glory of the
Lord is his work." And even pagan writings attest to it; this is
Lucan in the ninth book: "Jupiter is whatever you see, wherever
you move."[21]

[23] And so the author says well when he writes that the divine
ray, or divine glory, "penetrates through the universe and shines,"
for it penetrates, as the beginning of essence, and shines, as the
beginning of being. What he adds about "more and less" is clearly
true, since we see that on a scale of excellence, one essence will be
higher, while another is lower, as is obvious in the case of heaven
and the elements, one of which is incorruptible, while the others are
corruptible.

19. Pseudo-Dionysius *On the Celestial Hierarchies* 3.2. It should be noted that in
this work, as in *On Causes* (above and below), intelligence is personified, and means
an active agent of some sort (like an angel) responsible for the essence and motion
of the heavens. Some of the obscurity of this passage in Dante arises from the
ambiguity of the word.

20. *On Causes*, prop. 10.

21. Jeremiah 23:24; Psalm 138:7–9 (139:7–9 in the King James version);
Wisdom 1:7; Ecclesiasticus 42:16; Lucan *Pharsalia* 9.580.

[24] And after having set forth this truth, he follows it with a circumlocution for Paradise, saying that he was in that heaven which received more abundantly the light, or glory, of God. By this heaven he means to be understood to refer to the highest heaven, that one which contains all the bodies in the universe and is contained by none, within which all bodies move while it remains in perpetual rest,[22] receiving its virtue from no corporeal substance And it is called the empyrean, which is as much as to say, the heaven glowing with its own fire or heat. These words do not refer to material fire or heat, but to spiritual, which is to say, holy love or charity.

[25] That it does receive more of the divine light can be proved, first, on the basis of its containing all things and being contained by none, and, second, on the basis of its perpetual rest or peace. The first proof is of this form: In its natural position, the container stands in relation to the thing contained as a formative to the thing formed, as it is asserted in the fourth book of the *Physics*.[23] Since the natural position of the first heaven with relation to the whole universe is that of the container, it therefore is related to all things as the formative to that which is formed, which is to be in the relation of cause and effect. And since all causative force is a kind of ray emanating from the first cause, which is God, that heaven which is to the greatest extent causative must obviously receive most of the divine light.

[26] The second proof goes this way: Anything which moves is moved because of something which it does not have, which thereby constitutes the end of its motion. The heaven of the moon, for instance, moves because some part of itself has not that position toward which it is moving; and since no part of it whatsoever ever reaches such a position (for it cannot), it moves to another position. For this reason it is always in motion and never at rest, and this constitutes its appetite. And what I assert about the heaven of the moon is true of all the heavens except the first. Anything which moves, then, is deficient in some way, not having the whole of its being at any one time. Therefore that heaven which does not move

22. There may be a gap in the text here, since the balance of clauses is lost: the sentence seems to require something like, "giving its virtue to all other things." Several of the manuscripts have other words in this place.

23. Aristotle *Physics* 4.4.

because of anything else must have complete in itself and in every part of itself whatever is necessary to its being, so that it does not need to move in order to reach perfection. And since all perfection is a ray of the first perfection, which is perfection in the highest degree, the first heaven obviously must receive most of the first light, which is God. This reasoning, however, has the appearance of an argument based on the denial of the antecedent; it is not absolutely valid and in accord with syllogistic form.[24] But it is valid because of the nature of its content. For it deals with something eternal, and assumes that it could be eternally deficient. Therefore, if God did not give it motion, it follows that he did not give it material in any way deficient. And on this assumption, the argument is valid because of its content. The same principle would hold were I to argue, "Since he is a man, he is capable of laughing"; for in every reversible proposition, the same reasoning is valid because of the nature of the content. Therefore it is clear that, when the author says, "In that heaven which receives more of the light of God," he intends a circumlocution for Paradise, or the empyrean heaven.

[27] The Philosopher presents an argument consonant with the above in the first book of *On Heaven*, where he says that a heaven "has material more honorable than that of other heavens beneath it to the extent that it is more distant than they from the earth." And to this might be added what the Apostle told the Ephesians concerning Christ, "who ascended above all the heavens, that he might fill all things." This is the heaven of the Lord's pleasures, to which pleasures Ezechiel refers in accusing Lucifer, "Thou wast the seal of resemblance, full of wisdom, and perfect in beauty. Thou wast in the pleasures of the paradise of God."[25]

[28] And after having said in his circumlocution that he was in

24. That is, it is of the form, "If A is B, then C is D; but A is not B, therefore C is not D." ("A thing which moves is not satisfied; but the first heaven is not moved, and therefore must be satisfied.") Such an argument is, as Dante says, not valid unless its content makes the propositions reversible, as would be true where the content of the proposition is something eternal. The lower spheres are always moving and the empyrean is always still, so the propositions contain all the possibilities.

25. Aristotle *De Caelo* 1.2; Ephesians 4:10; Ezechiel 28:12–13.

that part of Paradise, he continues by stating that he saw things which he who descends cannot relate. And he gives the cause of this, saying that the "intellect goes so deeply" into "its desire" itself, which is God, "that the memory cannot follow." To understand what this means, it should be noted that, in this life, the human intellect, because of the affinity it has for the separated intellectual substance with which it shares its nature, reaches such a height of exaltation, when it is exalted, that, upon its return to itself, having transcended the ordinary capacity of man, memory fails. And this idea is implied to us by the Apostle, addressing the Corinthians, where he writes: "I know a man (whether in the body, or out of the body, I know not; God knoweth), [who was] caught up to the third heaven, and [who] heard secret words, which it is not granted to man to utter." See, when the intellect had passed beyond the bounds of human capacity in its exaltation, it could not remember what happened outside these bounds. And the same idea is implied to us in Matthew, where the three disciples fell down on their faces, and told nothing about it afterwards, as if they had forgotten. And it is written in Ezechiel: "I saw, and I fell upon my face." [26] But if these passages do not satisfy the skeptical, let them read Richard of St. Victor in his book, *On Contemplation*, or Bernard in his book *On Consideration*, or Augustine in his book *On the Capacity of the Soul*,[27] and they will be no longer skeptical. Or if they should bark out against the possibility of such exaltation because of the sinfulness of the speaker, they should read Daniel, where they would find that even Nebuchadnezzar, by divine permission, saw something which was a warning to sinners, and then forgot it.[28] For he "who maketh his sun to rise upon the good and bad, and raineth upon the just and the unjust,"[29] manifests his glory to all the living, no matter how evil they are, sometimes mercifully, for the sake of their conversion, sometimes harshly, as a punishment, and to a greater or lesser degree, according to his will.

26. 2 Corinthians 12:2–4 (Dante has left out certain of the phrases in the passage); Matthew 17:1–8; Ezechiel 2:1 (1:28 in the King James version).

27. *De Contemplatione* is also known as *Benjamin Major*; the relevant passage is in 4.23. In Saint Bernard's book the relevant passage is 5.2.3, in Augustine's, 33.76.

28. Daniel 2:3–5.

29. Matthew 5:45.

[29] And so the author saw, as he says, something he on returning "neither knows how nor is able to relate." Now it should be carefully noted that he says that he "neither knows how nor is able"; he does not know how because it was forgotten, he is unable because even if he had remembered and could retain the content [of his vision], the words would be lacking. For we see many things with the intellect for which there are no verbal signs. This fact Plato makes plain enough by the use he makes of metaphors in his books: for he saw many things by the light of the intellect which he was unable to express in the appropriate words.

[30] Next the author goes on to say that he will tell about those things which he was able to retain concerning the kingdom of heaven; and he calls this the "matter" of his work. The nature and extent of these things are to be made explicit in the executive part.

[31] Next he makes his invocation, beginning with the line, "O good Apollo . . . ." And this part is divided into two parts. In the first, he makes his petition in a formal invocation [of the god]; in the second, he tries to persuade Apollo to grant the petition by promising him a certain recompense. The second part begins with the line, "O divine virtue . . . ." The first part is itself divided into two parts: the first, his petition for divine aid, the second, his allusion to the necessity of his being granted the petition, which is its justification. This second part begins with the line, "Up to this point one summit of Parnassus . . . ."

[32] This is the meaning in general of the second part of the prologue. But I will not at present explicate it in particular; anxiety about personal matters weighs upon me, and so I must put aside this and other works useful to the common good. But I hope that your Magnificence will grant me opportunity at another time to continue this useful exposition.

[33] Concerning the executive part which, in the division of the whole, is coordinate with the prologue, I shall not say anything further, either about its divisions or its meaning, except that it proceeds throughout by telling about the ascension from one heaven to another, and about the blessed souls to be found in each of these heavens; and that their true blessedness consists in their perception of the Origin of Truth. This is clear from the book of John, which

says, "Now this is eternal life: that they may know thee, the only true God," and so forth; and from the third book of the *Consolation* of Boethius, where it says, "To behold thee is the end." [30] Thus it is that, in order to show the glory of their blessedness, many things must be asked of these souls, as of those who have the vision of all truth, the answers to which are, to the greatest extent, both delightful and useful. And since, having reached the beginning or first cause, which is God, there is nothing further to seek, he being Alpha and Omega, or the first and the last (as he is designated in John's vision),[31] the treatise comes to an end in God himself, who is blessed in the world without end.

30. John 17:3; Boethius *The Consolation of Philosophy* 3, met. 9.
31. Apocalypse (Revelation) 1:8; 21:6; 22:13.

The Four Levels of Interpretation

Dante's description of the method of allegorical interpretation in the
Banquet, *some ten years earlier than the* Letter to Can Grande, *differs
from that of the letter in making a distinction between the allegory of the poets
and that of the theologians. (See above, p. xliii.) But what is most obvious
in the two passages is the continuity of Dante's thought, represented in his
insistence upon the necessity of expounding the literal level before proceeding to
the allegorical, and upon the usefulness of the moral level.*

[2] I say, as declared in the first chapter, that the interpretation
should be both literal and allegorical. For the understanding of this,
it should be realized that texts can be understood and should be
explicated primarily on four levels. [3] The first of these is called the
literal level, the level which does not extend beyond the letter of the
fictive discourse, which is what the fables of the poets are. The
second is called allegorical, and is hidden under the cloak of these
fables, a truth disguised under a beautiful lie; as for example when
Ovid says that Orpheus with his lyre made the wild beasts tame, and
caused the trees and the stones to move,[1] this means that the wise
man with the instrument of his voice makes cruel hearts tame and
humble, and causes the wills of those who do not have a life of
learning and art to be moved (for those who do not possess the life
of reason are like stones). [4] The reason why the wise [poets] invented this hidden sense will be discussed in the next-to-last treatise.
Of course, the theologians understand this sense in another way than
do the poets. But because my purpose is to follow the mode of the
poets, I understand the allegorical sense as it is used by poets.

[5] The third sense is called the moral, and it is this one which
teachers should seek out with most diligence when going through

---

1. Ovid *Metamorphoses* 10.86–105, 143–47; 11.1–2.

texts, because of its usefulness to them and to their pupils. One may discover, for example, from the Gospel,[2] that when Christ went up to the mountain to be transfigured, he took only three of the twelve disciples with him: this may be interpreted morally to mean that in the most secret affairs we should have few companions.

[6] The fourth sense is called the anagogical, or the "sense beyond." This sense occurs when a spiritual interpretation is to be given a text which, even though it is true on the literal level, represents the supreme things belonging to eternal glory by means of the things it represents. It may be perceived in that song of the Prophet which says that, in the departure of the people of Israel from Egypt, Judea was made holy and free.[3] [7] For even though the literal truth of this passage is clear, what it means spiritually is no less true, that in the departure of the soul from sin, it is made holy and free in its power. [8] In bringing out this meaning, the literal sense should always come first, it being the meaning in which the others are contained and without which it would be impossible and irrational to come to an understanding of the others, particularly the allegorical. [9] It would be impossible because, in the case of anything which has an outside and an inside, it is impossible to come to the inside without first coming to the outside. Thus, since in a text the literal meaning is always the outside, it is impossible to come to the others, particularly the allegorical, without first coming to the literal. [10] It would also be impossible because in everything, both natural and artificial, it is impossible to proceed to the form without having first prepared the subject upon which the form is to be based, just as it is impossible for the form of gold to appear unless the material, which is its subject, has been refined and made ready, or the form of an ark to appear unless the material, that is the wood, has been shaped and made ready. [11] Thus it is that since the literal meaning is always the subject or material for the others, particularly the allegorical, it is impossible to come to a knowledge of the others before the literal. [12] Furthermore, it is impossible because with anything, either natural or artificial, it is impossible to advance the work without first constructing the foundation, as is true in the case

2. Matthew 17:1–8; Mark 9:1–7; Luke 9:28–36.
3. Psalm 113:3; see the *Letter to Can Grande* 7.

of houses or of areas of study. And so, since the establishment of meaning is something constructed by systematic study, and since the establishment of the literal meaning is the foundation of the other meanings, particularly the allegorical, it is impossible to arrive at the others before the literal.

[13] Furthermore, even were it possible, it would be irrational, that is, out of the proper order, and therefore a tiring and erratic process. For, as the Philosopher says in the first book of the *Physics*, Nature wishes our procedure of discovery to be orderly, proceeding from what we know well to what we know not so well.[4] I say that "nature wishes" it because this mode of discovery is an innate gift of nature. [14] And therefore if the other senses besides the literal are less well understood—and that they are seems quite clear—it would be irrational to proceed to establish them until the literal has already been established. [15] For these reasons, then, I shall by all means first discuss the literal meaning of each *canzone*, and afterwards discuss its allegory, or hidden sense. And sometimes I shall touch upon the other senses in passing as time and space permit.
Banquet 2.1.2–15

4. This principle is attributed to Aristotle by Saint Thomas Aquinas in his commentary on the *Physics* 1.1.

The Interpretation of Poetic
Figures and Fictions

In the middle of The New Life, *Dante pauses to explain, in almost naive terms, the nature of that poetic license which allows him to speak of love as if it were a person; in the process, he claims for himself along with other vernacular writers that license (see the first selection below). The prime qualification for this license is the rationality of its employment: a poet must be able to explain in plain terms what he expresses through figures. Dante's explanations of his own figures demonstrate the sort of rationality he asks for. The "noble lady" of his* canzoni, *he explains (in the first two selections below from the* Banquet*), was philosophy, whose followers have made it the supreme object of their love. The gods and goddesses of the poets were figures for what the philosophers called ideas or intelligences; the actions of the gods are parallel in form to the operations of the intelligences (the third selection from the* Banquet, *below). The function of the sun in the material world is like the function of God in the spiritual world, so that the sun becomes the most worthy figure for God himself (the fourth selection below from the* Banquet*). Furthermore, so "rational" are poetic figures that the ancient poets, without realizing it, had represented in their fiction of the Golden Age the earthly paradise of the true Christian revelation (the selection below from* Purgatory*). The proper interpretation of myths and figures, like their proper use in poetry, accords them a place in the rational and intelligible system of truth.*

[1] At this point a person whose perplexities are worth the clearing up may be perplexed, and this is what would perplex him: that I speak of Love as if it were a thing in itself, not only an intelligent substance, but as if it were a corporeal substance. Scientifically speaking, this is false, since Love does not exist by itself as a substance, being rather an attribute of a substance. [2] And that I speak of it as

115

if it were a body, and even as if it were a man, appears in three statements I make about it. I say that I saw him coming; therefore, since in fact "coming" implies motion in space, and since, according to the Philosopher, only bodies may move in space of themselves.[1] I clearly assume that Love is a body. I also say of him that he laughs, and even that he speaks. These activities are obviously peculiar to man, especially to have the capacity for laughter; therefore I clearly assume that he is a man. [3] To clear up such a puzzle, as is fitting at this point, it must first be understood that among the ancients there were no writers dealing with love in the vernacular tongue, although there were writers dealing with love, certain poets, in the Latin tongue. I refer to our own nation, although the same state of affairs—learned, but not vernacular, poets dealing with such subjects—may have occurred, and may still occur, among other peoples, as, for instance, in Greece. [4] And it was not a great many years ago that poets first appeared who wrote in the vernacular; for to write with rhyme in the vernacular is equivalent to writing metrical lines in Latin. The evidence that this occurred only a short time ago is that, were we to try to search for such writings in either Provençal or Italian, we would not find any which are any earlier than one hundred and fifty years ago. [5] The reason why certain crude writers acquired the reputation for skillful writing is that they were almost the first to write in Italian. [6] The first person who began to write as a vernacular poet was motivated by the desire to make his words understood by a woman to whom the understanding of Latin verse was too difficult. This fact argues against those who would use rhyme for other subjects since the truth is that such a mode of discourse was originally invented to write about love. [7] Furthermore, since poets have been granted a greater license than writers in prose, and since writers using rhyme are simply vernacular poets, it is appropriate and reasonable that they be granted greater license in their writings than is granted to other vernacular writers. So if any rhetorical figure or color is granted to poets, it is also granted to those who use rhyme. [8] And then if we observe that poets have addressed inanimate things as if they had sense and reason, and even had these things speak; if we observe that they do this not only

1. This principle is implied in *Physics* 3. 1–3.

with real, but even with unreal things, having written, for example, that noncorporeal things spoke, or written that many attributes of things spoke as if they were substantial and human, then it is appropriate that writers who use rhyme do similar things, not purposelessly, but with a purpose which they could later explain in prose. [9] That poets have spoken in that manner I said is evident, for example, in Virgil. He says that Juno, a goddess inimical to the Trojans, addressed Aeolus, the lord of the winds. The passage is in the first book of the *Aeneid*, beginning, "Eole, namque tibi." He goes on to say that this lord answered her, saying, "Tuus, o regina, quid optes explorare labor; / mihi iussa capessere fas est." [2] In this same poet, an inanimate thing is made to address animate things, as when (Apollo addresses the Trojans): "Dardanidae duri." [3] In Lucan an animate thing addresses an inanimate one, where (the poet speaks to the city of Rome): "Multum, Roma, tamen debes civilibus armis." [4] In Horace, a man addresses his own learning as if it were another person; and these are not just Horace's words, but are written as if quoted from the great Homer. The passage from the *Art of Poetry* goes, "Dic michi, Musa, virum." [5] In Ovid, Love speaks as if he were a human person at the beginning of a book called *The Book of the Remedy for Love*: "Bella michi, video, bella parantur, ait." [6] This should clear up any perplexities raised by any part of my little book. [10] But to prevent any crude persons from drawing any wrong inferences, I say that the poets did not write this way lacking a purpose, nor should those who use rhyme write in this manner without there being a purpose behind what they say. For it would be a disgrace to someone who dressed his rhymes in the figures or colors of rhetoric if later, on demand, he could not strip his discourse

---

2. *Aeneid* 1.65: "Aeolus, for to you [has the father of the gods and king of men / given the power to calm and raise the waves with your winds . . .]"; *Aeneid* 1.76–77: "Your job, oh queen, is to decide what you wish; my duty is to fulfill your commands."

3. *Aeneid* 3.94: "O fierce sons of Dardanus . . . ."

4. Lucan *Pharsalia* 1.44: "A great deal, Rome, you nevertheless owe to civil war . . ." (or "to arms employed by your citizens").

5. Horace *Art of Poetry* 141: "Tell me, Muse, of the man . . . ."

6. Ovid *Remedia Amoris* 1: "'Wars against me, I see, wars are being prepared,' he said."

of this dress to show what he had really meant. My best friend[7] and I are quite aware that there are those who write rhymes in this stupid manner.
The New Life 25

[5] And as it often happens that a man who was looking for silver finds, without his having intended it, gold which some secret cause has put in his way, perhaps not without divine planning; so I, who was seeking consolation, found not only the remedy for my tears, but also the words of authors, and of learning, and of books. In looking over these words, I correctly judged that Philosophy, who was the lady of these authors, of this learning, and of these books, must be a very exalted thing. [6] So I imagined her under the form of a noble lady, and I could not imagine her engaged in any other kind of act than a merciful one. And, in truth, in this form my senses so eagerly marveled at her that I could hardly turn away from her. [7] And starting with this act of imagination, I began to frequent those places where she showed herself in her true form, which is to say, the schools of the Religious orders and the disputations of the philosophizers. As a result, in a short time, perhaps thirty months, I began to feel her sweetness so strongly that my love for her drove away and destroyed every other thought. [8] And thus it happened that, feeling myself raised above the thought of my first love to the power of this new one, I opened my mouth as if in amazement with the words of the *canzone* written above, displaying my condition under the figure of something else. I did this because rhyme in the vernacular was not worthy of treating openly in poetry the lady with whom I was in love, nor were my readers properly prepared to understand easily words which were not fictive. They also would not have believed the true meaning as readily as the fictive because, indeed, everyone believed in my disposition toward the earlier love, but would not have believed in the later.
Banquet 2.12.5–8

[1] As the order requires, I return once again to the beginning [of the *canzone*[8]] and say that the lady to whom I refer is that lady of

7. Probably Cavalcanti.
8. For the text of this *canzone*, see p. 168.

the intellect who is called Philosophy. But because praise naturally gives rise to the desire of making the acquaintance of the person who has been praised; and since acquaintance with a thing consists in knowing what it is when it is looked at in itself and as a function of all of its causes, as the Philosopher says at the beginning of the *Physics*;[9] and since this knowledge is not to be found in the name, but rather in what the names signifies, as he says in the fourth book of the *Metaphysics* (where he states that a definition is the conception signified by a name),[10] I must here, before proceeding further in the displaying of her praise, first state what it is which is called Philosophy, that is, what this name signifies. [2] Having demonstrated this, I may more effectively discuss the allegory of the present poem. I will first tell who first gave it this name; then I will proceed to its significance.
Banquet 3.11.1–2

[4] There were others, including Plato, a most eminent man, who posited not only as many Intelligences as there are movements of heaven, but even as many as there are species of things (which is to say, types of things), all men belonging to one species, all gold to another, and all measurements to another, and so on with all other things. [5] He had it that just as the Intelligences of the heavens are the generators of them, each one of its own heaven, so these others are generators and the exemplars of other things, each one of its own species; and Plato called them "ideas," which is to say, universal forms and natures. [6] The pagans called them gods and goddesses, not understanding them so philosophically as Plato, and adored the images of these, and even built splendid temples for them. They built them, for example, for Juno, said to be the goddess of power; and for Pallas, or rather Minerva, called the goddess of wisdom; for Vulcan, called the god of fire, and for Ceres, the goddess of wheat. [7] That these opinions were held is clear on the testimony of the poets, who everywhere represent the custom of the pagans both in their sacrifices and in their beliefs. It is also clear in the many ancient names which have remained either as the names or as the

9. Aristotle *Physics* 1.1.
10. Aristotle *Metaphysics* 1.4.16.

surnames of places and ancient buildings, as anyone who wishes may discover.

Banquet 2.4.4–7

[6] Now I shall proceed to the second stanza, where the discussion actually begins. I say there, "The sun, which circles all the world, does not see . . . ." Here one should understand that, just as it is appropriate to discuss objects of sense in order to discuss objects which the senses cannot perceive, so it is appropriate to discuss intelligible things as a means of dealing with things which the intellect cannot grasp. Therefore, just as I began my literal exposition by speaking of the sensible and material sun, so now I must discuss the spiritual and intelligible sun, which is God. [7] No sensible thing in the entire world is more deserving of being made a type of God than is the sun. It first illuminates itself and then all of the heavenly bodies and the elements with sensible light just as God first illuminates himself, and then the creatures of heaven and the other intelligible creatures with intellectual light. [8] The sun gives life to all things with its heat, and if anything decays, this is not because of any intention in the cause, but is an accidental effect. So God gives life to all things in goodness, and if anything becomes evil thereby, this did not follow from the divine purpose, but rather happens as an accidental result of the fulfilling of the intended purpose. [9] For if God made both the good and the bad angels, he did not make both of them on purpose, but only the good. The viciousness of the evil ones followed outside of his intention. But it was not outside of his intention in that God was not capable of predicting in himself their viciousness; rather his desire to produce spiritual creatures was so great that even his foreknowledge that some of them would come to a bad end should not have and could not prevent God from producing them. [10] It would not be to the credit of nature if, knowing ahead of time that a certain number of a tree's flowers would be lost, it produced no flowers on that tree, and abandoned the production of the fruitful ones for the sake of those which would bear no fruit. [11] Thus it is that I say that God, who understands each thing (his "circling" meaning his "understanding"), does not see

any thing among all the things he sees so noble as when he gazes at
that place where Philosophy is to be found.
Banquet 3.12.6–11

At this point, Mathilda is telling Dante about the streams of the Earthly
Paradise.

> "And although it—your thirst—may be satisfied
> Without my revealing anything else,
> I will grant you another little present as a favor;
> I do not believe that my words will be less dear to you
> For having exceeded my promise to you.
> Those who in ancient times wrote poetry
> About the Golden Age and its state of happiness
> May have dreamed on Parnassus of this place.
> Here the root of humanity was innocent;
> Here it was always spring, and there was every fruit;
> This [stream] is the nectar of which they all spoke."
> I turned myself all the way around
> Facing my Poet,[11] and saw that with a smile
> He had heard this last passage.
> Then I turned my face toward the beautiful lady.

Purgatory 28.134–48

11. That is, Virgil, whose *Fourth Eclogue* tells of the Golden Age.

Interpretations of Scripture and Poetry

The canzone *upon which Dante comments in Book 4 of his* Banquet *defines, on its literal level, the qualities of nobility; it takes the form of an answer to Frederick II's offhand assertion that nobility was the product of "ancient wealth." Though Dante's definition is straightforward and literal, his commentary is rather ingenious and allegorical. His definition, he asserts, is consonant with Scripture and with ancient epic, the two prime sources of the concept of nobility; and, to demonstrate this consonance, he must interpret these documents both in accord with the general tradition of commentary and so as to fit the specific assertions of his poem. Thus his interpretation of the coming of the women to the tomb of Christ on Easter morning follows the general lines of traditional interpretation, wherein the tomb stands for the world of fleshly life, and Galilee for the world of spiritual life and contemplation. But Dante, in the first passage below, identifies the angel as "our nobility" and the three women as the three principal philosophic sects, a reading which gives specificity to the general outline of an exegesis which makes the angel stand for the perfection of human nature and the three women for the fleshly discernment not yet enlightened by the resurrection.*

Similarly, Dante's interpretations of the Latin epic writers, which gives precedent for his assertions about the qualities of nobility appropriate to the various ages of man, follows standard exegetical practice. His reading of Statius merely lays bare the passions which motivate a particular passage, making them the constituents of adolescence. In the case of Virgil, Dante accepts the Fulgentian tradition that the Aeneid *describes allegorically the ages of man, and thus explains how Aeneas' activities, in Books 4–6, are representative of the virtues of young manhood. Ovid's story of Cephalus and Aeacus, according to Dante, shows the qualities of maturity; the digression concerning the Myrmidons may be explained as a way of allowing for a full representation of all four qualities listed in Dante's* canzone. *As for Lucan, he had represented in Cato a God-like figure; his wife's return to him, therefore, may be understood as a recapitulation of all the virtues appropriate to*

122

the various ages, given significance by the necessity of facing the end of life.
Thus Dante's allegorical interpretations, if indeed these be such, preserve
quite clearly the structure and intentions of both the original passages and the
exegetical tradition. If they are overingenious, it is because they are brought
forth in support of a new poem, having its own structure and intentions.

A. Scripture

[13] And truly, of these two ways of employing the mind, one of
them, the speculative, is more full of blessedness than the other,
since it makes use of our noblest part without any mixture of any
other part: that part—the intellect—which is particularly the object
of that radical love of which I have spoken. This part cannot have
its most perfect use—the contemplation of God, the most exalted
of intelligible things—in this life except insofar as it contemplates
and admires him in his works. [14] And that we should seek this
blessedness in the higher, and not the other, way, not in the active
life, is taught us by the Gospel of Mark, if we examine it closely.
Mark says that Mary Magdalene and Mary the mother of James and
Mary Salome went to find the Savior in the sepulcher, but did not
find him. Rather they found a young man dressed in white who
told them, "You seek the Savior, and I tell you that he is not here;
therefore, be not affrighted, but go, and tell his disciples and Peter
that he goeth before you into Galilee; there you shall see him, as he
told you."[1] [15] By these three women may be understood the
three schools of the active life, the Epicureans, the Stoics, and the
Peripatetics, who go to the sepulcher, the present world, which is a
receptacle for corruptible things, and seek the Savior, or blessedness, without finding it. Rather they find a young man in white
clothes who is, according to the testimony of Matthew and the others
as well, an angel of God, for Matthew says, "An angel of God descended from heaven, and coming, rolled back the stone, and sat
upon it. And his countenance was like lightning, and his raiment
as snow."[2]

[16] This angel is that nobility of ours which, as I said, comes

1. Mark 16.
2. Matthew 28:2–3.

from God, and speaks to us in our reason, saying to each of these schools which come seeking blessedness in the active life: "It is not here; but go, and say this to the disciples and to Peter," to those who come seeking it and to those who have gotten off the track like Peter, who had denied Him, that "He will go before them into Galilee," which is to say, blessedness will go before us into Galilee, meaning into speculation. [17] Galilee is the equivalent of whiteness. Whiteness is the color containing more visible light than any other color, just as contemplation contains more spiritual light than the other things which we do on earth. But he says, "He will go before you," and not, "He will be with you," from which it is to be understood that in our contemplation, God always goes before, nor can we catch up with him who is our highest blessedness in this life. Then the angel says, "There you shall see him, as he told you." This means, there you will have some of his sweetness, or happiness, as has been promised you here, that is, it has been established that you will be able to possess it. [18] Thus it is clear that our blessedness (this happiness of which I have been speaking) may first be found in an imperfect form in the active life, that is, in the exercise of the moral virtues, and then all but perfectly in the exercise of the intellectual virtues. These two exercises are the quickest and most direct paths leading to the highest blessedness which we cannot possess in this life, as is clear from what I have said.

Banquet 4.22.13–18

B. Poetry

1. *Statius*

[5] For awe is a certain bewilderment of mind caused by seeing or hearing of, or sensing in some manner, great and marvelous things. To the extent that they are great, they make whoever senses them reverent toward them; and to the extent that they seem marvelous, they make him desirous of learning more about them. It was for this reason that ancient kings had constructed in their palaces magnificent works of gold and stone and elaborate workmanship, so that those who viewed them would be awestruck and thus reverent, and would seek to know more about the honorable estate of the

king. [6] And thus Statius, the sweet poet, says in the first book of his *Theban History* that when Adrastus, king of the Argives, saw Polynices draped in a lion's skin, and saw Tydeus draped in the hide of a wild boar, and recalled the response which Apollo had given concerning his daughters, he was awestruck, and consequently more reverent and more desirous of knowing.[3]

[7] Modesty is the withdrawal of the mind from things which are ugly combined with a fear of falling into them. We see it in virgins and virtuous ladies and adolescents, who are so modest that their faces are entirely covered by a pallid or a red color not just when they are propositioned or tempted to commit a fault, but even when they may have some imagination of the fulfillment of sexual desire. [8] Thus this poet I mentioned above says in the first book of Thebes, just cited, that when Aceste, the nurse of King Adrastus's daughters, Argia and Deiphile, led them before the eyes of their revered father and of the two wanderers, Polynices and Tydeus, the virgins became pale and red, their eyes fleeing from the gazes of all others and fixing themselves on their father's face, as if in safety.[4] [9] Ah, of how many faults is modesty the bridle! How many dishonest things and demands does it silence! How many dishonest desires rein in! How many temptations to evil does it discourage, not only in the modest person himself, but also in those who look on him! how many foul words does it hold back! For as Cicero says in the first book of *On Moral Duties*, no act is foul which it is not also foul to name.[5] For this reason no modest and noble man will speak·that which would not be honest in the speech of a lady. Ah, how unbecoming it is in a noble man who goes in quest of honor to mention something which would be unbecoming in the mouth of any lady!

[10] Shame is the fear of being dishonored by some fault already committed. From this fear there arises a penitence concerning the

3. Statius *Thebaid* 1.490–91: "Stupet omine tanto / defixus senior" ("Awe-struck, the old man stands motionless at so great an omen"). Dante's term in Italian is *stupore*, here translated "awe," but derived from the Latin word (*stupet*) used in this passage.

4. Statius *Thebaid* 1.527 ff.

5. Cicero *De officiis* 1.35. Dante's phrasing, however, corresponds more closely to the paraphrase of Cicero found in Brunetto Latini's *Trésor*, Book 1, part 1, chapter 56.1.

fault, bitter enough to serve as a warning against further commission of the fault. So this same poet in the same section of his poem says that Polynices was at first fearful about speaking when asked by Adrastus who he was, both out of shame over what he had committed against his father, and out of shame over what his father had committed, which obviously had survived as a shame to his son. He does not give his father's name, but rather those of his ancestors, his land, and his mother. From this it is evident that shame is necessary to this stage in life.

Banquet 4.25.5–10

2. *Virgil*

[5] Here should be recalled to mind what I discussed above in the twenty-second chapter of this treatise concerning the appetite which is born with us at the beginning. This appetite never does anything else but to pursue and to flee. Whenever it pursues what it ought to pursue, or flees from what it ought to flee, a man stays within the bounds of his perfection. [6] This appetite, however, must be ridden by the reason. If it is not, it will be like an unbridled horse which, however noble its nature might be, cannot guide himself rightly without a good rider. What we call the irascible and concupiscible appetite, however noble it might be, must obey the reason which guides it with the bridle and with spurs, like a skilled rider. [7] Reason uses the bridle when pursuing, and this bridle is called temperance, which points out the limits within which the pursuit should take place. The spur is used in fleeing, and is called courage, or rather magnanimity. This virtue points out where to take a stand and to fight. [8] And Virgil, our greatest poet, shows that Aeneas was so bridled in that section where he figures forth this state of life. This section includes the fourth, fifth, and sixth books of the *Aeneid*. How well bridled he was when, after having received so many benefits from Dido, which I will tell about in the seventh treatise, and after having experienced so much pleasure with her, he departed from her, as the fourth book of the *Aeneid* tells it, in order to follow an honest, praiseworthy, and fruitful path! [9] How well spurred on he was, when this same Aeneas endured alone with the Sibyl, against so many perils, the descent into Hell in search of the

spirit of his father Anchises, as this same story tells in the sixth book! This shows that in our young manhood it belongs to our perfection to be "temperate and courageous," as the text expressly says.[6]

[10] Furthermore, it is required of this stage of life, for its perfection, to be loving; for at this age one should look both forward and backward, as if on the meridian of a circle. One should love one's elders from whom one has received existence and nurture and teaching, so as not to appear ungrateful. One should love one's juniors so that, having given them benefits out of love, one will be sustained and honored by them later when one's prosperity is the less. [11] This same poet, in the fifth book of this same work, shows that Aeneas possesses this love, both when he leaves the elder Trojans on Sicily in the care of Acestes, sparing them the fatigue of the journey, and when he gives instruction in arms, in that same place, to his young son Ascanius and the other adolescents. This demonstrates that, as the text says, love is required of this stage of life.

[12] It is also required of this stage of life to be courteous, for although having courteous manners is attractive at any stage, it is particularly required at this one. Adolescence deserves easy pardon for a lack of courtesy, on the grounds of the fewness of its years, while maturity cannot have such manners because of the seriousness and severity required of it; and the same reasoning applies more strongly to old age. [13] And this same most exalted poet shows (in the sixth book) that Aeneas possesses this same courtesy, when he says that King Aeneas—in order to honor the body of the dead Misenus, who had been Hector's herald, and had later recommended himself to the king—girded himself and took up an axe to help cut wood for the fire on which they were going to burn the dead body (as was their custom). In this it is apparent how necessary courtesy is to young manhood; consequently, the noble spirit, as I say, shows itself in the exercise of it.

[14] Finally, it is required of this stage of life to be loyal.[7] Loyalty

6. "The text" is that of the *canzone* upon which the Fourth Treatise of the *Banquet* is a commentary; the quotation is from line 129: "In young manhood, [he will be] temperate and brave."

7. The meaning which Dante gives this term is based upon its derivation from the word for "law" (Fr. *loi*).

is the following and the putting into effect of what the law says, which is particularly necessary to young manhood. An adolescent, as I said, deserves easy pardon because of the fewness of his years, while a mature man because of his great experience, should simply be just, and not a scrupulous follower of the laws (since his own upright judgment and the law are practically the same thing, so that, without any laws, he ought to judge himself justly, as the young man cannot do). It is enough for the young man to be a follower of the law, and have his delight in that following. This the aforesaid poet says that Aeneas did when he held the games in Sicily on the anniversary of his father's death, as described in the fifth book: whatever he promised for a victory, he afterwards loyally gave it to the victor, in accord with their ancient practice, this constituting for them a law. [15] In this it is clear that this stage of life requires loyalty, as well as courtesy, love, courage, and temperance, as the text we are discussing at present says; consequently, the noble spirit will display them all.
Banquet 4.26.5–15

3. *Ovid*

[17] Ovid teaches us that all four of these qualities—prudence, justice, generosity, and affability—are fitting to this stage in life [maturity] in the seventh book of the *Metamorphoses*, where he writes the fable concerning the visit to Aeacus by Cephalus of Athens, seeking aid in the war in which Athens was engaged with Crete. He shows that the mature Aeacus was prudent when, having lost almost all his people through a pestilence of corrupt air, he wisely had recourse to God, and asked him to restore his dead nation. Through his good sense, which fortified him in patience and caused him to turn his face to God, his people were restored to him in greater number than they had been before. [18] Ovid shows that he was just, when he says that he divided and distributed his empty country to the new people. He shows that he was generous when he has him say to Cephalus in answer to the request for aid, "O Athens, do not ask for aid from me, but take it; and do not hesitate to consider the forces of this island your own. And this is what my state of affairs provides: forces are not lacking; rather there are

more than enough for us. And the enemy is strong, but times are prosperous for giving, and there is no excuse." [8] [19] Ah, how many things are worth noticing in this reply! But for someone who understands subtly, it is enough to set it down here in the same form which Ovid set it down. He shows that he was affable when he says that Aeacus related to Cephalus carefully and in a long speech[9] the story of the pestilence which attacked his people and of their restoration. [20] This should make it clear enough that these four qualities are required of this stage of life; consequently, the noble spirit will, as our text says, display them. But to make the example I gave more memorable, I will add that Aeacus was the father of Telamon, of Peleus, and of Phocus, and that from Telamon Ajax was born, from Peleus, Achilles.

Banquet 4.27.17–20

4. *Lucan*

[13]And that these two things—the return to God, and the blessing of the way one has come—are required of old age, is shown figuratively by that great poet, Lucan, in the second book of the *Pharsalia*,[10] where he says that Marcia returned to Cato, asking and entreating him that he should take her back in her exhausted state. In this, Marcia stands for the noble spirit; and we may thus show the correspondence of the figure to the truth. [14] Marcia was a virgin, and in that state stands for adolescence. Then she was married to Cato, and in that state stands for young womanhood. At this time she had children, who stand for the virtues which were said above to belong to the young. She departed from Cato, and was married to Hortensius, by which is meant that she departed from young womanhood and entered maturity. She also had children by him, these standing for the virtues which were said above to be required of maturity. [15] Hortensius died, by which is meant the end of maturity, and having become a widow—widowhood standing for old age—Marcia returned to Cato at the beginning of her widow-

8. Ovid *Metamorphoses* 7.507–11. Dante's paraphrase departs rather considerably from the text available in modern editions.

9. *Metamorphoses* 7.518–660.

10. 2. 326 ff.

hood, which corresponds to the noble spirit returning to God at the beginning of old age. And what earthly man is more worthy of being made to stand for God than Cato? None, for sure.

[16] And what does Marcia tell Cato? "While I had blood in me," that is, young womanhood, and "while I had in me the capacity for motherhood," that is, maturity, which is truly the mother of the highest virtues, as was demonstrated above, "I carried out," says Marcia, "and fulfilled all of your commandments," which means that the soul persevered in the activities of a citizen. She adds, "And I took two husbands," that is, I have been fruitful at two stages of life. [17] "Now," Marcia says, "that my womb is tired, and now that I am barren in that part, I return to you, no longer being fit to be given to another husband." This means that the noble spirit, knowing that it no longer has a womb which can be fruitful, that is, feeling that its members have reached a state of feebleness, turns to God, he who has no need of bodily members. And Marcia adds, "Give me the contract of our former marriage bed, give me only the name of a married woman." This is as much as to say that the noble spirit says to God, "Give me, my Lord, at least your repose; grant me, at least, that I in whatever remains of my life may be called yours." [18] And Marcia says, "Two causes move me to ask for this. The first is that when I am gone it may be said that I died the wife of Cato. The second, that when I am gone it may be said that you did not cast me off, but rather gave me in marriage with your good will." [19] The noble spirit is also moved by these two causes. It wishes to depart from this life the spouse of God, and it wishes to make it known that its actions were pleasing to God. Oh, you unfortunate and ill-born ones, who would be willing to depart from this life bearing the name of Hortensius rather than Cato! It is a beautiful touch to end what ought to be said about the signs of nobility with the name of Cato, since in him nobility displayed all of these signs in all of the stages of his life.

Banquet 4.28.13–19

ON POETS AND THE EFFECTS
OF POETRY

Dante's Comedy *may, from one point of view, be regarded as an essay in literary history. Every mythological and fictional person included among the residents of Hell, Purgatory, and Paradise gains his significance by an act of interpretation; whatever such a person had meant in earlier work must lead plausibly to his position in the* Comedy. *More importantly, the poets who play various parts in the action, and who comment on their own poetry, express that continuity of ancient and vernacular art which makes possible and explains the art of the* Comedy *itself. Dante's meetings with the father of Cavalcanti* (Inferno *10), with Brunetto Latini* (Inferno *15), with Buonagiunta Orbicciani* (Purgatory *24; see above, p. 72), and with Guido Guinizelli and Arnault Daniel* (Purgatory *26, below) express the varying degrees of dependence and transcendence which Dante felt with respect to the vernacular tradition. On the other hand, his tribute to Virgil and his acknowledgment of Virgil's responsibility for his own poetic development* (Inferno *1); his being asked to join the circle of ancient great poets* (Inferno *3); and his observation of the meetings between Virgil and Sordello* (Purgatory *6–8) and between Virgil and Statius* (Purgatory *22, below): these establish relations between ancient and modern poetry which make plausible the transition between pagan and Christian modes of practicing poetry. In general, poets make advances in style when they follow a more authentic and universal inspiration; and the development of style makes possible the participation by poets in the establishment of a just society. Dante's own purposes are most directly proclaimed by his ancestor Cacciaguida (below the selection from* Paradise), *who tells Dante not to hold back for fear of offending the great, since his own purposes are so high. Literary culture, that joining of the classical and vernacular exemplified in the poem, has made such high ambition possible.*

133

Comments on His Own Contemporaries

"If perhaps you wish to know who we are by name,
  There is not time to tell, and I could not do it.   90
But I will, indeed, rid you of your curiosity about mine.
  I am Guido Guinizelli, and am now being purged
  Because I repented before the end."
As during the grief of Lycurgus
  Her two sons acted upon seeing their mother again,[1]   95
  So I acted (but did not reach so far),[2]
When I heard named the very one who was the father
  Of me, and of others who are my betters, we who still
  Employ the sweet and pleasant rhymes of love;
And without hearing or speaking I paced thoughtfully   100
  For a long time, staring amazedly at him,
  But did not go any closer because of the fire there.
Then when with looking I had been satisfied,
  I put myself entirely at his service,
  With an assurance which another could trust.   105
And he said to me, "You make such an impression,
  So clear (through that which I hear),
  That Lethe could not erase it or make it dim.
But if your oath is in words of truth,
  Tell me what is the cause for your showing   110
  In words and in looks that you hold me dear?"
And I said to him, "Your sweet writings
  Which, so long as the practice of the moderns lasts,
  Will make dear even the ink in which they are written."
"O my brother," he said, "that one which I point out to you   115

1. Hypsipyle had been the nurse of Lycurgus's child, whom she left behind in order to show the Argives, led by Adrastus, a spring. The child was killed by a serpent in her absence, and Lycurgus, in his grief, had ordered her death, until her two sons ran to embrace her. See Statius *Thebaid* 5.718 ff.

2. Dante cannot "reach so far" to embrace Guido because of the fire in which Guido is being purged.

With my finger"—and he indicated a spirit in front of me—
   "Was the better craftsman in the mother tongue.
In verses of love and in prose of romance
   He outdid all others; let the fools say
   That he of Limousin should be considered the best.[3]   120
On report rather than on truth they build these structures,
   And thus make firm their opinion
   Before having heard what reason and art would tell them.
Many of the older generation did the same concerning Guittone,[4]
   From one rumor to another giving him the prize,   125
   Until it had conquered the truth in many persons.
But if you have such a wide privilege
   That you are allowed to wander in that cloister
   In which Christ is the abbot of the college,
Recite to him for me a Pater Noster,   130
   Such as we of this realm have need,
   Where we can no more commit a sin."
Then, perhaps to leave a space meant for another,
   Who had pressed upon him, he disappeared into the fire,
   Like a fish in the water diving to the bottom.   135
I advanced a little toward the spirit he had pointed out,
   And said that for his name my desire
   Had prepared a place of welcome.
He began to speak freely:[5]
   "So much delights me your courteous request,   140
   That I cannot, nor do I wish to, hide myself from you.
I am Arnault, who weep and sing out.
   With sadness I look on the follies of the past,
   And look joyously on the joy for which I hope, before me.
Now I beg you, by that power   145
   Which guides you to the top of the stairway,
   Take heed, while there is still time, of my sorrow."
Then he hid himself in the fire which refines.

Purgatory 26.89–148

3. Probably Girautz de Borneilh, although there were several other poets from Limousin.

4. Guittone d'Arezzo.

5. Arnault Daniel's following speech is in Provençal.

I then say that God alone places this gift [nobility] in the soul which he sees exists complete in its own person, fitted and disposed to receive this divine action. For, as the Philosopher says in the second section of *On the Soul*, "things must be disposed for their agents and for the reception of their actions." 6 Thus were the soul imperfectly disposed, it would not be disposed to receive this blessed and divine infusion, just as a pearl, were it badly, or rather imperfectly, placed, could not receive its power from heaven, as the noble Guido Guinizelli states in one of his *canzone* which begins, "To the gentle heart Love always takes refuge."
Banquet 4.20.7

6. Aristotle *De Anima* 1.2.2.

The Transmission of Culture:
Virgil and Statius

. . . Virgil began, "Love,   10
  When kindled by virtue, always kindles another
  Merely by the flame's appearing openly.
Thus, from the time when among us descended
  Into the Limbo of Hell that Juvenal
  Who made known to me his affection for you,   15
My good feeling towards you has been such
  That never a stronger bound someone to a person he has never
    seen,
  So that to me this ascent seemed short.
But tell me, and pardon me as a friend
  If with too much confidence I loosen the reins,   20
  And as well discuss it with me as a friend;
How could avarice within your breast
  Find a place, among the quantity of good sense
  With which, because of your zeal, you must be filled?"
These words caused Statius to be moved   25
  At first to a little smile, and then to an answer:
  "Each word you say is a dear token of love.
Truly, quite often things have an appearance
  Which provides material for false suspicions,
  While the true cause remains hidden.   30
Your request assures me that your belief
  Is that I was a miser in my former life,
  Perhaps because of the circle[1] where I have been.
But know, that I was separated from avarice
  By too great a distance, and that for this excess   35
  I have been punished for thousands of months.
If it had not been that I set right my desires
  By what I understood from that passage where you cried out

1. That is, he had been in the circle of Purgatory reserved for misers.

As if tortured by the thought of human nature,
'Why do you not govern, oh blessed hunger   40
    For gold, the appetite of mortals?'[2]
    Rolling [a weight], I should now be engaged in the dismal
       jousts.[3]
But later I perceived that spending hands
    Can spread their wings too far, and repented
    For this evil as for the other.   45
How many there are who will be raised up with cropped hair[4]
    Out of ignorance, which prevents repentance
    For this sin during and at the end of life!
And know also that the fault which pushes out
    By headlong opposition any sin   50
    Here with its opposite has its green dried out.
Thus, if I have been placed among those people
    Who weep because of their avarice, this befell me
    In order to purge myself of their contrary."
"Then when you sang of the savage strife   55
    Of Jocasta's double grief,"[5]
    Said the singer of the bucolic songs,
"Judging from the song that Clio[6] plays with you there,
    It does not seem that you had yet made yourself faithful
    To the faith without which it is useless to do well.   60
If this is the case, what sun or what candle
    Dispelled the shadows, so that you could raise up
    Your sails at a later time behind the Fisherman?"
And the other answered him, "You first set me on the way

2. The passage in Virgil is *Aeneid* 3.56–57: "Quid non mortalia pectora cogis, /
Auri sacra fames," which is usually translated, "To what do you not drive mortal
hearts, / Cursed hunger for gold!" But since *quid* may mean "why" as well as "to
what," *cogis* may mean "govern" as well as "drive," and *sacra* can mean "blessed"
(in this case with the implication "temperate") as well as "cursed," Dante's
translation is possible, if not so fitting to the original context. It may be that Dante
intended to show that Statius saw deeper into the passage than its most obvious
meaning—as he also does in interpreting the new age of the *Fourth Eclogue*, below.

3. The "dismal jousts" are those engaged in by the spendthrifts and misers in
Inferno 7.25–30.

4. Cropped hair is a sign of prodigality: *Inferno* 7.56–57.

5. Jocasta's double grief is her two sons, whose strife was savage because between brothers.

6. Clio, the muse responsible for Statius's "Theban history."

Toward Parnassus to drink from its springs,   65
  And you first lighted me the way to God.
You accomplished the same thing as one who walks in the night
  Carrying behind him a lamp which, if he cannot use it himself,
  Makes the people coming behind him aware,
When you said, 'The world renews itself;   70
  Justice returns, and the first age of man,
  And an offspring descends from a new heaven.'[7]
Through you I became a poet, through you a Christian!
  But because I know much more than this outline tells,
  I will put forth my hand to fill it in.   75
Already the world was as if completely impregnated
  With the true faith, the seeds having been spread
  By the messengers of the eternal kingdom,
And your speech, which I mentioned earlier,
  Accorded well with the new preachers;   80
  So I took up the practice of frequenting them.
Then they came to seem to me such holy people
  That, when Domitian persecuted them,
  Their cries brought tears from me.
And as long as I remained down there,   85
  I remembered them, and their upright practices
  Made me disparage all other sects;
And before the time that I conducted the Greeks to the river
  Of Thebes, in my poetry, I received baptism;
  But out of fear I remained a secret Christian,   90
For a long time showing paganism outwardly;
  And this lukewarmness made me go around
  The fourth circle more than four hundred years.
But now you, who have lifted up the cover
  Which hid from me that great good of which I have spoken,   95
  Since we have some spare time in this ascent,
May tell me where our ancient Terence is,
  And Caecilius, Plautus, and Varius, if you know.
  Tell me if they are damned, and in what lane."
"All of these, and Persius, and I, and others as well,"   100
  My leader replied, "are, along with that Greek
  Whom the Muses nourished more than any other,[8]

7. Virgil *Fourth Eclogue* 5–7.
8. Homer.

In the first belt of the blind prison.
    Many times we converse about that mountain
    Which always has our nurses on it.   105
Euripides is known there, and Antiphon,
    Simonides, Agathon, and many more Greeks
    Who earlier had their temples crowned with laurel.
Here also your people can be seen:
    Antigone, Deiphile, and Argia,   110
    And Ismene, with the same grief.
She who pointed out the Langria can be seen,
    The daughter of Tiresias is there, and Thetis,
    And, along with her sisters, Deïdamia."[9]

Purgatory 22.10–114

9. Hypsipyle is "she who pointed out the Langria" to the Argive army (*Thebaid* 4). The daughter of Tiresias is Manto. Deïdamia and her sisters were daughters of King Lyomedes of Syros, with whom Thetis hid Achilles. Achilles later loved Deïdamia.

On His Own *Comedy*

I began, like one who longs for,
   In his perplexity, the counsel of a person
   Who discerns, and wills uprightly, and loves: 105
"I well perceive, my father,[1] how Time
   Spurs upon me, to give me blows
   Of a sort which are hardest upon one who is least careful;
Therefore it would be good to arm myself with foresight,
   So that if the place [Florence] which is most dear to me is taken
      away from me,   110
   I will not, through my verses, lose all other places.
Through the world down there which is bitter without end,
   And through the mountain whose peak is beautiful
   The eyes of my lady have raised me,
And afterwards through the heavens from planet to planet,   115
   Where I have learned such things that, were I to tell them,
   They would have a strongly sour taste to many people;
But if I were to be a timid friend to truth,
   I fear losing my life among those
   Who will call the present time ancient."   120
The light in which my treasure laughed,
   He whom I found there, at first shone
   Like a mirror of gold in the rays of the sun:
Then he answered: "Only a conscience darkened,
   Either by its own or by another's disgrace   125
   Will feel that your words are harsh.
But nevertheless, avoid all lying,
   Bring all of your vision out in the open,
   And let only those scratch who feel an itch!
For if your words will be unpleasant   130
   At the first taste, vital nourishment
   They will leave behind when they are digested.

1. Cacciaguida, Dante's great-great-grandfather and his most prominent ancestor, who was a crusader, and knighted by the Emperor.

This your report will behave like the wind,
  Which beats most strongly the highest peaks;
  And for this reason will be no little proof of your honor.   135
You have been shown, in these spheres,
  On the mountain, and in the sorrowful valley
  Only those spirits who are well known to fame,
Because the spirit of him who will hear will not put
  Firm faith in examples which have   140
  Their roots unknown and hidden,
Nor in arguments other than those which are plain."

Paradise 17.103–42

On His Refusal to Write in Latin

Giovanni del Virgilio, whose name honors his Virgilian studies (and who wrote a commentary on Ovid as well), was noted as both a poet and a scholar. In a Latin epistle, he invites Dante to Bologna, where he teaches the liberal arts at a university noted for its training of lawyers, and urges Dante to write Latin poetry, assuring his stature among those whose judgment is educated, and his fame throughout all ages. Dante's reply is not only in Latin and in poetry, but also takes the form of an Eclogue. Dante thus outdoes Giovanni as a Latinist, and uses the most paradoxically appropriate medium for an argument in favor of the vernacular.

We saw in black letters borne up by the white paper
The harmonious song, milked for us from the Pierian breast.[1]
    At this time it happened that, while as usual counting
Our pastured goats, Meliboeus and I were under an oak.
He said (for he wished to know the content of the song)   5
"Tityrus, what does Mopsus, what does he want?[2] Tell me."

I smiled, Mopsus; but he pressed me harder and harder.
Overcome by love for him, and hardly suppressing a smile,
I finally said, "Fool! what is this madness? Your care, the goats,
Rather demand your attention, though upset by poor feeding.   10
There are pastures[3] unknown to you, which Maenalus, its high

1. The Muses were called the Pierides after King Pieres, who named his daughters after the Muses; they were reputed to nurse poets.

2. Meliboeus probably stands for ser Dino Perini, a Florentine, and Dante's companion in exile. Tityrus: Dante himself; Virgil had represented himself under this name in the *Eclogues*, from which the other names Dante uses are also derived. Mopsus: Giovanni del Virgilio.

3. These pastures are Bologna, where Giovanni del Virgilio was the sole teacher of poetry, among a great many teachers of law, at the university. It is also possible that these "pastures" are deep and learned poems, where the truth is obscured in allegory.

143

Peaks concealing the declining sun, overshadows,
Adorned with the various colors of grasses and flowers.
There winds through this place a humble stream bed covered over
With willow leaves, splashing its banks with continuous waves   15
From its brimming surface; it willingly makes itself the gentle path
For the waters which the mountain lets loose from above.
Mopsus, in the midst of all this, while his cattle play
In the waving grass, contemplates in exaltation the works of men
   and gods;

Then he lets out through the blown reeds his inner joy,   20
So that even the herds follow his sweet melody,
And lions, made tame, run down the mountain to the fields,
The waves flow backwards, and even Maenalus bends its foliage."
   Then he said, "Tityrus, though Mopsus sings in fields
Unknown, still, I could learn his unknown songs,   25
If you show me, for the sake of my wandering goats."
   What could I do now, since he so breathlessly insisted?
"Meliboeus, Mopsus has for years dedicated himself to the
Aonian Mountains, while others have been devoted to learning
Law for the courts, and he has grown pale in the shade of   30
The sacred groves;[4] laved in the bard-making waters, carrying
A belly filled with the milk of song, filled even up to his palate,
He calls me to receive the leaves which sprang from the transformed
   Peneid."[5]
   "What will you do?" Meliboeus asked, "Will you, a shepherd[6]
In the pastures, have your temples always unadorned with laurel?"   35
   "Oh Meliboeus, the honor due a poet, even the name of poet,
Have vanished into air; the Muse is overtaxed even in giving us
Wakeful Mopsus," I replied, as indignation gave me a voice:
"With how many bleatings the hills and fields would echo
Were I to draw out a paean[7] on my lyre with my hair bound in
   green!—   40

4. The Aonian Mountains are the dwelling place of the Muses. Giovanni del Virgilio was apparently not well paid for his teachings, hence his pallor.

5. The "transformed Peneid" is Daphne, daughter of the river-god Peneus. The leaves which sprang from her were laurel.

6. By implication, a poet in the vernacular, since shepherds' songs, eclogues, were assumed to be "low" in comparison to the epic style just as the vernacular is low in comparison to Latin.

7. A hymn to Apollo, therefore a high-style poem in Latin.

But let me fear the valleys and countryside which do not know the
    gods.[8]
Would it not be better to fix my hair in triumph, and hide my
Now white, but once growing gold, hair with the interlaced leaves[9]
Along my native Arno, if ever I am able to return?"
    He said, "Who could question that? But look, Tityrus, how   45
Swift the time goes; for those goats have grown old
To whose mothers we mated he-goats before they were conceiced."
    Then I said, "When the bodies which float around the
        world,[10]
And the dwellers on the stars,[11] are shown forth in my song
Along with the lower regions,[12] then it will be a joy to bind my
    head   50
In ivy and laurel; Mopsus will allow it."
                                        "Mopsus," he said,
"How does it concern him?"
                            "Do you not see how he objects to the
                            words
Of comedy, since they are sounded tritely on the lips of women,
And since the Castalian sisters[13] are ashamed to acknowledge
    them?"
Thus I answered him, and read once again your verses,   55
Mopsus.
    Then he shrugged his shoulders, and said, "Then,
What will we do, to win over Mopsus's good will?"
    "I have one ewe—you know which one—of great charm," I
        said,
"Who can hardly carry her udders, so filled they are with milk.
Even now she is browsing on cropped grass under a huge rock.   60
She has never run with the herd, and never grown used to the pen;
She comes by herself to the milking-pail, never driven by force.
I am getting ready to milk her with skilled hands;

8. Probably meaning a city which does not recognize the Emperor, which
would therefore not be receptive to Dante and his party.
9. Laurel.
10. The heavenly bodies.
11. The blessed souls—the subject of Dante's *Paradise*.
12. Hell and Purgatory.
13. The Muses.

I will fill ten pails to be sent to Mopsus.[14]
You in the meantime tend to your wanton goats,[15]   65
And learn to use your teeth on hard crusts."
    Then did Meliboeus and I sing under an oak,
While some barley was being cooked for us in our little hut.

The Eclogue of Dante to Giovanni del Virgilio

14. Probably the first ten cantos of the *Paradise*; the ewe is thus the subject matter of the last canticle of the *Comedy*.

15. The political adversaries of Dante and Dino Perini, those who are thus responsible for the "hard crusts" of exile, and those whom Dante is also thinking about as suitable for condemnation in his poem.

Appendix A
Illustrations of Dante's Principles of Construction and Prosody

The poems printed and translated below are those referred to by Dante in On Eloquence in the Vernacular 2.6.6. *Only the first stanza of each* canzone *is printed and analyzed (the given stanza of no. 9—Cavalcanti—is the entire* canzone*). Since the texts here printed are taken from modern editions, they occasionally differ in orthography and even wording from those found in Dante's text. The terms used in explaining the arrangement and construction of the poems are defined in Dante's treatise and in the glossary which follows. It should be noted that, in counting the syllables in a line, I have followed Dante's practice and assumed that a line with an even number of syllables has the form of the next-highest odd number* (On Eloquence 2.5.7).

1. Girautz de Borneilh

> Si per mon Sobretotz no fos
> que·m ditz qu'ieu chant e sia gays,
> ja·l suaus temps quan l'erba nais,
> ni pratz ni rams ni bosc ni flors,
> ni durs senhers ni van'amors
> no·m pogram metre en eslays:
>   mas d'aisso·m tenc ab lui
> que, pos joys falh e fui,
> merma pretz e barnatz,
> e pois las poestatz
> s'estraigneron de jay,
> de quan que·l piegers fay
> no fon per mi lausatz;
> qu'aissi·m suy cosseillatz,
> que nul ric non envey
> que trop mal senhorey.

Text: H. J. Chaytor, *The Troubadours of Dante* (Oxford: Clarendon Press, 1902).

Arrangement: *Fronte* of six lines, diesis after line 6, five verses of two lines each. Nine syllables in lines of *fronte*, for a total of 54; seven syllables in lines of verses, for a total of 70. First line unmatched.

1.

> If it were not for my All-excelling one
> who tells me that I should sing and be gay,
> even during the sweet season when the grass is born,
> neither fields nor branches nor bushes nor flowers,
> and not cruel lords or vain loves
> would be able to put me in motion:
> but by him I am kept from them,
> which, when joys fail and flee,
> prowess and nobility decay,
> and when the great themselves
> are alienated from joy,
> and however many things do badly,
> will draw no praise from me;
> for by him I am consoled,
> and so envy no powerful one
> who rules badly.

Construction

Flavor: two periodic sentences, followed in each case by an antithesis.

Elevation: the assertion implied in this stanza, and more fully expressed in later stanzas, that great poetry depends upon the existence of nobility; this poem can be written only because there exists one "all-excelling" example thereof, whose presence thus elevates the poem.

2. Folquetz of Marseilles

> Tant m'abellis l'amoros pessamens
> que s'es vengutz e mon fin cor assire
> per que no'i pot nuills autre pes caber
> ni mais negus no m'es dous ni plazens,
> qu'adonc viu sas quan m'aucizo'l cossire
> e fin'amors aleuja·m mo martire
> que·m promet joi, mas trop lo·m dona len,
> qu'ap bel semblan m'a trainat longamen.

Text: *Le Troubadour Folquet de Marseille*, ed. Stanislaw Stronski (Geneva: Slatkine Rprts., 1968), pp. 15–16.

Arrangement: *Fronte* of four lines, diesis after line 4, two verses of two lines each. All lines of eleven syllables, forty-four syllables and four lines in both *fronte* and verses. Third line unmatched.

2.

> The cares of love so greatly delight me,
> which have come and fixed themselves in my faithful heart,
> that no other thought can find a place there,
> nor can anything else be so sweet or pleasant to me;
> for now my life is such that the cares are killing me,
> and refined love relieves my suffering;
> it promises joy, though giving too little of it,
> for I have been led on at length by pleasant appearances.

Construction

Flavor: the extended periodic sentences of this stanza and of the others as well; the nesting of adjectival clauses in conditional sentences, with the result that the clauses are parallel in form, but not in meaning.

Charm: the personification of the "amorous thought," which both tortures and pleases the mind; the oxymorons and oppositions which express the qualities of love.

Elevation: the treatment of the subject of a cruel mistress with such refinement and art as to raise it to a level of nobility.

3. Arnault Daniel

> Sols sui qui sai lo sobreafan, que·m sortz
> al cor, d'amor, sofren per sobramar,
> car mos volers es tant ferms et entiers
> c'anc no s'esduis de celliei ni s'estors
> cui encubic al prim vezer e puois:
> qu'ades ses lieis dic a lieis cochos motz,
> pois quan la vei non sai, tant l'ai, que dire.

Text: H. C. Chaytor, *The Troubadours of Dante* (Oxford: Clarendon Press, 1902), p. 52.

Arrangement: Continuous melodic line, unrhymed. Stanzas of seven lines, all of eleven syllables.

3.

> I am the only one who knows the superfrustration of love
> which issues from the heart when suffering from superlove;
> for my desire is so steadfast and full,
> which can never escape from or resist her
> whom it has coveted from the first sight and since,
> that apart from her I say to her ardent words,
> yet when I see her I don't know, I have so many [words],
>   what to say.

Construction

Flavor: the single periodic sentence, with elaborate hyperbatons (lines 2 and 7) and with the balancing of parallel constructions within clauses (lines 3, 4, 6, and 7).

Charm: the invention of such concepts as "superfrustration" and "superlove"; puns (*sobreafan* and *sobramar*); alliteration (lines 1 and 2); internal rhyme (line 7); assonance (*cochos motz*).

Elevation: the hyperbole whereby love transcends the ordinary human condition by being most strongly expressed in its non-expression.

4. Aimeric de Belenoi

Nulls hom no pot complir adrechamen
So qu'a en cor, si tot quan el eis fai
No·l sembla pauc, ni am'ab cor veray,
Pus que cuja amar trop finamen:
Qu'aytals cujars descreys, e l'autr'enansa,
Mas ieu non am ges per aital semblansa,
Ans jur per lieys cui tenc a·l cor plus car,
Qu'on plus fort l'am, la cug petit amar.

Text: *Poésies du Troubadour Aimeric de Belenoi*, ed. M. Dumitrescu, Société des Anciens Textes Français (Paris, 1935), p. 85.

Arrangement: Two feet of two lines each, diesis after line 4, two verses of two lines each. All lines of eleven syllables, for a total of forty-four syllables in feet, forty-four syllables in verses.

4.

> No man can satisfactorily fulfill
> what he wishes in his heart, if when he has done it,
> it does not seem to him a small thing; or love with a true heart
> if he intends to love perfectly;
> for the one intention humbles, the other makes proud;
> but I have never loved in such a manner,
> but rather swear by her whom I hold most dear in my heart,
> that the greater my love, the less I believe I love her.

Construction

Flavor: periodic structure with balance of clauses.

Charm: variations on the forms of *cujar* and *amar* ("intend" and "love"); puns (*cor* and *car*, line 7); the beginning with a rhetorical *sententia*.

Elevation: argues the nobility of love on the paradoxical grounds that the very inability to fulfill the demands of love satisfactorily makes it nobler in its suffering than anything else is in its acting.

5. Aimeric de Pegulhan

> Si cum l'arbres que, per sobrecargar,
> Frang se meteys e pert son frug e se,
> Ai perduda ma belha dona e me
> E mon entier sen frag, per sobramar.
> Pero, sitot me suy apoderatz,
> Anc jorn no fi mon dan ad escien;
> Enans cug far tot so que fatz ab sen,
> Mas ar conosc que trop sobra·l foudatz.

Text: *The Poems of Aimeric de Peguilhan*, ed. W. Shepard and F. Chambers (Evanston, Ill.: Northwestern University Press, 1950), p. 233.

Arrangement: Two feet of two lines each, diesis after line 4, two verses of two lines each. Rhymes reversed in both feet and verses. All lines of eleven syllables, forty-four syllables in feet and forty-four syllables in verses.

5.

> Just like the tree which, from being overloaded,
> breaks itself and loses its fruit and itself,
> so I have lost my beautiful lady and myself,
> and broken my whole sense, from excess of love.
> Yet, although I have been overpowered,
> at no time did I knowingly do myself harm;
> rather I intended to do everything with good sense,
> but know now that folly is the stronger.

Construction

Flavor: the balancing (endings of lines 1 and 4, 2 and 3) and reversing (beginnings of lines 2 and 4) of parallel clauses.

Charm: the elaboration of the comparison between the overloaded tree and the overloving lover.

Elevation: the psychological subtlety of this rejection of the folly of love.

6. Gace Brulé (attributed by Dante to Thibaut of Champagne)

> Ire d'amour qui en mon cuer repaire
> Ne me lest tant que de chanter me tiengne.
> Grant merveille est se chançon en puis traire,
> Ne je ne sai don l'ocheson me veingne;
> Car li desirs et la grant volontez,
> Dont je sui si pensis et esgarez,
> M'ont si mené, ce vous puis je bien dire,
> Qu'a paines sai conoistre joie d'ire.

Text: *Les Chançons de Gace Brulé*, ed. G. Huet, Société des Anciens Textes Français (Paris, 1902), p. 33.

Arrangement: Two feet of two lines each, diesis after line 4, two verses of two lines each. All lines of eleven syllables, forty-four syllables in feet, forty-four syllables in verses.

6.

> The disdain of love, who dwells in my heart,
> by no means leaves me when I set about to sing.
> It is a great wonder if I can still produce a song,
> I don't know where the power to do so comes from;
> for the desire and the strong will
> because of which I am thoughtful and distressed,
> have so confused me, I can tell you,
> that I cannot distinguish joy from disdain.

Construction

Flavor: the *inclusio*, whereby the stanza begins and ends with the same word; the use (more obvious in other stanzas) of exclamations and questions.

Elevation: the complex analysis of the contradictions inherent in jealousy and disdain.

7. Guido delle Colonne

> Ancor che l'aigua per lo foco lassi
> la sua grande freddura,
> non cangerea natura
> s'alcun vasello in mezzo non vi stasse;
> anzi averria senza lunga dimora
> che lo foco astutasse
> o che l'aigua seccasse,
> ma per lo mezzo l'uno e l'autro dura.
> Cusì, gentil criatura,
> in me ha mostrato Amore
> l'ardente suo valore,
> chè senza amore er'aigua fredda e ghiaccia:
> ma Amor m'ha allumato
> di fiamma che m'abraccia,
> ch'eo fora consumato,
> se voi, donna sovrana,
> non fustici mezzana
> infra l'Amore e meve,
> che fa lo foco nascere di neve.

Text: *Poeti del Duecento*, ed. Gianfranco Contini (R. Ricciardi, 1965), 1:107.

Arrangement: Two feet of four lines each, diesis with concatenation across it after line 8, coda or sirma of eleven lines. Lines of eleven and seven syllables, seventy-two syllables in feet, eighty-five in coda. Echo rhyme in fourth line of coda. Coupling of last two lines.

7.

   Although some water might have lost, because of fire,
its extreme coldness,
it will not change its nature
when no vessel is placed in between;
thus it happens that, without long delay,
either the fire will be quenched
or the water will evaporate;
but with a vessel between them both of them will last.
   Thus, noble creature,
in me Love has shown
its great heating power
who would be without Love cold and icy water:
but Love has so lit me up
with flames that embrace me
that I would be consumed
unless you, sovereign lady,
make yourself the vessel
between Love and myself,
you, who make fire issue from the snow.

Construction

   Flavor: the balancing of two periodic sentences, with almost perfect, but surprising, correspondences between the parallel clauses.

   Charm: the elaboration of the comparison (in this as well as the other stanzas); the play of sound in the rhymes; the hyperbole of the last line.

8. Guido Guinizelli

> Tegno de folle'impres', a lo ver dire,
> chi s'abandona inver' troppo possente,
>   sì como gli occhi miei che fér'esmire
> incontr'a quelli de la più avenente,
>   che sol per lor èn vinti
> senza ch'altre bellezze li dian forza:
> ché a ciò far son pinti,
> si come gran baronia di segnore,
> quando vuol usar forza,
> tutta s'apresta in donarli valore.

Text: Contini (see above, no. 7), vol. 2, p. 450.

Arrangement: Two feet of two lines each, diesis after line 4, three verses of two lines each. Eleven syllables in lines of feet, eleven and seven in lines of verses; forty-four syllables in feet, fifty-four syllables in verses.

8.

> I told him of foolish daring, to tell the truth,
> who places himself at the mercy of a great power,
> in the manner of my eyes which have been struck with wonder
> on meeting those of the most attractive one,
>   which were conquered by these alone,
> without other beauties adding to their force;
> which are as eager to do so
> as the troops of a lord
> who, when he wishes to bring his forces into play,
> are all in readiness to add to his strength.

Construction

Flavor: produced by a single sentence containing elaborate qualifying clauses.

Charm: the extended comparison of a lady's beauties to a lord's military forces.

Elevation: the development of the nobility and heroism of love on the analogy of military heroism.

9. Guido Cavalcanti

Poi che di doglia cor conven ch'i'porti
e senta di piacere ardente foco
e di virtù mi traggo a sì vil loco,
dirò com'ho perduto ogni valore.
E dico che'miei spiriti son morti
e 'l cor che tanto ha guerra e vita poco;
e se non fosse che'l morir m'è gioco
far'ne di pietà pianger Amore.
Ma, per lo folle tempo che m'ha giunto,
mi cangio di mia ferma opinïone
in altrui condizione,
sì ch'io non mostro quant'io sento affano:
là 'nd'eo ricevo inganno,
ché dentro da lo cor mi pass' Amanza
che se ne porta tutta mia possanza.

Text: Contini (see above, no. 7), vol. 2, p. 504.

Arrangement: Two feet of four lines each, diesis after line 8, coda or *sirma* of seven lines. Lines of eleven syllables in feet, of eleven and seven in coda; total of eighty-eight syllables in feet, sixty-nine syllables in coda. First line of coda unmatched; last two lines coupled.

9.

Since it has happened that I bear a heart of sorrow,
and that I feel the burning fire of desire,
and am dragged from virtue into a very vile place,
I will tell how I have lost all my worth.
And I say that my spirits have died,
and also my heart, which has a great struggle and little life;
and if my own death had not become a joy to me,
I would make Love for pity complain of it.
But because of this season of folly which has come upon me,
I have changed my fixed opinion
about the condition of other people,
so that I do not make known how depleted I feel:
for this reason I remain in pain,
because love passes through my heart
who bears away from it all my powers.

Construction

Flavor: produced by the fitting of the syntax to the arrangement, and by
the *inclusio*, wherein the stanza ends with the *cor* and *porto* with which it
began.

Charm: the elaboration of the figure, in which the heart becomes the
locus of love's activity.

Elevation: the opposition between love and virtue.

10. Cino da Pistoia (addressed to Dante)

> Aveegna ched el m'aggia piú per tempo
> per voi richesto Pietate e Amore
> per confortar la vostra grave vita,
> non è ancor sí trapassato il tempo
> che 'l mio sermon non trovi il vostro core
> piangendo star con l'anima smarrita,
>   fra sé dicendo: "Già sete in ciel gita,
> beata gioia, com chiamava il nome!"
> Lasso me! quando e come
> veder vi potrò io visibilmente?
> sí ch'ancora a presente
> vi posso fare di conforto aita.
> Donque m'odite, poi ch'io parlo a posta
> d'Amor, a li sospir ponendo sosta.

Text: *Le Rime di Cino di Pistoia*, ed. G. Zaccagnini (Pistoia: Tariffi, 1936), p. 27.

Arrangement: Two feet of three lines each, diesis after line 6 with concatenation across it, coda or *sirma* of eight lines. Lines of eleven syllables in feet, eleven and seven in coda; total of sixty-six syllables in feet, eighty in coda. Echo rhymes in lines 3 and 7 of coda; last two lines coupled.

10.

Although it has been a very long time
since Pity and Love have requested for your sake
that I give comfort to your heavy life,
it has only been a short passage of time
in which my words did not find your heart
standing and crying, with your spirit disordered,
    saying within itself, "Already you are in heaven,
blessed joy, as your name signifies!"
Alas for me! when and how
will I be able to see you visibly?
so that at last in the present
I will be able to give you the aid of comfort.
Therefore listen, for I speak at the command
of Love, and put aside your sighs.

Construction

Flavor: lines 1–12 a single periodic sentence, given variety by the
quotation, and by the questions, commands, and exclamations of which it
is composed.

Charm: the personification of Love and Pity; the disguised pun on the
name of "Beatrice," line 2 of coda; the alliteration of lines 3, 4, 10, 13, and
14.

Elevation: the high and noble conceptions of friendship, love, and
consolation to which it gives expression.

11. Dante Alighieri

> Amor che ne la mente mi ragiona
> de la mia donna disiosamente,
> move cose di lei meco sovente,
> che lo 'ntelletto sovr'esse disvia.
> Lo suo parlar sì dolcemente sona,
> che l'anima ch'ascolta e che lo sente
> dice: "O me lassa! ch'io non son possente
> di dir quel ch'odo di la donna mia!"
> E certo e' mi conven lasciare in pria
> s'io vo' trattar di quel ch'odo di lei,
> ciò che lo mio intelletto non comprende;
> e di quel che s'intende
> gran parte, perchè dirlo non savrei.
> Però, se le mie rime avran difetto
> ch'entreran ne la loda di costei,
> di ciò si biasmi il debole intelletto
> e 'l parlar nostro, che non ha valore
> di ritrar tutto ciò che dice Amore.

Text: *Convivio*, ed. G. Busnelli and G. Vandelli (Florence: Felice le Monnier), 1:253.

Arrangement: Two feet of four lines each, diesis after line 8 with concatenation across it, coda or *sirma* of ten lines. Lines of eleven syllables in feet, of eleven and seven in coda; total of eighty-eight syllables in feet, one hundred and six in coda. Last two lines coupled.

11.

Love, who in my mind discourses with me
concerning my love, with enthusiasm,
often urges things concerning her with me
such that my intellect, overcome, gets lost.
His speech so sweetly sounds,
that my soul, which listens and which hears him,
says, "Alas for me! for it is beyond my capacity
to utter what I hear concerning my lady!"
And for certain I must leave behind,
when I wish to present what I have heard about her,
those things which the intellect cannot grasp;
and of those things which it does grasp,
the greater part, because I do not know how to say it.
Therefore, if there is any defect in those rhymes
which enter upon her praise,
the blame belongs to the feeble intellect,
and to our capacity for speech which lacks the power
to repeat all that Love says.

Construction

Flavor: produced by the neat adaptation of syntax to arrangement, and by the use of quotation and exclamation.

Charm: the elaborate conceit based upon the personification of Love as a "speaker" of transcendent power.

Elevation: the subject matter, those capacities of human intelligence which border on the superhuman, which, according to the *Letter to Can Grande*, are required for the plausibility of the fiction of the trip to Paradise which Dante reproduces in his *Comedy*.

Appendix B
Index of Poets and Poems Cited in Dante's Critical Writings

Those Italian poets whom Dante mentions whose works have survived are collected in Gianfranco Contini, ed., Poeti del Duecento, La letterature Italiana—Storia e testi, *no. 2, 2 vols. (Naples: R. Ricciardi, 1965), abbreviated "Contini" below. Medieval authors are entered under the first name.*

AIMERIC DE BELENOI (fl. 1217–1242; Provençal). "Nuls hom non pot complir addrechamen" cited as an example of excellence in construction (*Eloq.* 2.6.6; see Appendix A, no. 4); and as an example of a poem written entirely in lines of eleven syllables (*Eloq.* 2.12.3).

Edition: *Poésies du Troubadour Aimeric de Belenoi*, ed. M. Dumitrescu, Société des anciens textes français, no. 85 (Paris, 1935); with French translations of poems.

AIMERIC DE PEGUILHAN (fl. 1220; Provençal). "Si com l'arbres che per sobrecarcar" cited as an example of excellence in construction (*Eloq.* 2.6.6; see Appendix A, no. 5).

Edition: *The Poems of Aimeric de Peguilhan*, ed. W. Shepard and F. Chambers (Evanston, Ill.: Northwestern University Press, 1950); with English translations of poems.

ALDOBRANDINO DEI MEZZABATI DI PADOVA (d. 1297?; Italian). Mentioned as a Paduan who attempted to write a curial vernacular (*Eloq.* 1.14.7). His poetry has not survived.

ARNAULT DANIEL (fl. 1180–1210; Provençal). "L'aura amara fa·l bruol brancuz/ clarzir" cited as an example of a poem on the subject of love (*Eloq.* 2.2.9). "Sem fos Amor de joi donar" cited as a poem without rhyme (*Eloq.* 2.13.2). "Sols sui che sai lo sobraffan" cited as an example of excellence in construction (*Eloq.* 2.6.6; see Appendix A, no. 3). Arnault mentioned as using stanzas without division (*Eloq.* 2.10.2); addresses Dante in Provençal, after having been called by Guido Guinizelli "the better craftsman" (*Purg.* 26.140–47).

Edition: *La poésies du Troubadour Arnault Daniel,* ed. René Lavaud (Toulouse, 1910).

BERTRAN DA BORN (ca. 1140–1183; Provençal). Mentioned as a poet on the subject of arms, one of the three noble subjects, in his poem "No posc mudar" (*Eloq.* 2.2.9).

Edition: *Bertran von Born,* ed. A. Stimming, Romanische Bibliothek, no. 8 (Halle: S. M. Niemeyer, 1892).

BUONAGIUNTA ORBICCIANI DA LUCCA (fl. 1250–1297; Italian). Cited as one who believes that the Tuscan dialect is superior to the others, but as actually writing a municipal, not a curial, dialect (*Eloq.* 1.13.1); speaks to Dante about the difference between the old and new Italian poetic styles (*Purg.* 24.49–62).

Editions: *I rimatori lucchesi del secolo XIII,* ed. Amos Parducci (Bergramo, 1905); Contini, vol. 1, pp. 257 ff.

BRUNETTO (LATINI) OF FLORENCE (1220–1294; Italian). Mentioned as one of the Tuscan poets who believe they have the truly illustrious vernacular (*Eloq.* 1.13.1).

Edition: His one surviving *canzone,* "S'eo sono distretto innamoratamente," is published in Ernesto Monaci, *Crestomazia Italiana dei Primi Secoli,* new ed. (Rome: Società Editrice Dante Alighieri, 1955), pp. 269–70.

CINO DA PISTOIA (1270–1337; Italian). "Avegna che io aggia" cited as an example of excellence in construction (*Eloq.* 2.6.6; see Appendix A, no. 10). "Non spero che già mai" cited as a *canzone* beginning with a line of eleven syllables (*Eloq.* 2.5.4). Cino mentioned along with Dante as an Italian who has outdone the poets of France and Provençe in sweetness and depth (*Eloq.* 1.10.4); mentioned as one who knows, along with Dante, Lapo, and Cavalcanti, how to recognize vernacular excellence (*Eloq.* 1.13.3); his *canzoni* said to justify the term "illustrious" as applied to the highest vernacular (*Eloq.* 1.17.3); mentioned as a poet of love, one of the three subjects suited to the "tragic" style (*Eloq.* 2.2.9).

Editions: *Le Rime di Cino di Pistoia,* ed. G. Zaccagnini (Florence, 1921); Contini, vol. 2, pp. 629 ff.

DANTE ALIGHIERI (1265–1321; Italian). "Al poco giorno e al gran cerchio d'ombra" cited as a stanza without rhyme, an imitation in this respect of Arnault Daniel (*Eloq.* 2.10.2, 2.13.2). "Amor, che movi" cited as a *canzone* beginning with a line of eleven syllables (*Eloq.* 2.5.4); and as an example of a *canzone* where the feet exceed the coda or *sirma* in the number of their syllables and lines (*Eloq.* 2.11.7). "Amor che ne la mente mi ragiona" cited as an example of excellence in construction (*Eloq.* 2.6.6; see Appendix A, no. 11); last stanza translated and commented upon (*Banq.* 3.9.1–4). "Amore, tu vedi ben" cited as a young work, claiming novelty in art by using excessive repetition of the same rhymes (*Eloq.* 2.13.12). "Doglia mi reca" cited as an example of a poem on rectitude, one of the three noble subjects (*Eloq.* 2.2.9). "Le dolci rime d'amor ch'i solia" (subject of commentary in *Banq.* 4), first stanza translated (*Banq.* 4.2.11–16); lines 112–20 translated (*Banq.* 4.20.19–20). "Donna pietosa e di novella etate" cited as a stanza where the coda or *sirma* exceeds the feet in the number of its lines and syllables (*Eloq.* 2.11.8). "Donne, che avete intellecto d'amore" translated and divided (*New Life* 19); cited as a model of the art of the *canzone* (*Eloq.* 2.8.8); cited as a stanza made up entirely of lines of eleven syllables (*Eloq.* 2.12.3); used by Buonagiunta Orbicciani to identify Dante as a poet (*Purg.* 24.50). "Poschia ch'Amor" cited as using internal rhyme (*Eloq.* 2.12.8). "Tragemi de la mente" cited as an example of a poem where the verses exceed the *fronte* in the number of their syllables and lines (*Eloq.* 2.11.5). "Tutti le miei penser" translated and divided (*New Life* 13). "Voi che'ntendendo il terzo ciel movete" (subject of commentary in *Banq.* 2), *tornado* translated (*Banq.* 2.11.1–9). Dante mentioned as one exiled unjustly, but still a lover of his native Florence (*Eloq.* 1.6.3); as a poet whose excellence argues for the superiority of the Italian vernacular (*Eloq.* 1.10.4); as "one other" who understands excellence in the vernacular (*Eloq.* 1.13.3); as one who, along with Cino, has exalted the art of poetry in the vernacular (*Eloq.* 1.17.3); as an example of a poet for whom the glory of poetry makes an exile less harsh (*Eloq.* 1.17.6); as a poet of rectitude (*Eloq.* 2.2.9). His *Paradise* 1.1–37 subject of commentary (*Letter* 17–31).

Fabruzzo di tommassino dei lambertazzi (d. ca. 1300; Italian). "Lo meo lontano gire" cited as an example of an excellent poem written by a Bolognese (*Eloq.* 1.15.6); and as a *canzone* beginning with a line of seven syllables, but slightly tinged with elegy (*Eloq.* 2.12.6). Neither this nor any other of his poems have survived.

Folquetz of marseilles (fl. 1180–1195, d. 1231; Provençal). "Tan m'abellis" cited as an example of excellence in construction (*Eloq.* 2.6.6; see Appendix A, no. 2).

Edition: *Le Troubadour Folquet de Marseille*, ed. Stanislaw Stronski (Geneva: Slatkine Rprts., 1968).

[GACE BRULÉ] (fl. 1220–1250; French). "Ire d'amor qui en mon cor repaire" cited as an example of excellence in construction, though attributed to Thibaut of Champagne (*Eloq.* 2.6.6; see Appendix A, no. 6).

Edition: *Les Chançons de Gace Brulé*, ed. G. Huet, Société des Anciens Textes Français (Paris, 1902).

GIOVANNI DEL VIRGILIO (fl. 1319; Latin). The "Mopsus" of Dante's poetic epistle to him (*Eclogue* 1).

Editions: *Dante and Giovanni del Virgilio*, ed. P. Wicksteed and E. Gardner (Westminster: A. Constable, 1902); *La Correspondenza Poetica di Danti Alighieri e Giovanni del Virgilio*, ed. E. Bolisani and M. Valgimigli (Florence: L. S. Olschki, 1963).

GALLO (GALLETTO) OF PISA (fl. 1274; Italian). One of the famous Tuscans who are cited as wrongly believing that the Tuscan dialect, as used in their poetry, is the illustrious vernacular (*Eloq.* 1.13.1).

Edition: Two surviving *canzone* are published in G. Zaccagnini and A. Parducci, *Rimatori siculi-toscani del Dugento* (Bari: Laterza, 1915), pp. 135 ff.

GIRAUTZ DE BORNEILH (fl. 1165–1200; Provençal). "Ara ausirez encabilitz" cited as a poem which begins with a line of eleven syllables (*Eloq.* 2.5.4). "Per solaz reveillar" cited as an example of a poem on rectitude, one of the three noble subjects (*Eloq.* 2.2.9). "Sim sentis fezelz" cited as an example of a poem in Provençal using the word *amor* (*Eloq.* 1.9.3). "Si per mon Sobretots" cited as an example of excellence in construction (*Eloq.* 2.6.6; see Appendix A, no. 1). Girautz is probably "he of Limousin" thought by some to be superior to Arnault Daniel (*Purg.* 26.120).

Edition: *Sämtliche Lieder des Trobadors Giraut de Bornelh*, ed. A. Kolsen (Halle: Verlag von Max Niemeyer, 1907).

GOTTO OF MANTUA (fl. 1300?; Italian). A poet who read his poems, which made use of the "key," to Dante (*Eloq.* 2.13.4). Nothing outside of this reference is known about Gotto.

GUIDO CAVALCANTI (d. 1301; Italian). "Donna me prega" cited as a poem with stanzas entirely in lines of eleven syllables (*Eloq.* 2.12.3); and as a poem with internal rhymes (*Eloq.* 2.12.8). "Poi che de doglia" cited as an example of excellence in construction (*Eloq.* 2.6.6; see Appendix A, no. 9)." Guido mentioned along with Cino, Lapo, and Dante as one who knows what is excellent in the vernacular (*Eloq.* 1.13.3); mentioned as Dante's "best friend" who is also aware that there are poets who use figures without rational purpose (*New Life* 25.11).

Editions: *Le Rime de Guido Cavalcanti*, ed. Guido Favati, Documenti di Filologia, no. 1 (Milan and Naples: R. Ricciardi, 1957); Contini, vol. 2, pp. 487 ff.

GUIDO ("GUITTONE") D'AREZZO (fl. ca. 1250; Italian). Mentioned as a poet who never attempted the curial language (*Eloq.* 1.13.1); as the leader of a sect of poets who used plebeian rather than noble constructions (*Eloq.* 2.6.8); as among those poets who, not hearing the voice of love, never attained to the sweet new style (*Purg.* 24.56); as one given an undeserved reputation for his poetry (*Purg.* 26.124); probably among those referred to by Dante as known to him and to his best friend for a poet who writes figurative language without being able to explain his figures in ordinary language (*New Life* 25.11).

Edition: Contini, vol. 1,   pp. 189–255.

GUIDO DELLE COLONNE ("The Judge of Messina"; fl. 1257–1280; Italian). "Amor, che lungiamente" and "Anchor che l'aigua" cited as excellent poems in the "Sicilian" manner (*Eloq.* 1.12.2). "Amor, che lungiamente" cited as a poem beginning with a line of eleven syllables (*Eloq.* 2.5.4). "Anchor che l'aigua" cited as an example of excellence in construction (*Eloq.* 2.6.6; see Appendix A, no. 7).

Editions: "Rime," ed. Gianfranco Contini, in *Bollettino, Centro di Studi Filologici et Linguistici Siciliani* 2:178–200; Contini, vol. 1, pp. 95 ff.

GUIDO GHISILIERI (d. 1280; Italian). "Donna, lo fermo core" cited as a poem by an excellent poet from Bologna (*Eloq.* 1.15.6); and as a *canzone* beginning with a line of seven syllables, but tinged with elegy (*Eloq.* 2.12.6). His poetry has not survived.

GUIDO GUINIZELLI (1240–1276; Italian). "Al cor gentil repara sempre amore" cited (lines 3–4) as using the word *amor* in Italian (*Eloq.* 1.9.3); cited as a *canzone* beginning with a line of eleven syllables (*Eloq.* 2.5.4); cited as an authoritative discussion of the nature of *gentilizza* (*Banq.* 4.20.7). "De fermo sofferire" cited as a poem beginning with a line of seven syllables, but tinged with elegy (*Eloq.* 2.12.6). "Madonna, lo fino amor" cited as the work of an excellent poet among the Bolognese (*Eloq.* 1.15.6). "Tegno de folle 'impresa" cited as an example of excellence in construction (*Eloq.* 2.6.6; see Appendix A, no. 8). Guinizelli speaks to Dante about poets and poetry (*Purg.* 26.89–132).

Editions: *I rimatori bolognesi del secolo XIII*, ed. G. Zaccagnini (Milan:

Società editi *Vitae pensiero*, 1933); *I rimatori del dolce stil novo*, ed. Luigi di Benedetto, Scrittori d'Italia, no. 192 (Bari, 1939); Contini, vol. 2, pp. 447 ff.

GUITTONE. See GUIDO D'AREZZO.

HOMER (9th century B.C.; Greek). His not having been translated into Latin cited as proof of the untranslatibility of poetry *(Banq.* 1.7.15); his address to the Muses, quoted by Horace, cited as authority for using in poetry figures which make nonexistent things human *(New Life* 25.9).

HORACE (Q. Horatius Flaccus; 65–68 B.C.; Latin). *Art of Poetry*, lines 38 ff., cited as authority for the necessity of suiting the matter to a poet's ability and style *(Eloq.* 2.4.4); lines 93–96 quoted as implying the necessity of matching style to genre *(Letter* 10). Horace cited as the source of Dante's list of genres *(Letter* 10).

JACOPO DA LENTINO ("Il Notario"; d. 1250; Italian). "Madonna dire vi voglio" cited (without attribution) as a composition in illustrious diction by an Apulian *(Eloq.* 1.12.8); "The Notary" mentioned as a poet who, along with Guittone, failed to achieve the sweet new style *(Purg.* 24.56).

Editions: *The Poetry of Giacomo da Lentino, Sicilian Poet of the Thirteenth Century*, ed. Ernest F. Langley (Cambridge, Mass.: Harvard University Press, 1915); Contini, vol. 1, pp. 49 ff.

LAPO GIANNI (1275–1328; Italian). Mentioned, along with Cavalcanti, Cino, and Dante, as knowing what is excellent in the vernacular *(Eloq.* 1.13.3).

Edition: *I rimatori del dolce stil novo*, ed. Luigi di Benedetto, Scrittori d'Italia, no. 192 (Bari, 1939).

LATINI. See BRUNETTO

LUCAN (M. Annaeus Lucanus; A.D. 39–65; Latin). *Pharsalia* 1.44 quoted as an example of a poet addressing something inanimate *(New Life* 25.9); *Phar.* 2.326 ff., concerning the return of Marcia to Cato, the subject of commentary *(Banq.* 4.28.13–19); *Phar.* 2.396 ff. cited as a model for the description of rivers flowing from the Apennines *(Eloq.* 1.10.6); *Phar.* 9.580 quoted as an example of pagan knowledge of God's true universality *(Letter* 22). Lucan mentioned as an authority for excellence in construction *(Eloq.* 2.6.7).

MINO (BARTOLOMEO) MOCATI OF SIENA (fl. 1282?; Italian). One of the famous Tuscans cited as believing that the Tuscan dialect of his poetry is the truly illustrious Italian vernacular *(Eloq.* 1.13.1). His poetry has not survived.

ONESTO DEGLI ONESTI (1240–1301 [?03]; Italian). Mentioned as an excellent poet of Bologna (*Eloq.* 2.15.6).

Edition: One poem, "Messer Onesto a Messer Cino," has survived, and is edited by Contini, vol. 2, p. 255.

OVID (P. Ovidius Naso; 43 B.C.–A.D. 17; Latin). *Remedies of Love*, line 1, cited as an example of an abstraction speaking in poetry (*New Life* 25.9); *Metamorphoses* 5.294 ff. the source of the story of speaking magpies (*Eloq.* 1.2.7); *Meta.* 7, esp. lines 507–11, the source of the story of the meeting between Cephalus and Aeacus, which contains the virtues of maturity (*Banq.* 4.27.17–20); *Meta.* 10.86–105, 143–47, and 11.1–2 the source of the story of Orpheus, used to explain the nature of poetic allegory (*Banq.* 2.1.3). Ovid in *Metamorphoses* cited as a model of excellence in construction (*Eloq.* 2.6.7).

PEIRE D'ALVERNHE (fl. 1150–1180; Provençal). Cited as one of the most ancient experts in vernacular composition, and therefore as evidence for the precedence of Provençal among the three members of the Romance language-group (*Eloq.* 1.10.3). (In fact, there were several troubadours before Peire, including William VII, Count of Poitiers, Jaufré Rudel, and Marcabrun; Dante was either unfamiliar with them, or thought them to be contemporaries of Peire.)

Edition: *Liriche*, ed. Alberto del Monte, Collezione di 'Filologia romanza,' no. 1 (Turin, 1955).

RINALDO D'AQUINO (d. 1279 [?81]; Italian). "Per fino amore vo si letamente" cited as a poem using noble diction written by an Apulian (*Eloq.* 1.12.8); cited as a *canzone* beginning with a line of eleven syllables (*Eloq.* 2.5.4).

Editions: "Rime," ed. O. J. Tallgren in *Mémoires de la Société néo-Philologique de Helsingfors* 6 (1917): 175–303; Contini, vol. 1, p. 111.

SORDELLO DI MANTOVA (d. 1269; Italian-Provençal). Mentioned as a poet who, by choosing to write in Provençal, proved the impossibility of harmonizing the dialects of the cities surrounding Mantua (*Eloq.* 1.15.2).

Editions: *Vita e poesie di Sordello di Goito*, ed. C. De Lollis (Halle: M. Niemeyer, 1896); *Poesie di Sordello*, ed. Marco Boni (Bologna: Libreria Antiquaria *Palmaverde*, 1954); Contini, vol. 1, p. 501.

STATIUS, P. PAPINUS (A.D. 40–79; Latin). Mentioned as a model of excellence in construction (*Eloq.* 2.6.7). His *Thebaid* 1.490 ff., containing the qualities of noble youth, the subject of commentary (*Banq.* 4.25.5–10). His meeting with Virgil described (*Purg.* 22.5–114).

THIBAUT DE CHAMPAGNE ("The King of Navarre"; 1201–1253; French). "De fin'amor si vient sen et bonté" cited as an example of the use of the word *amor* in French (*Eloq.* 1.9.3); cited as an example of a *canzone* beginning with a line of eleven syllables (*Eloq.* 2.5.4). *Ire d'amour* falsely attributed to him (*Eloq.* 2.6.6): see GACE BRULÉ. Edition: *Les Chansons de Thibaut de Champagne*, ed. A. Wallensköld, Société des Anciens Textes Français (Paris: Champion, 1925).

TOMASSO FAENTINI (fl. 1267–1274; Italian). Mentioned as a poet departing from the effeminacy of his native Romagnolese dialect (*Eloq.* 1.14.3). Edition: His only surviving poem "Tenzone with Monte Andrea," may be found in Contini, vol. 1, pp. 453 ff.

UGOLINO BUCCIOLI DEI MANFREDI (d. 1301; Italian). Mentioned as a Romagnolese who, like Tomasso, wrote poetry departing from the effeminacy of his native dialect (*Eloq.* 1.14.3). His poetry has not survived.

VIRGIL (P. Virgilius Maro; 70–19 B.C.; Latin). *Aeneid* 1.1 cited as using *cano* in an active sense, with the writer as subject (*Eloq.* 2.8.4); *Aen.* 1.65 and 76–77 cited as examples of noncorporeal things or attributes of things speaking as if human (*New Life* 25.9); *Aen.* 3.94 cited as an example of an inanimate thing addressing an animate one (*New Life* 25.9); *Aen.* 6.126–30, referring to those who are "favorites of gods," applied by Dante to poets who make the greatest use of their genius and art (*Eloq.* 2.4.10); various passages of *Aeneid*, Books 4–6, exemplifying the virtues of young manhood, subject to commentary (*Banq.* 4.26.8–15). Virgil mentioned as a model of excellence in construction (*Eloq.* 2.6.7); his conversation with Statius recorded, in which the latter attributes to Virgil both his becoming a poet and his becoming a Christian (*Purg.* 22.10–114); he is shown as pleased with Mathilda's revelation that poets who had spoken of the Golden Age had been referring to the Terrestrial Paradise (*Purg.* 28.146–47).

Glossary of Technical Critical Terms

The following list contains those words which are used technically in either the discussion of poetic art or in the establishment of the nature of poetic language. It therefore does not contain common critical terms where Dante's use does not depart from the ordinary meaning. Each word is followed by the Latin or Italian it translates; by its various meanings in key passages; and by references to passages where Dante himself defines or discusses the term. —Italicized words are cross-references to other terms defined in the glossary.

L. = Latin; I. = Italian

ALLEGORY, ALLEGORICAL LEVEL (L. *allegoria, allegoricus*; I. *allegorico*). The *sense* or meaning contained in or hidden in the *literal level* of scripture or poetry; also, one of three such meanings, distinguished from the *moral* and the *anagogical*, taking the form, in Scripture, of a belief, and in poetry, of a general philosophical principle. Defined *Letter* 7; *Banq.* 2.1.3.

ANAGOGIC, ANAGOGICAL LEVEL (L. *anagogicus*; I. *anagogico*). That *allegorical* meaning which refers to the spiritual qualities of eternal glory; that is, to salvation and damnation, the Second Coming, or other last things. Defined *Letter* 7; *Banq.* 2.1.6.

ARRANGEMENT (L. *habitudo*). The disposition of the parts of a stanza in order and in numerical relation to each other, as in *Eloq.* 2.11.

AUTHORITY; AUTHORITATIVE IDEAS (L. *auctoritas*, I. *authoritade*). One of the two sources of true principles, the other being reason; "pronouncements worthy of faith and obedience" (*Banq.* 4.6.5, not found in this volume), or those writers and works making such pronouncements.

BARBARISM (L. *barbarismus*). A term in grammar referring to irregularities in inflection, pronunciation, or the combination of roots.

CANTICLE (L. *cantica*). One of the three larger *divisions* (*Hell, Purgatory,* or *Paradise*) of the *Divine Comedy*.

CANTO (L. *cantus*). Literally, a song; used by Dante to refer to the middle of the three *divisions* in his *Divine Comedy*, between the *canticles* and the *rhymed units*.

CANZONE (L. *cantio*). The major form in *vernacular* poetry, defined by Dante (*Eloq.* 2.8.8) as the "linking together in the *tragic style* of equal stanzas without a *reprise* with the meaning expressed as a unity." An ode.

CANZONETTA (L. *cantilena*). A shorter and low-style form of the *canzone*, the art of which Dante intended to describe in the later portion of his treatise *On Eloquence in the Vernacular*. See *Eloq.* 2.8.8.

CARDINAL (L. *cardinalis*). Basic and controlling, as a hinge (L. *cardo*) is to a door; one of the qualities of the most excellent poetic language. Defined *Eloq.* 1.18.1.

CHARM (CHARMING) (L. *venustas, venustus*). That quality imparted to discourse by the presence of figurative language; complementary to *flavor*, and the precondition of *elevation*. Defined *Eloq.* 2.6.5.

CODA (L. *cauda*). The term describing the section of a stanza in a *canzone* which comes after the *diesis* when the *melodic line* is not repeated. From the Latin for "tail"; the same thing as a *sirma*. Defined *Eloq.* 2.10.4.

COMEDY (L. *comedia*). The classical genre distinguished by the wretched beginning and happy ending of its plot, and by the low style of its diction. Derived from the Greek for "rustic song." Defined *Letter* 10.

CONCATENATION (L. *concatenatio*). The rhyming of the lines immediately before and after the *diesis*, as a means of joining the sections of a *canzone*; regarded by Dante as an allowable grace even when violating some other rule of *arrangement*. Defined *Eloq.* 2.13.6.

CONSTRUCTION (L. *constructio*). The building of a discourse according to the rules of grammar and rhetoric, ending at a level where the resulting sentence is *flavorless, flavorful, charming,* or *elevated*. Defined *Eloq.* 2.6.2.

COUPLING (L. *combinatio*). The ending of a stanza with a rhymed couplet, allowed even when such a rhyme might violate some rule for the *arrangement* of rhymes. Defined *Eloq.* 2.18.7.

COURTLY (L. *aulicus*). Belonging to the royal court or palace; hence, elegant and sublime. One of the terms describing the most excellent poetic language. Defined *Eloq.* 1.18.2–3.

CURIAL (L. *curialis*). Pertaining to the judicial and administrative offices of a government; hence, the result of a formal and ordered procedural judgment. One of the terms describing the most excellent poetic language. Defined *Eloq.* 1.18.4.

DEFINITION, CONSISTING IN (L. *definitivus*). The putting forth in poetry of formal definitions of concepts. One of Dante's ten terms for the treatment of a treatise. See *Letter* 9.

DESCRIPTIVE (L. *descriptivus*). Making use of that formal rhetorical figure ("descriptio") which consists of making some object, scene, or person seem to be present to the poet and his audience. One of Dante's ten terms for the treatment of a treatise. See *Letter* 9.

DIALECT. *See* SPEECH

DIESIS (L. *diesis*). The point of transition between *melodic lines* in the stanza of a *canzone*, called "volta" in Italian. Defined *Eloq.* 2.10.2.

DIGRESSIVE (L. *digressivus*). The introduction of material into a poem not directly necessary to its argument. One of Dante's ten terms for the treatment of a treatise. See *Letter* 9.

DIVISION, (CONSISTING IN) (L. *dividio, divisivus*). A constituent part of a rhetorical argument, marked by some change in subject matter, speaker, mode, or rhetorical figure; the artful use of such divisions, one of Dante's ten terms for the treatment of a treatise. See *Letter* 9.

DOCTRINES (L. *doctrina*). The basic principles of an art or science, formulated and ordered for the teaching of that art or science.

ELEGY (L. *elegia*). A classical genre of lyric poetry, which Dante says is characterized by a tone of lament or complaint. See *Eloq.* 2.12.6.

ELEVATION, ELEVATED (L. *elevatio, elevatus*). The quality of a discourse which is not only *flavorful* and *charming*, but also expressed so as to contain a grave or profound thought. Defined *Eloq.* 2.6.5.

ELOQUENCE (L. *eloquentia*). Speech or written discourse which follows the rules of art; the quality of such a discourse; the rules of the art itself.

EXECUTIVE PART (L. *pars executivus*). The main body of a poem or argument, where the promises of the *prologue* are carried out. See *Letter* 17.

EXORDIUM. *See* PROLOGUE

EXPERTS (L. *doctores*). Those capable of providing authoritative instruction or example in a field of learning; used by Dante to refer to the masters of *eloquence* in both *grammar* and the *vernacular*.

FICTIVE (L. *fictivus*). Invented or made up for purposive use in a work of art. Containing such inventions. One of Dante's ten terms for the treatment of a treatise. See *Letter* 9.

FLAVOR (FLAVORFUL, FLAVORLESS) (L. *sapor, sapidus, insipidus*). The quality imparted to a grammatically correct but also "flavorless" sentence by the introduction of rhetorical schemes, or artful departures from normal syntactic order. Complements *charm*, and is a constituent of *elevation*. See *Eloq.* 2.6.4–5.

FOOT (L. *pes*). Each division of the stanza of a *canzone* repeated before the *diesis*, and therefore fitted to the repetition of the *melodic line*. Defined *Eloq.* 2.10.4. Dante notes (*Eloq.* 2.11.12) that the congruence and difference between vernacular and Latin prosody is indicated in the fact that, in the one, feet are made up of lines, while in the other, lines are made up of feet.

FRONTE (L. *frontis*). The division of the stanza of a *canzone* before the *diesis* which is not repeated, and which therefore fits a single continuous *melodic line*. Defined *Eloq.* 2.10.4.

GRAMMAR (L. *grammatica*). A language whose rules of agreement, *paradigms*, and morphology have been regularized and must therefore be learned, in contrast with a *vernacular*, acquired by imitation and subject to variation over time and geographical area, from which a grammar follows as a secondary acquisition. Defined *Eloq.* 1.1.3.

HISTORICAL SENSE (L. *historalis*). The "story" or sense indicated by the *literal* level of Scripture or poetry; the fundamental and primary sense which contains or hides the *allegorical* levels of meaning.

ILLUSTRIOUS (L. *illustre*). Most worthy of dignity; containing and conferring illumination and luster. One of the four qualities of the most excellent poetic language. Defined *Eloq.* 1.17.2.

JOINING TOGETHER (L. *coniugatio*). That art which unites all of the other arts in the composition of a discourse. See *Eloq.* 2.6.2.

KEY (L. *clavis*). The use of a rhyme, in a *canzone*, which has no mate in its own stanza, but in some subsequent stanza. Defined *Eloq.* 2.13.4.

LANGUAGE. *See* SPEECH

LETTER, LITERAL LEVEL (L. *litera, literalis*; I. *lettura*). The basic and surface sense of Scripture or poetry, which contains or hides the *allegorical* senses. Same as the *historical sense*. Defined *Letter* 7, *Banq.* 2.1.3.

LINE, POETIC LINE (L. *carmina*). The elemental unit in the *arrangement* of a stanza, defined by the number of its syllables, and fitting into a scheme of *divisions* and rhymes.

LITERAL LEVEL. *See* LETTER

MATTER, SUBJECT-MATTER (L. *materia*). The plot, or myth, about which a poem is composed. Identical with the *subject* when a poem is considered the product of the Aristotelian causes.

MEANING (MEANING EXPRESSED AS A UNITY) (L. *sententia* [*ad unam*]). The formulation of a signification, derived from the surface *sense* of a discourse, but carrying that sense to a universal and practical level. In the *canzone*, the meaning must be "expressed as a unity," or, in other words, be capable of formulation in a single set of related propositions. See *Eloq.* 2.8.8.

MELODIC LINE (L. *oda*). The *musical setting, tune, notation*, or *melody* to which the words of a poem have been fitted. The change in a melodic line is indicated by a *diesis*, and is determined by the melodic line's repetition. Also, the Greek form of the word is the root of *comedy* and *tragedy*.

MELODY (L. *melos*). *See* MELODIC LINE

METER (L. *numeris*, I. *numero*). The measure of a poetic *line*, defined in vernacular poetry by the number of its syllables. The same term is translated, *Eloq.* 2.5.7, as "number," since Dante seems to have in mind here the Pythagorean idea of the underlying primacy of odd numbers. But the translation "meter" would have made equal sense.

METRICAL FORM (L. *modus*). The features of rhythm and *meter* by which poems of particular kinds are distinguished from other poetic kinds.

MORAL, MORAL SENSE (L. *moralis*, I. *morale*). One of the three *allegorical* senses, or senses beyond the *literal*, which teaches something useful to behavior. Defined *Letter* 7; *Banq.* 2.1.5.

MUSICAL SETTING (L. *modulatio*). Synonymous with *melodic line*; more particularly, the determinant of the *metrical form* ("modus") of a poem.

NOTATION (L. *nota*). *See* MELODIC LINE

NUMBER. *See* METER

PARADIGM (L. *prolatio*). An ordered list of inflectional endings which determine case, tense, aspect, and number, along with the relations of agreement, in a *grammar* or a form of *speech*. The same term is translated, *Eloq.* 1.14.2, as "pronunciation."

PASTORAL VERSE (L. *carmen bucolicum*). Mentioned by Dante as one of the principal genres of classical poetry. See *Letter* 10.

POET (POETIC, POETRY) (L. *poeta, poeticus, poetria*). The term for a writer in *grammar* who uses the classical meters, a term which Dante appropriates for *vernacular* writers who use rhyme, *New Life* 25; the term refers to a poet's use of the rules of his art, rules which allow him to make figures and fictions which would be out of place in other kinds of discourse; the use of this license makes a treatise *poetic*, and this term is one of Dante's ten for the treatment of a treatise.

POETIC LINE. *See* LINE

POLYSEMOUS (L. *polysemus*). Having more than one *sense*, or meaning, particularly if these senses are on different levels. Defined *Letter* 7.

PROEM. *See* PROLOGUE

PROLOGUE (L. *prologus*). The opening section of a poem, corresponding to the proem or exordium of an oration, and distinguished from the *executive part* of the argument, which fulfills the promises of the prologue. Besides announcing the *subject* of a work, the prologue also has as its purpose to render the audience attentive, well disposed, and willing to learn. Defined *Letter* 18.

PRONUNCIATION. *See* PARADIGM

PROOF, CONSISTING IN (L. *probativus*). The employment of formal procedures for deriving conclusions from a set of propositions; one of Dante's terms for the treatment of a treatise. See *Letter* 9.

REFUTATION, CONSISTING IN (L. *reprobativus*). The employment of formal procedures for the invalidation of propositions; one of Dante's terms for the treatment of a treatise. See *Letter* 9.

REPRISE (L. *responsorio*). The repetition, during or after the stanzas of a poem, of a certain line or lines; not allowed, according to Dante, in a *canzone*. See *Eloq.* 2.8.8.

RHYME, RHYMED UNITS (L. *rithimus*, I. *rima*). The phonetic correspondence (in Italian) of the last two syllables of those words which end *poetic lines*, or divisions of *poetic lines*; the defining characteristic, equivalent to *meter* in Latin, of vernacular poetry; in the *Divine Comedy*, the smallest of the formal *divisions* of the poem.

SENSE (L. *sensus*). The immediate understanding of a passage, distinguished from its more general and abstract *meaning*; a level of interpretation.

SIRMA (L. *sirma*). *See* CODA

SPEECH; LANGUAGE [GROUP]; TONGUE; DIALECT (L. *locutio, ydiomate, lingua, vox, loquela*). The medium of human communication, consisting of a (sensible) sound and an (intelligible) meaning; the capacity for producing speech; the speech of a particular geographic area or political subdivision; a group of languages related to each other historically; a dialect. (Note: Dante's use of these terms is not entirely consistent or systematic; therefore, with the exception of "loquela," which is always translated "dialect," there is not, in this translation, a uniform equivalence between the English and Latin words, though the order of their listing above corresponds to the general practice in the translation.)

SUBJECT (L. *subiectum*). The topic of a work of poetry, usually identical with its story or myth; the term is therefore sometimes synonymous with *matter*.

TONGUE. *See* SPEECH

TRAGEDY (TRAGIC STYLE) (L. *tragedia, tragica*). That ancient genre distinguished by a plot with a prosperous beginning and unhappy ending, and by its high-style diction; etymologically derived from the Greek for "goat song" (*Letter* 10). Hence the highest style of poetry, requiring the most excellent poetic language, is called the "tragic style."

TRANSUMPTIVE (L. *transumptivus*). Figurative; metaphorical. One of Dante's ten terms for the treatment of a treatise. See *Letter* 9.

TUNE (L. *tonus*). *See* MELODIC LINE.

VERNACULAR (L. *vulgarus*; I. *vulgare*). The language spoken by the common people ("vulgus"), including women and children, as against the language of the learned; that language learned by each person in childhood through imitation, in contrast to a *grammar*, which is based upon the vernacular, but must be acquired by study. Defined *Eloq.* 1.1.2.

VERSE (L. *versus*; I. *volta*). In the *canzone*, one of the repeated sections of a stanza coming after the *diesis*, and therefore fitted to a repetition of the *melodic line*. Defined *Eloq.* 2.10.4.

WRITING (HIGH-STYLE WRITING) (L. *dictaman, magna dictamen*). A composition which follows the rules of art. High-style writings, since they deal with more important subjects, follow more elaborate rules than other writings. See, for example, *Eloq.* 2.12.7.

Acknowledgments

Thanks are due the following publishers for permission to use copyrighted material as a basis for translation:

Società Dantesca Italiana for *Vita Nuova*, ed. M. Barbi, in *Le Opere di Dante*.

Felice le Monnier for *De Vulgari Eloquentia*, ed. Aristide Marigo; and *Convivio*, ed. G. Busnelli and G. Vandelli.

D. C. Heath and Company, for Grandgent: *La Divina Commedia di Dante Alighieri* (Lexington, Mass.: D. C. Heath and Company, 1933). Used by permission of the publisher.

Oxford University Press, for *Epistola ad Canem Grandem*, in *Dantis Alagherii Epistolae*, ed. Paget Toynbee. © Oxford University Press 1966. By permission of the Clarendon Press, Oxford.

Leo S. Olschki for *Ecloga* in *La corrispondenza poetica di Dante Alighieri e Giovanni del Virgilio*, ed. E. Bolisani and M. Valgimigli.

Thanks are also due the following publishers for permission to use copyrighted material in its original form:

Clarendon Press, Oxford, for H. J. Chaytor, *The Troubadours of Dante*.

Slatkine Reprints for *Le Troubadour Folquet de Marseille*, ed. Stanislaw Stronski.

Société des Anciens Textes Français for *Poésies du troubadour Aimeric de Belenoi*, ed. M. Dumitrescu.

Northwestern University Press for *The Poems of Aimeric de Peguilhan*, ed. W. Shepard and F. Chambers.

Riccardo Ricciardi Editore for *Poeti del Duecento*, ed. Gianfranco Contini.

Tariffi for *Le Rime di Cino di Pistoia*, ed. G. Zaccagnini.

Casa Editrice Felice le Monnier for *Convivio*, ed. G. Busnelli and G. Vandelli.

Index

THE WORKS OF DANTE

The numbers preceding the colon indicate the portion of the work printed or extracted; those following the colon indicate the page numbers in this volume.

GENERAL INDEX

Medieval authors are entered under the first name.